Shortage of Victory

Shortage of Victory

CAUSE AND CURE

By GABRIEL JAVSICAS

D. APPLETON-CENTURY COMPANY
Incorporated
NEW YORK   1943   LONDON

To
Erma Rockhill,
Michèle, and John Peter

Foreword

THE liberation of French Africa, which was made possible by the British victory in Egypt, the counter-offensive of the Russian armies following the opening of a Mediterranean front, and the magnificent defiance of German might by the French Navy at Toulon furnish a happy climax to the story told in this book.

The deceptive victory of 1918 notwithstanding, the shortage of victory for the democracies has now lasted some twenty-five years. During the long retreat of the western powers before the onslaught of German and Japanese arms there was much confused thinking on the decisive factors in this war. It was said that the armies of France were defeated because of French decadence, political and military treason; after the loss of Tobruk by the British in the summer of 1942, Mr. Harold J. Laski expressed the opinion that the defeat was due to the conservatism of the Churchill government; and failure to open a second front in Europe gave rise to widespread suspicion that a spirit of solidarity was lacking among the United Nations.

Now, however, the democracies, more efficient in the production of armaments than the totalitarians, have turned the tide. From now on it is likely that the armament industries of the United Nations will rapidly outstrip the Axis powers in the quantity and quality of the sinews of war. The democracies have just begun to fight, and the shoe is already on the other foot.

The battle could not have turned in favor of the democracies a day earlier than it did. Before a counter-offensive against a well-prepared totalitarian state can be launched, it is obviously necessary to switch over from the mass production of consumer goods to the mass production of armaments. But democratic governments can obtain the consent of the governed for such a radical change in the national economy only when the enemy, fully prepared, launches the assault.

All history is a conflict between forces of liberation and forces of oppression. Our own time is but a variation on this theme. While the theme is as old as mankind, there are nevertheless constant variations in the theme, and these are determined by material forces.

The industrial revolution during the long armistice, brought about by the development of the conveyer belt in industry, has thus a direct bearing on the as yet unrecognized or unadmitted necessity of formulating new principles of international relationships. Hitherto it has been axiomatic that an act of aggression was committed only when the armies of the aggressor invaded some neighboring territory. But this doctrine has been rendered obsolete by the development of mass production in industry. The history of our times compels the conclusion that any nation which gives itself a totalitarian form of government has thereby committed an act of aggression against its neighbors—in renouncing liberty, a nation gives its government a clear mandate to wage war.

The totalitarian state, when unhampered by either internal or external forces, makes full use of that mandate. Wherever and whenever a totalitarian state has come into being and no matter under what pretext, it has invariably increased the means of warfare and decreased for the common man the means of satisfying his economic needs. From the moment of its creation it is possible to calculate with a high degree of probability the year, and even the month, when the totalitarian state will assault its neighbors. Moreover, with the constant progress of industry and invention, it must become increasingly difficult to organize a defense against the well-prepared armies of the aggressor. As long as the peaceful people of this world adhere to the principle of non-intervention in the internal affairs of sovereign states, the totalitarian state will always have the time to develop a war economy while remaining nominally at peace with its neighbors. Well-prepared, it invariably wins the first battles. In the future it may succeed in making that first battle the last and thus win final victory.

The final battle is no longer likely to be gained by the Axis powers. From now on the title of this book applies to the enemy as well as to the United Nations. Nevertheless it will never be possible for the defense to time its own war production so as to be ready for the enemy when he attacks. The initiative must remain with the aggressive totalitarian state unless it is attacked and destroyed at its inception.

In making use of the potentialities of assembly-line production to the end of world conquest, Germany set the pace, emerging as the principal force in the constellation of modern tyranny. Great Britain, owing to her geographical position and the internal structure of her state and empire, emerged as the nucleus of resistance, a position she has held against all continental conquerors on the European scene. With the shrinkage of space, the struggle has become a global struggle; and in this fourth year of the Second World War the United States is the last fortress of liberty, around which all nations resisting aggression in Europe and Asia must group themselves for survival.

If there be any panacea for human suffering and the errors and evils of our time, it is, to-day, as it has always been, universal liberation from all forms of tyranny. Without liberty there can be no peace, no justice, no charity, no wealth, and no well-being. I have not, however, attempted to write a Utopia. In writing the history of our time I have had in mind the principle of Macaulay: A knowledge of the past is the best guide for the solution of the problems of the present. The story as told in this book suggests only the solution for the worst scourge of mankind, the barbarism of total warfare.

The cause of the democratic defeats suggests the cure: In the future a time differential must be applied in international relations. That is to say, a nation must be designated the aggressor as soon as, renouncing all individual liberty, its people submit or are subjected to a totalitarian form of government. In the development of this idea I have followed a principle first enunciated by the National Convention of the French Revolution.

The advent of the totalitarian state is not to my mind a revolution but a counter-revolution, a movement of expanding oppression. Apart from the association of the word "revolution" with radical changes in industry and trade, I have used the term only in the sense of liberating movements such as the American and the French revolutions.

All history is written with the future in mind. The preoccupation of the present must necessarily be with victory, but a military victory has no lasting quality. It failed to last after 1918. It will fail again unless this time it is won over the spirit of darkness which has descended upon regions of this world, threatening to engulf it. The defeat of the armies of the enemy is but a necessary step, in itself by no means decisive, toward a better future which, if it is to last and expand, this time must embrace all inhabitants of this earth.

Since prevention is better than cure, it will be imperative after victory is won to set up a world-wide system of checks and balances designed to prevent the rise of dictatorship anywhere in the world.

In telling the story of our time I have drawn not only upon the social sciences but also to some extent upon the imaginative literature of the world. As this story is in many ways fabulous, I have recalled some of the fables of Æsop and La Fontaine, which are as fresh and conclusive to-day as when they were first written. Fables are in the nature of understatements, and understatements are in order for all contemporary writers because our immediate predecessors have used up the entire stock of invective at the disposal of language to stigmatize the lesser evils of an age gone by.

GABRIEL JAVSICAS

Acknowledgments

Professor Allan Nevins of Columbia University has read the manuscript and has made many valuable suggestions, doubly helpful to one who was writing a first book.

Equal thanks are due to my wife, Erma Rockhill, for her active collaboration, particularly in the French and American chapters.

The introductory chapter of this book, entitled "Of Space And Time," has appeared in the magazine *The Nation* as two separate articles entitled, respectively, "War's Fourth Dimension" and "The 'Raw Materials' Hoax." Keith Hutchinson of *The Nation* read the chapters on anti-Semitism and psychological warfare when they were as yet in embryo. He nursed them as they grew to completion.

Acknowledgments are due to the International Publishers for permission to quote from the poem of Alexander Blok, "The Scythians."

Contents

"But while our politicians and economists dispute whether or not there is a shortage of rubber, no one with a heart or head disputes that there is certainly a Shortage of Victory."

CLARE BOOTHE
August 5, 1942

Messenger. . . . Never such a power
For any foreign preparation
Was levied in the body of a land. . . .
    King John. O, where hath our intelligence
            been drunk?
Where hath it slept?

SHAKESPEARE

Of Space and Time

THE world has long been led to believe that the territory occupied by the Axis nations is too small for them and their economic needs. The Kaiser demanded a place in the sun for Germany; the Nazis developed this theme by claiming more *Lebensraum* and access to raw materials. Japan and Italy joined in the chorus. During the flourishing days of appeasement a sympathetic ear was lent to this claim abroad. Socialists and conservatives alike, endeavoring to understand the causes of recurrent German aggression, found the economic explanation offered by the Nazis a plausible one.

The specific promise of access to raw materials to the vanquished, contained in the Atlantic Charter, Point 4, has naturally enough been seized upon by the Nazis as an implied admission that hitherto Germany has had no such opportunity. Yet that claim is without basis in fact. Switzerland, more densely populated, with few natural resources, and without access to the sea, finds sufficient creative ability among her people to enjoy the highest per capita income in Europe next to Sweden. Sweden in turn has a higher per capita income than the United States with her virtually unlimited resources and thinly populated territories.

Obviously the size of a country and the number of its inhabitants bear little relation to the wealth and well-being of its people. The economic structure of a country, the organization of production and distribution, is the important factor. Highly industrialized capitalist countries experience periodic unemployment and suffer from poverty amid plenty, but the people of a totalitarian state are forced to divert all their resources and energy to the production of armament and in consequence suffer chronic deprivation. The contrast between nations organized for peace and those dedicated to war is most pronounced in their treatment of the problem of raw materials.

In a liberal world economy, in time of peace, all states, great and small, do in fact enjoy "free access to the raw materials of the world, on equal terms." Obstacles which interfere with the free play of supply and demand affect all nations alike. The commodity markets of the world know no racial, national, or religious distinctions. Export quotas may be adopted at the place of origin to halt a disastrous fall in prices. Great Britain may establish preferential duties within the Empire: the price of the commodity is still the same to all buyers regardless of the sovereignty under which they carry on their trade. The British merchant pays the same price for a pound of British rubber as the German, Japanese, or Italian merchant.

If the countries exporting raw materials offer a higher yield on invested capital, capital can flow to these countries; the individual investor is free to participate in the risks and profits of the companies exploiting the mines and plantations by buying their shares on the exchanges of the world. Nor is economic control limited to raw materials. For example, German capital virtually controlled the optical industry in the Americas, many pharmaceutical and other chemical concerns everywhere in the world, and furthermore, through patent agreements in international cartels, even branched out into other industries penetrating all national economies. There is no discrimination based upon the nationality of the investor. For all practical purposes, in time of peace, the only limitation to free access to raw materials is the buying power of the importing countries and of their individual merchants. That buying power in turn depends upon the ability of the nation to husband its resources.

The "Raw Materials" Hoax

This was substantially the situation before the development of the totalitarian state. Nations which had no intention of conquering the world or even of robbing their neighbors of a bit of territory in the good old-fashioned way had little cause to complain about lack of access to raw materials. They could afford to pay for what they needed with the product of their labor. In time of peace even the totalitarian countries, despite the insatiable demands of their war industries, had no difficulty in obtaining more raw material than was good for the peace of the world. Until Japan invaded Indo-China, the United States was sending Japan sufficient supplies to enable her to conquer a great part of China and to build a fleet almost as large as that of the United States itself. Germany managed to accumulate enough raw materials to conquer eighteen nations, keep a badly beaten Italy in the war, and still, after three years of blockade, to threaten two continents with conquest. Does this argue any lack of access to raw materials?

Before this world war access to raw materials was in fact so easy for the aggressor nations that puzzled and perturbed democratic countries began to suspect their own governments of connivance in the totalitarian schemes. But a more effective interference with the free flow of raw materials would have exacted a high price from the citizens of the democracies: they would have been obliged to submit in time of peace to government control of all imports and exports. The interdependence of all countries is clearly visible in this dilemma. Curtailment of economic liberty anywhere in the world threatens liberty everywhere in the world.

While the democratic nations were loath to practise the kind of interference with economic liberty that the use of raw materials as a political weapon would have entailed, the totalitarian governments had no such scruples. Of all collective human enterprise modern war is the least spontaneous. It requires the mustering of all resources of the nation, material and human, and their dedication to a single purpose. Years before a government bent on aggression goes to war, it must accumulate vast stocks for the mass production of armaments. In the process of changing over from peace production to war production, and after, the totalitarian government makes the life of the individual merchant, importer, and producer miserable with ever more stringent rules and regulations.

The obstacles in the way of his free access to raw materials do not come, in time of peace, from abroad, but from within, from his own government. Through its absolute control of foreign currency and of all imports and exports, the totalitarian government starves the producers of consumers' goods of all raw materials while it furnishes ample supplies to the war industries. Furthermore, in order to render the country blockade-proof, the government places high import duties on various products—rubber, gasoline, and the like—in order to stimulate the production of *Ersatz* goods. Thus the totalitarian state cuts off its subjects from free and equal access to raw materials and then broadcasts to the world jeremiads about unfair treatment by the plutocratic democracies.

Complaints about lack of access to raw materials have not come from peaceful nations or even from individual German, Japanese, or Italian merchants, but only from the governments of the totalitarian countries. The reason is obvious. It is a political demand, not an economic one. The Nazis did not go to war in order to obtain raw materials; they needed raw materials in order to be able to wage war. When they clamor for access to raw materials they mean access in time of war, not in time of peace. In time of peace they *have* access, but in time of war the devil needs more than his due.

In time of war the totalitarian constellation is at a grave geographical disadvantage, for some of the most vital raw materials can be obtained only from overseas. Even if Germany and Italy had been given all the colonies which produce these materials, Great Britain and the United States would still have ruled the seas, and could bar their enemies from access to these colonies in time of war. The German and Japanese demand for *Lebensraum* was therefore tantamount to asking England and America to scuttle their fleets. Nor should it be forgotten how perilously near the German war machine came to achieving this Nazi wish. Alone at first, it soon gained the support of the Japanese and Italian navies in a common cause. The American neutrality law held out a promise, long kept, of non-intervention in European affairs. In 1940 the French fleet scuttled itself for all practical purposes. There remained only the British fleet; and no one can doubt that, but for Britain, Germany and Japan would by now have access to all the raw materials in the world for a final campaign against the last obstacle in their path—the Western hemisphere.

Every nation the Nazis and the Japanese have conquered to date they have stripped of its resources in order to obtain material for the next conquest. They boast that they have already obtained more than the cost of their entire war effort. But even literally free access to the raw materials and the accumulated wealth of the conquered nations has not solved their economic problem. The Germans, the Japanese, and the Italians, are still among the have-nots. As long as their merchants operated on a free home market they imported and produced goods which they could sell to the consumer at a profit. Now the government is their only buyer, dictating what goods shall be produced and fixing the price. They have been deprived of that saving grace of capitalist society—the individual liberty of its members—without which it can not function.

Lack of access to raw materials, imperative need for *Lebensraum*—these are myths which the totalitarians have used to serve their ends. What Germany, Italy, and Japan really need is not access to raw materials, but a priority program in favor of a consumers'-goods industry, severely restricting the supply of raw materials for the production of the implements of war. They have proved that they know how to husband their resources for the business of war. As long as their peoples are unwilling or unable to husband those same resources for peace, the impulse will have to be provided from without.

War's Fourth Dimension

No matter how much raw material, industrial resources and skilled labor are at the disposal of any nation, the totalitarian state feeds them into the insatiable industries geared to mass production of implements of war, and leaves no more than a minimum to provide for the food, clothing, and shelter of the nation.

Assembly-line production in industry introduced into modern warfare a new element as revolutionary in its import as the invention of the steam engine, which brought about the Industrial Revolution of the nineteenth century. As the airplane added a third dimension to war, the conveyer belt introduced the fourth—the space-time element. During 1914–18 time already played an important rôle; with the development of mass-production methods it has become the decisive factor. It deprives war of all spontaneity. No longer can a nation rise as one man and smite the enemy. The conveyer belt has made war a long-premeditated enterprise, chained to time.

In 1914 war fervor could be stirred up in a few weeks and an army mobilized in a few days. Equipment for the armies was on hand or could be produced in sufficient quantities by established war industries. Peace industries could quickly switch over to war production. Even so, the very complete preparations of Germany would have defeated France but for the breathing spell gained for French war industries by the victory of the Marne.

In the machine production brought in by the Industrial Revolution a finished article is produced not directly, by a craftsman or a number of workers, but indirectly, through the intermediate process of constructing a power-driven tool or machine. This method lengthens the time needed for the manufacture of one article, but materially reduces the time needed for manufacturing it in quantity. The conveyer belt developed during the long armistice since 1918, while it speeded up mass production, increased the time required for the construction of the first finished implement of war from months to years, and thereby made modern war a matter of long and careful premeditation. Thus it placed almost all the trump cards in the hands of the determined aggressor. *Blitzkrieg* is a misleading word. The surprise attack may look like lightning out of the blue, but actually it is the result of years of intensive preparation.

Terrible as is the destruction inflicted by the weight of the aggressor's accumulated material, the havoc wrought upon the time at the disposal of the defense is even more fatal. Only as the enemy attacks does he reveal the nature of the weapons which he has developed in years of secret preparation. It is then too late for the defense to produce the weapons with which it might resist these new offensive methods. With rare exceptions, such as the degaussing cable invented by the English to combat the magnetic mine, effective defensive weapons can be produced in quantity only on the assembly line. The invention and mass production of weapons that can stop the dive-bomber or pierce the heavy armor of a tank require months or even years in time of peace; in time of war the decisive battle may be lost, as the Battle of France was lost, before the blue-print can be put upon paper. Hence under the conditions created by the time element, the offensive is not only the best defense but virtually the only possible defense.

Because the war planes produced on the conveyer belt can fly at 300 miles an hour while the land army is provided with fast motorized vehicles the totalitarian war machine, once set in motion, devours space with unprecedented speed. Only China and Russia, with vast space at their disposal, could retreat before the onslaught of the *Blitz* and thus gain time for themselves and their future allies, but the totalitarian attack is instantly fatal for countries which have little space at their disposal, and which are unprotected by the sea, such as the small democracies of Europe and metropolitan France.

Before 1914 arms and ammunition could be accumulated leisurely over a period of years on a yearly war budget; they did not have to be used in offensive warfare in order not to be wasted. New types of arms were invented, but the new machinery required could be built under peace-time conditions while business continued as usual. Arms and ammunition used in the Boer War and earlier were still serviceable in 1914. Since it now takes from three to five years of intensive work and planning to make modern implements of war come off the assembly lines in appreciable quantities, the aggressor must plan the moment of his attacks years ahead. The Nazi war machine knew the approximate day on which its tanks, planes, and guns would come off the belt in sufficient quantities to conquer Europe.

Nevertheless, modern industry also contains an element which, properly used, could defeat the aggressor in the long run. Capitalism differs from any system of economy which preceded it in being revolutionary in tendency, whereas the others were static. The same horse-drawn cart served the Roman economy and medieval feudalism. In an industrial economy, however, machines and the product of machinery grow obsolete in shorter and shorter periods of time. Each year industry must retool for the mass production of ever-improved motor-cars. This process is greatly accelerated under the pressure of war. Implements of war grow obsolete much faster than motor-cars. Because Great Britain froze her war-plane models later than Germany she gained an edge in quality which enabled her to defend the British Isles successfully against invasion. Germany was aware that the United States might throw in her productive capacity on the side of the victims of German aggression. She knew, therefore, that she would be compelled to go to war as soon as she was ready or the initial advantage which she enjoyed, of being able to coördinate the mass production of all implements of war for the chosen day of attack, would be lost. To delay risked making all her preparations useless by rendering her weapons obsolete. The non-aggressive nations could have no such foreknowledge. It is true that German rearmament was no secret, and theoretically the United States, Great Britain and France were in a position to counter the German armament program by one of their own, but practically the difficulties, both material and psychological, proved insurmountable.

General Mitchell in the United States and General Charles

de Gaulle in France saw the importance of planes and tanks, and De Gaulle worked out the idea of mechanized warfare later adopted by the Germans. But neither of them were industrial experts. If they realized the task which the adoption of these instruments of warfare would impose upon industry, they considered it beyond the scope of their competence and did not occupy themselves with it. Inasmuch as their suggestions were rejected by the army bureaucracy and as the antimilitarist world in which they lived failed to support them, the problem of gearing industry to the quantity production of planes and tanks did not come up for consideration.

The French Government had a dim realization of the difficulty, and after the remilitarization of the Rhineland in 1936, the inadequacy of plane production was debated in the French Parliament. On the ground that plane models grow obsolete in a very short time, it was decided that France should not go in for mass production of war planes until war became imminent. The complications that were bound to arise when it became necessary to freeze the models and start mass production were not taken into account. No one, apparently, had any conception of the time that would be required to conquer these difficulties. In this respect the course of action of France and even Great Britain was as little related to practical experience as the speculations of the ancient Greeks were to the experimental method of modern science.

Germany, however, having accepted the principles of modern warfare developed by De Gaulle in 1934 in his book *Vers l'Armée de Métier*, acted upon them. It took Germany about six years to build a modern army. It may be assumed that she could have accomplished this in half the time if some other country had done the pioneering. Once Germany had passed the experimental stage and had built the necessary new factories, its intended victims could describe their own defensive efforts only as "too little and too late." When Hitler remilitarized the Rhineland, German industry was well advanced in the mass production of planes and tanks, while France was totally unprepared in spite of her large standing army.

From then on the trump card, adequate industrial preparation for war, remained in the hand of Hitler. It conferred such
tremendous advantages upon the Nazis that all their apparently reckless words and actions now look in retrospect like
models of moderation and caution. Conversely, United States
isolationism and Britain's traditional policy of maintaining a
balance of power on the Continent, her cautious wait-and-see
attitude, now appear as the height of fool-hardiness. Englishmen still thought France was wielding the big stick in Europe, while in reality Germany had seized that weapon. They
failed to perceive that the time factor was shifting the balance
in favor of Germany.

The purely technical difficulties imposed by the time factor
upon the nations dedicated to defense were enhanced by psychological complications. A nation could not make the effort
for total defense while its government was straining every re-
source to appease the enemy. As long as they hoped that war
might be avoided, the people of the United States, England
and France could not be expected to renounce all social progress in order to prepare for war. It is not easy to grapple with
a hypothetical danger several years ahead of time. The more
peaceful a people is, the less likely it is to attribute bellicose
intentions to another people. And our energies fail where our
imagination does not reach. Two million men in Great Britain
took a solemn oath that under no conceivable circumstances
would they go to war. In such an atmosphere Liddell Hart's
theory of the superiority of defense over offense fell on willing
ears.

As British statesmen indulged in the luxury of spending
their week-ends away from their desks, and as French democracy habitually reshuffled the Cabinet every six months or so,
Hitler seemed to choose these moments for action, and the
legend grew that he had an unfailing sense of timing. But
country week-ends and fallen Cabinets were only superficially
the cause of democratic inaction. Actually any day was propitious for any of Hitler's undertakings, since he was always
several years ahead in his preparations for war. The United

States, England, and France had missed the bus in Europe in 1933, and in Asia the bus was missed in 1931, when Japan attacked Manchuria.

To-day, a determined United States is slowly turning the tables on the Axis powers by drawing upon the experience of the British and the German war industries. The comparative value of the various modern implements of war in actual battle is no longer a secret. The struggle for Crete and the sinking of the *Bismarck* have solved the problem of sea power versus air power by emphasizing coördination, with a sharp edge in favor of air power. The question of land power versus air power was settled by the Battle of France, likewise in favor of coördination, with the air force as the decisive factor.

The United States, Great Britain, and Russia have tabulated the time required for the production of each implement of war now needed to defeat Germany and Japan. It became imperative to create a coördinating body of all the armed services and of industrial experts to work out a schedule which would make all the needed equipment ready at the same time. Since battleships could not be completed as quickly as the rest of the program, and since they can no longer be effective against land-based aviation, it was found wiser to build flying fortresses instead. At the same time an expeditionary force is being trained and sent overseas to the strategic regions of this world. That force should be trained and ready to fight as its equipment comes rolling off the assembly lines. In the preparation of this force the important point is, of course, its striking power. The thin end of the wedge must be exceedingly sharp—a condition which, according to De Gaulle, calls for a concentration of one hundred thousand combat planes and fifty thousand tanks, in the decisive theater of war. The concentration of such a force demands time, not only because of production but also because of the vast distances over which man-power and machines have to be shipped.

The fourth dimension of modern war, the time-space element, has created for the democracies the problem which they

failed to solve: to designate the enemy and to seize the offensive without waiting for an act of aggression. No task is
more difficult for a peaceful people than to resolve to fight
before it has been attacked. Of that the Nazis and the Japanese were well aware. Reliance upon the will to peace of
their victims gave them the impetus to prepare their conquests,
and at the same time sustained the morale of their peoples.

The outcome of the last battle in this global war depends
upon the ability of United States industry to overtake the axis
powers in the quantity and quality of the sinews of war, and
in the ability of the American and British navy and air force
to conquer the problem of space, to transport the arms to
their point of destination where they can do the most harm
to the enemy, before China and Russia are lost.

Chinese, British, and Russian resistance furnished the United
States with that most precious of all commodities in a totalitarian world: Time. Upon the use the United States makes of
this commodity depends the outcome of the last battle.

It remains to be seen whether the peaceful people after victory is won will develop that spirit of solidarity which alone
can justify to their own conscience a well-timed simultaneous
intervention against the creation of any totalitarian state in
the future. For unless such a state is attacked and destroyed
forthwith, at its inception, the inhabitants of this globe indubitably will be reduced to slaves in the life-time of our
children, if our children are allowed to live at all.

2

Genesis of the German Totalitarian State

THE rise of Nazi Germany to the greatest military power in history in the relatively short span of six years' time can not be explained in terms of raw materials, industrial capacity, skilled mechanics, time and space alone. These material resources at the disposal of a nation are potential means which can be used as readily for peace and economic development as for war and destruction. Assembly-line industry is innocent of moral values. It is a device which can be used for the production of motor-cars for business and pleasure, and for refrigerators and washing-machines to reduce the labor of the housewife. It makes the mass production of labor-saving devices possible while reducing the cost of each finished article. Theoretically, under an ideal system of economy, it would eliminate all pain from labor and make the satisfying of the material needs of man as easy as a hobby.

But at the service of a mighty state which uses labor and capital as its slaves, the conveyer belt, given time, can produce enough implements of war to move the conquest of the world within the reach of a single man, if that man be dictator over a docile nation skilled in warfare and ready to do his bidding. In either case assembly-line production remains but a means to an end, an end conceived and executed by man and the spirit which moves him. It serves the good and the wicked with equal impartiality, but like man himself it can not serve two gods at the same time. Its use for total war production, by definition, precludes the satisfaction of economic needs beyond a minimum.

Obviously no nation imposes upon itself voluntarily the

13

heavy sacrifices which total preparation for war entails. Either its very existence must be threatened by forces from without or its government must be independent of the public will and powerful enough to devise and execute a totalitarian plan for a war of aggression. But in this latter case the nation must be virtually unanimous in supporting the ultimate aim of the state, world conquest, if the plan is to find a measure of realization.

The Defeat and Humiliation of 1918

In the popular view, the Treaty of Versailles and its imperfections were the primary cause which drove Germany into the strait-jacket of the totalitarian state. But the Treaty of Versailles was itself preceded by the defeat of Imperial Germany, and it is that defeat rather than the treaty which ate into the heart of Germany and slowly corroded whatever reason, justice, and humanity had flourished before in that country. To the defeated, no treaty is a good treaty. Those who are attacked and vanquished without provocation can see defeat as a misfortune which may be borne with honor. But a defeated aggressor can find no consolation in the knowledge of his innocence. Nations, like individuals, are not deceived by their own hypocrisy. A very distinct atmosphere of ridicule attaches itself to the man who falls into the trap which he has prepared for others. No other humiliation can cut so deep and leave such lasting wounds. The indignation of the cheater who is cheated, the thief who is caught, the liar who is exposed, is of a different flavor from the indignation of an honest man who, subjected to injustice, may be ennobled by it.

Prussian militarism had no cause in 1914 to seek revenge or redress for injustice done to Germany. On the contrary, as a result of victories (from 1864 to 1871) over Denmark, Austria, and France, the German states, united into a confederacy under the hegemony of Prussia, had become the most powerful military empire on the continent; German industries prospered, and foreign trade expanded with unprecedented rapidity.

The power which Germany exercised on the continent had gone to the head of her ruling class and of her megalomaniac Kaiser in particular, who styled himself a "warlord" and believed that he was destined to rule the world. The attack on the Archduke of Austria at Sarajevo provided the pretext to go to war at a time when Germany believed herself fully armed and able to defeat the "decadent" countries, particularly France. The Kaiser and his general staff were so certain of victory that they hardly bothered to disguise their desire for conquest behind the claim that Germany had been attacked or threatened with encirclement. The emphasis was put upon the "right" of Germany, by virtue of her moral and military superiority, to establish a hegemony over Europe.

When the defeat came, there was, therefore, neither a moral nor a military excuse that the Kaiser and his government could offer to the people of Germany whom they had misled. Neither the Kaiser nor his commander-in-chief, Ludendorff, had the moral courage to face the consequences. The Kaiser fled to Holland, and Ludendorff put on a pair of dark spectacles, adopted the name Lindstroem, and bolted to Sweden. Ludendorff never recovered from the shock of his fall and of his own cowardice. The realization that he might have stayed and received the honors later bestowed upon Hindenburg destroyed his sanity and made him turn for comfort to the Germanic gods of old.

The militarists who remained resented their defeat just as vehemently. The defeat had frightened their leaders badly enough to make them take to their heels, thus leaving the way open for the weak and uncertain forces of German democracy. No treaty, either milder or more harsh, could have altered the consequences of the defeat for the military masters of Germany. It was the defeat which ousted them.

Great Britain had been particularly guilty in crossing their plans and bringing about their downfall. They had not planned on England's entering the war. The traditional British reluctance to cross bridges before coming to them made her foreign minister refuse to state beforehand whether or not Britain would come to the assistance of France and Russia. Germany confidently expected her to acquiesce in the violation of Belgian neutrality and the consequent threat to the British channel ports. But instead of falling in with the German plans, Britain declared war.

The authoritarian mind is necessarily a narrow mind. It must remain closed to another's point of view lest it fall victim to the spirit of tolerance. Britain's unforeseen intervention in 1914 was therefore interpreted in Germany as something quite different from the purely military challenge that France and Russia presented. The action of these two powers had been foreseen, and they were consequently acting as they should. But England was not under direct attack, and her refusal to wait until her turn would come was regarded by the German High Command as something very much akin to insubordination, not to say treason. The malediction, *"Gott Strafe England,"* therefore, came from the heart.

The consequences of Britain's intervention and the blockade were not immediately apparent. Before the entry of the United States into the war of 1914–18 clinched the victory for the Allies, Germany celebrated an almost unbroken string of victories, as a result of which she was able to impose two peace treaties of her own, the Treaty of Brest-Litovsk and the Treaty of Bucharest. By comparison with these, the Versailles Treaty reads like an act of friendship and conciliation. The treaty dictated to Russia gave Germany the richest agricultural and industrial provinces of that country, including the Ukraine, and by the Treaty of Bucharest Germany simply annexed all of Romania.

The United States was already at war with Germany and transporting millions of fresh troops to the Western Front when Russia was forced to sign the Treaty of Brest-Litovsk. The Romanian treaty likewise was concluded only a few months before the German debacle. Yet both treaties show Germany to have been free of any evil foreboding. The maxim, "Do as you would be done by," had no place at the conference tables where Germany dictated terms on the principle of "woe to the vanquished."

The humiliation was all the greater when defeat came. Among her greatest losses Germany counted the fruits which she had hoped to harvest from her victories. Throughout the war, wherever there had been a German soldier Germany had been victorious, and toward the end she had held Russia and the Balkans within her grasp, only to lose them (and more) when she was beaten in the west. Her military rulers had seen their powers extended beyond the Reich and had already distributed high positions in the conquered provinces among themselves, their relatives and friends. They had counted on making the western powers with their great wealth pay for the war which had drained the resources of Germany. All these high hopes were crushed by the defeat.

The Treaty of Versailles may still loom large in the imagination of the western world as the cause which brought the Nazis into power in Germany, but in Germany itself it served the disappointed and humiliated conquerors as a screen behind which they could hide their defeat. The defeat itself was an unalterable fact for the time being, but the treaty was subject to abrogation. In the German view it was consequently judged expedient to treat the year 1919 as Anno I of a new era: an era of unjust oppression and humiliation which Germany suffered at the hands of the Allies, while all that had preceded the Treaty of Versailles—the provocation and the defeat—were conveniently passed over in silence or vehemently denied.

The Stab in the Back

On the second of October, 1918, more than a month before the armistice, Prince Max von Baden was scheduled to take over the Chancellorship. In conformity with the wishes of the supreme command he was to ask the Allies for an armistice since the military situation was desperate:

"He wanted to gain time before all things. He had hopes of Ludendorff coming to his senses, and then of his feeling sorry for having howled for mercy from his enemies in this abject way. . . . It appeared that Ludendorff was foolish enough to think that the enemy would grant him a breathing space and then he hoped to be able to fight on again and stem the tide. . . . The Prince in his distress had summoned the Hamburg banker Warburg, who advised him not to accept the Chancellorship, as he would be powerless under existing circumstances: 'If the Supreme Command regard the position so despairingly they should go across with the white flag.' "

The Socialist Phillip Scheidemann, who tells this story in his *The Making of the New Germany*, adds the following comment:

"(Hear, hear!) That [Mr. Warburg's view] was my point of view until Fritz Ebert [later President of the Weimar Republic] got the better of me at the Section meeting [of the Socialist party]."

The people of Germany, Socialists, Democrats, and Conservatives alike, supported the militarists and their program of conquest throughout the war and up to the end. As long as the armies were victorious there was no thought of revolution. Only after the Imperial government had fled did the Socialists and Democrats take over. Thus even the "Revolutionists" had failed to dissociate themselves in time from a share in the responsibility for war and defeat. They had desired a victory for German arms as ardently as their masters, and their disappointment was equally great. There was consequently no joy at being liberated from the yoke of militarism and absolutism. Democracy in Germany was not the result of a revolutionary movement against oppression and inequality. It had not been hardened in the fire of a heroic struggle against the reaction within. To the German people it came as a gift from the outside world which had defeated their rulers for them. For that reason it was little appreciated. Throughout the Weimar epoch, freedom from governmental oppression was to remain a poor substitute for a glorious victory over the enemy without. A new generation, the children born during the last war, grew up with the conviction that defeat and democracy were as intimately related as cause and effect. To them the Weimar Republic with its liberal institutions was under suspicion as an alien form of government which had been imposed upon Germany by the enemy to keep her weak and humiliated.

The people of Germany had seen their armies in retreat before a foe grown overwhelmingly superior in man-power and equipment; they had seen the Hindenburg line broken, Ludendorff begging for an armistice, and the Kaiser in flight.

Nevertheless, the fairy-tale of a dagger thrust in the back of the victorious German armies by the Revolution at home found wide credence. It was a tale which originated in the fertile though diseased brain of Ludendorff, who thought to regain his prestige by a subterfuge worthy of a school-boy. This originator of the totalitarian theory of warfare argued that Germany had not been "honorably defeated in open battle."

Woodrow Wilson's "lying propaganda," his tricky fourteen-point peace offer and the British blockade which "starved innocent women and children" had so weakened home morale as to lower the resistance of the civilian population to the treacherous Socialist Revolution. "Just when the victorious German army stood on the threshold of victory, the Revolution at home deprived it of the ammunition with which to clinch that victory." In the same breath Ludendorff affirmed that when Germany laid down her arms, she did so not because of any military necessity but in good faith that the fourteen points would be the basis for the peace treaty. This good faith had been betrayed. Once again, in the drawing up of the peace treaty, the treacherous Socialists and Democrats had connived with the enemy to devise a constitution for Germany which would enable them to guarantee to the Allies fulfilment of the unjust Treaty of Versailles.

Hitler acquired his conviction that the masses will believe any lie if it is big enough and repeated often enough, when he saw with what eagerness this story was accepted by a people who had themselves witnessed the true sequence of events. But it was precisely the failure of the German people and the German army to stage the Revolution before they were beaten which made them eager to believe that they had been tricked into submission. Had they really helped to defeat the régime of the Kaiser, they could have hailed the enemy's victory as their own. Had they not identified themselves with that régime they could have cheerfully concurred in the Allied view that Imperial Germany was guilty of beginning the war, instead of resenting the war-guilt clause in the Treaty of Versailles as an unjust accusation against their former government.

The German Revolution of 1918 came too late to save the nation from the humiliation of defeat, and it also failed to effect any profound changes in the structure of the German state. Though it dethroned the crowned heads of the German states, it left them, including the Kaiser and his family, in possession of their vast private properties. The Junkers, some 15,000 families who owned practically all the arable and fertile land of Germany, remained undisturbed masters of their vast estates. No agrarian reform came to the rescue of the landless proletariat dependent for its economic existence upon the Junkers, who continued to rule over them like quasi-feudal lords.

In all rural districts the Junkers supervised the elections and had little difficulty inducing the peasants to think and vote in accordance with their wishes. The industrial and financial powers of the ruling capitalist class in the cities likewise retained all their privileges. The *economic* ideology of Imperial Germany had been as liberal as that of the western powers. Laissez-faire liberalism, in fact, was at the basis of the rapid industrialization of German economy from 1871 to 1914. The Weimar Republic neither liberated the bourgeoisie economically, nor did it in any radical way curtail their political powers. But while it gave them no more independence from government interference than they had enjoyed before, the defeat which the republic inherited from the preceding régime robbed them of the pride and glory of membership in a powerful state.

The political parties representing labor in parliament did little more for the working class than Imperial Germany had done. The first labor reforms of the Reich were introduced from above by Bismarck, who realized that contented labor makes contented soldiers, at least in Germany. Even after young William II dropped this pilot from the German ship of state, German labor legislation remained progressive. Unemployment and health insurance, shorter hours of work, and old-age pensions were granted to labor, and those measures steadily improved the standard of living of the German working man up to the outbreak of war in 1914.

Socialism maintained that capitalism caused war by looking for larger and more profitable markets abroad, with new populations to be exploited in the colonies and conquered countries. The Socialists of France under the leadership of Jean Jaurès, working upon this theory before the outbreak of war in 1914, asked the Socialists of Germany to join the workers of France in a common refusal to bear arms for the capitalist ruling class. But the German Socialists, even then more nationalist than socialist, informed their comrades in France that the Marxian doctrine was no longer applicable to Germany. Marx had called upon the working classes of the world to unite since they had nothing to lose but their chains. Since the days of Marx, however, German working men had obtained recognition for their trade unions, had gained shorter hours and higher wages, were represented in the Parliament of Imperial Germany by a strong Socialist Party, and consequently had more to lose than their chains. They would not let their fatherland be defeated by French and English capitalists and by the reactionary and absolutist government of Russia.

The revolution of 1918 accelerated the labor reforms in Germany. It granted labor enough advantages (such as the right to bargain collectively and the eight-hour day) to annoy the

capitalist class but not enough to win the enthusiastic allegiance of the working class to the Weimar Republic. Socialism,
confining itself in practice to ensuring certain reforms which
could be carried out without wrecking capitalist economy,
nevertheless taught labor to think of the capitalistic system as
inimical to the proletariat. In its democratic version Socialism
advocated the nationalization of all key industries, a program
which the Social Democratic Party promised to carry out as
soon as they could gain an absolute majority in Parliament.
The dictatorial version of the same program advocated by the
Communist Party urged revolution and violent overthrow of
the democratic régime as the only means for its realization.

Therefore, there was from the start no enthusiastic support for the Weimar Republic from any of the social classes
represented in Parliament. The parliamentary system was suffered as a makeshift until one or another of the revolutionary
movements could succeed in overthrowing it by force.

Early in 1919, a revolt inspired by the Bolshevik seizure of
power in Russia, the Spartacan movement, was crushed by a
coalition of the Social Democrats and rightist parties supported
by the army, not yet fully demobilized. A year later the Kapp
Putsch led by army officers met with the spontaneous resistance of the industrial workers, who succeeded in putting it
down by a general strike while the government fled Berlin.
But in 1923, the Ludendorff-Hitler beer-cellar Putsch in Munich no longer met with spontaneous public resistance. The
Putschists failed because they had started out without the
support of the Reichswehr, which, obeying government orders, made short work of the demonstraters. In the subsequent
investigation, General von Seeckt, Commander of the new
Reichswehr, limited to one hundred thousand men by the
Treaty of Versailles, confessed that he had refused his support to the Ludendorff-Hitler movement because they had
failed to show him a fifty-fifty chance of success. He did not
state the reasons for his skepticism. It was plain that the internal forces of democracy and the government would have
been too weak to resist the combined forces of the Reichs-

wehr and the reaction. What gave pause to General von Seeckt was the certainty of French intervention. In order to compel the payment of reparations in kind, France had occupied the Ruhr, and although the occupation failed in its objective because of the passive resistance of the working class, France was in no mood to tolerate a military dictatorship in Germany.

Currency Inflation

The Weimar Republic retained in office the personnel of the Imperial state. The parliamentary system was applied on the unaltered core of the Imperial state like a thin veneer. That core governed by its own rules. It sabotaged measures of the government which did not meet with its approval, and it developed schemes of its own which it could carry out without Parliament. It functioned like a state within the state, or, in present-day parlance, like a fifth column for the long arm of the past: the past of Prussian militarism, which was destined to return stronger than ever before and infuriated by fourteen years of frustration. But meanwhile, still too weak to begin the reconstruction of the German war machine on a large scale, this fifth column searched for equally deadly means of revenge. Thus it conceived the idea of destroying the value of the German currency, in order to rob the Allies of due reparations for the devastation caused by the German armies.

The management of the Reichsbank set the printing-press in motion, causing an inflation without parallel in the history of German finance. This financial disaster was deliberately engineered in order to present the Allies with the *fait accompli* of Germany's inability to pay. The democratic government welcomed the inflation for its external effect. Its desire for self-preservation was not so strong as its opposition to the Allied demand for reparations, and it let the inflation take its course at the risk of making the middle class its sworn enemy.

It is doubtful whether all members of government and

Parliament understood clearly the meaning and purpose of the inflation. The intricacies of the financial system in capitalist economics are a mystery to everybody but a financial expert. Even the various schools of economic science have not succeeded in fully elucidating its function to their mutual satisfaction. Socialist theoreticians before the First World War treated the whole subject of money with disdain. To them it was an unmitigated evil of which mankind would be freed with the arrival of Utopia.

As the inflation progressed it became apparent that the chief sufferers belonged to the middle class, particularly the rentiers, while labor, having no savings to lose, was relatively better off. Though wages did not go up as fast as the currency fell, nevertheless labor was fully employed and could make ends meet better than the professional classes and those who lived on their savings. For these last, Socialists had little sympathy, regarding them as parasites more reprehensible than the big capitalists. The industrialists and speculators made immense profits during the inflation, and a few of them were able to convert these profits into real values. The banks granted to big business unlimited credits, with which men like Stinnes, Thyssen, and their colleagues bought up factories, real estate, shipyards and mines, repaying their debts only after the money had lost all value. It was easy and safe to speculate in almost anything of real value. Factories, farms, and real estate could be bought like industrial shares on the stock-exchange with a down payment of ten per cent and with this additional advantage: so long as the inflation lasted their value could go only up, never down.

As a school-boy in Germany during the inflation years, I found that my pocket-money, which I received in dollars, gave me the exalted standing of a man of ample means. I could afford a season ticket for a box at the opera and a box at the theater. After that I had enough left over to become the most popular scholar in my class by treating my colleagues to a daily round of ice-cream. They had no pocket-money because they belonged to that middle class which, between the industrialists and the working class, was ground to pulp during the inflation. In justice to myself I should add that I was quite popular even before the inflation gave me an opportunity to play lady bountiful. Though I was an alien, two things militated in my favor: I was a poor scholar and the all-round athletic champion of my age group.

Throughout the inflation the liberal and enlightened press of Germany clamored for the dismissal of the Reichsbank management which the republic had inherited from the previous régime, but all such attempts were blocked by the reactionaries and the industrialists who hypocritically blamed the Allies and the Weimar constitution for the disaster which befell the middle classes. Consent to a stabilization of the mark was not given until the American dollar had reached the neat value of four billion marks. By that time the government had earned the undying hatred of the middle classes, holders of small savings, pensioned officers, and even a large class of very wealthy people, who in their simplicity never succeeded in freeing themselves from a lifetime of conservative habits which had been sound under a sound currency. Money put out on mortgages, invested in government bonds, or kept in the strong-box melted away until it was literally worth less than the paper on which it was printed. Unable to understand how this had happened or why, or who had engineered the inflation, the victims blamed the government which had failed to protect them, the Allies, and foreigners in their midst whose money was worth so much in comparison with their own. Even those who before had been merely indifferent to democracy now hated it with an all-consuming hatred. My classmates appeared at school with small pamphlets containing the text of the Versailles Treaty and veritable war-councils were held regularly during recess in the courtyard.

The basic material for the Nazi Party was formed during the war and by the defeat. Even before the inflation there were only two boys in my school who did not belong to the Nazi organization, but the inflation had a profound influence on the formulation of Nazi doctrine and ideas and many of my former colleagues are now high dignitaries of the totalitarian state. We had one liberal teacher, the head of the German department. He was cordially hated.

As a result of the inflation, the internal government debt was wiped out, but the backbone of democracy, the middle class, was destroyed. It is true that after stabilization and a return of prosperity, many of those who were ruined by the inflation managed to get back on their feet, but their traditional faith in law and order was gone.

Nor did the Republic gain the allegiance of those who benefited with the government from the organized banditry upon a trusting public ignorant of economic law. The German industrialists who retained the immense fortunes which had fallen into their laps nevertheless acquired no love for democracy. They had never understood, like their western colleagues, that freedom of speech, a free press, parliamentary institutions, and the rights of the individual against the state were basic principles essential to a liberal economy. Man does not live by bread alone. The fleshpots of the controlling class were full, but they continued to long for a powerful state under a new pharaoh who could give them even more power over an even more docile working class and who would confer upon them, as they thought, in the world at large, a standing on a par with the proud merchants and industrialists of the British Empire. The stock-market swindler looks with no more disdain upon the sucker who falls for his line than the Fritz Thyssens, Stinnes, and their friends looked upon the Weimar Republic which had allowed them to enrich themselves at the expense of the nation and the prestige of democracy. Members of the Association of German Industrialists dined often at my parents' home, and I had the privilege of being allowed to stay up and listen to their talk.

Credit Inflation

These men did not consent to a stabilization of the mark until they had drawn from the inflation the last ounce of economic and political benefits to themselves. Now, however, after having concentrated the entire national wealth into their own hands and having bankrupted the state and the middle classes, they found a new source of income from abroad. The Allies proved willing to grant new credits to the German govment in exchange for its promise to fulfil the German obligations under the Treaty of Versailles.

Under the Dawes Plan the reparations were removed from the realm of politics. Germany's ability to pay, not the magnitude of the destruction caused by her, was taken as a basis for calculating the amount she owed. The loans granted to Germany under the Dawes and the Young plans were to be used by the government to pay the industrialists for the delivery of manufactured goods and raw materials to the Allies. The arrangement promised to be very profitable, and the Association of Industrialists withdrew their objection to the fulfilment policy.

The influx of foreign capital produced a credit inflation in Germany which in the end proved more disastrous to democracy than the currency inflation.

Meanwhile, the money borrowed from the victors was used to increase to a maximum the productive capacity of German industry. All industrial plants were modernized and equipped with the latest and most efficient machinery. With renewed confidence in Germany and the revival of world trade, German cities were able to float loans in Germany and on the New York and London capital markets. These they used to construct magnificent municipal buildings, sport stadiums, etc. The wave of prosperity and the willingness to spend lavishly reached the trade unions, whose assembly halls began to rival the banking establishments in marble and metal fixtures.

The inevitable end to the credit inflation began with a crash on the Berlin stock-market in 1927 and ended in a German default on all foreign debts.

But while the foreign creditors were left holding the bag, having thrown good money after bad, German industries had converted all but four billion marks, of the thirty billions which were pumped into Germany, into industrial plants second to none in the world.

It is true that the deflation rendered the plants idle for want of a market for German products at home and abroad, and six million unemployed were thrown on the dole. But Germany now possessed an industrial war potential greater than she had when she went to war under the Kaiser in 1914.

The Comedy of Concessions

The treatment which Hitler received from the courts of the Weimar Republic after the failure of his Putsch in 1923 convinced him that power could be seized "legally" from a government which was unwilling to defend itself. The Weimar Republic, which had done nothing to stop the currency inflation, which had retained the civil servants of the old régime as well as its school-teachers and army officers, treated the leaders of the German counter-revolution with kindly tolerance. General Ludendorff, who had marched with Hitler in the beer cellar Putsch, was acquitted, while Hitler received five years of Festungshaft (confinement in a fortress town).

German Liberals and Socialists in the government and in Parliament saw in the reactionary movement of the Stahlhelm and the Nazi Party an additional means by which the Allies could be induced to make concessions. Pointing to the menace which these movements constituted to German democracy, they begged the victors to grant them support against the internal reaction. The need for such support to the young republic would, of course, be all the more convincing the stronger the reaction appeared to be. Consequently, the foreign agitator who had caused blood to flow in the streets of Munich was not shot, imprisoned, or expelled from the country.

Hitler's attempt to overthrow the democratic government by force was treated as a political offense, for which category the Weimar constitution reserved the mildest form of punishment. Inside his fortified town he was free to move about as he pleased, to receive any number of visitors, direct the Nazi movement, and dictate *Mein Kampf* to his friend Hess. Later, when as Chancellor of the Reich he was courting favor with the reactionary elements in France, he tried to explain away the more violent denunciations of France and the threat which he had made to exterminate "that nigger race," as having been inspired by the hardship which he was suffering in his solitary confinement. Actually, he had written only the first part during his "confinement." The reference to France in the second part was written after his liberation.

After he had served one year of his term, the government let him travel freely throughout the country denouncing the democrats as in the pay of the enemy, as traitors to the cause of Germany, as a product of the stab in the back and the Treaty of Versailles. Once he got into power, he would cause heads to roll, he told a German court when he appeared as a witness for one of his lieutenants, accused of murder. He organized storm troopers and élite guards, incited his followers to riot and murder, and yet met with no resistance from the established authorities. His party members owed allegiance only to him, but the government maintained the fiction that the National Socialist Party was a party like all other political parties and entitled to the same privileges. Although Hitler proclaimed that he meant to take power only by legal means, he at no time confined himself to obtaining followers by persuasion alone, nor did he make any secret of how he intended to govern. His followers demonstrated daily what his intentions were. Yet the men he promised to destroy "legally" opposed him by words only, while the German government addressed daily an S.O.S. to the outside world, appealing to the western democracies to witness their plight and to grant the demands of the German reaction in order to spare Germany and the world the horrors of resurrected German militarism.

Every concession the Allies granted was logically credited by the German people to the Nazis and bolstered the prestige of their leader. Hitler demanded and the Allies granted. While the German government, to gain good-will abroad, asserted that it was willing to fulfil to the letter its obligations under the Treaty of Versailles, Hitler was free to denounce that policy as the sincere expression of the enslavement of the German government to the will of the "enemy-league." Thus the German people were given convincing proof that Germany had not lost the war, since her reactionaries were strong enough to force concessions from the Allies, and that only the Weimar Republic stood in the way of complete and outright abrogation of the Treaty of Versailles. After every concession obtained, the Weimar government pronounced itself satisfied, while the appetite of the reaction grew apace. Long before Hitler seized power the comedy of the "very last demand" was already being played by democratic Germany, while the Allies unwittingly nursed the spirit of Nazism by an appeasement policy which did not yet go by that name and which was intended to act in support of German democracy, while in reality it served to undermine it.

The Nazi Liberals

By using the Nazi movement as a bugaboo to scare the Allies, German democrats raised a Frankenstein monster which destroyed their government and sent its leaders into exile, leaving the rank and file to shift for itself. These for the most part resigned themselves not without enthusiasm to the resurrection of Germany, or ended in the concentration camps.

It is clear that the German Liberals were not so far from Nazi doctrine as they would have the world believe to-day, when they are among its victims. They were Nazis without the brutality and the violence of the Nazis. They are to-day as national and socialist as they were while in power and while serving Nazi aims by winning outside sympathy for that "other Germany" of which they claimed to be the political representatives. To-day, as when they were at the helm of the state, they want the Allies to free Germany from the Nazi scourge and then hand the country back to them on a silver platter, as it were, with its frontiers intact, without any indemnities for the devastation which Germany has wrought upon the world, or the cities and the populations which she has destroyed.

Throughout this war German Liberals in exile have continued to write letters to the editors of American newspapers in which they insist that the Allies and the Allies alone are responsible for the rise of Hitler Germany. The Versailles Treaty was harsh, and it was not abrogated quickly enough. Never again must Germany be treated to a dose of her own medicine. Great Britain, while she still fought on alone, was warned that she must promise not to impose another Versailles Treaty; otherwise, the German people would remain loyal to Hitler. Before Germany attacked Russia there was even a hint that as a last resort fusion with Soviet Russia would be recommended as a way out. In all this recrimination against the western world, there was no *mea culpa* on the part of German liberalism; no suggestion that the only way to redeem Germany would be to overthrow Hitler from within, while the German armies were still victorious; no assurance to the people of Germany that no other fate could be as harsh for them as a continuation of this bloody rule of the Nazis.

To-day, after the entry of the United States into the war, Germans in exile are forming committees headed by such shining lights in the democratic world as Otto Strasser, once the confidant and friend of Hitler; Rauschnigg, who supported Nazism as long as he believed that Hitler might submit to the rule of the Junkers and the industrialists, and scores of others willing to take up where they were forced out by the Nazis. In their view, the rôle of the twenty-nine United Nations in the present struggle is to defeat the Nazis for the sole purpose of installing these "democrats" in exile as the rulers of Germany, preferably a powerful Germany, so that they can have a wide realm over which to rule.

Styling themselves the other Germany, the Germany of post-war pacifist literature, where the Germans were treated not only as quite as good as any other nationals, but even slightly better than the rest of the world, the German liberals in exile are running true to form. This liberalism is oblivious to the

fact that it has lost all prestige inside Germany through the
failure of German democrats to stand up and fight against
the "legal method" by which Hitler and his party seized power.
The contempt in which he held these spineless politicians of
the Weimar Republic Hitler has manifested nowhere more
clearly than in his conviction, constantly reiterated, that he
would become dictator without having to conquer in a civil
war.

When Hindenburg—yielding to the entreaties of his son,
implicated in the scandal resulting from government aid
to East Prussian Junkers who had bankrupted their estates
during the credit inflation—entrusted Hitler with the formation of a coalition government, the rank and file of the Democratic, Socialist and Communist parties in Germany were
sufficiently aroused to have put up a very good fight against
the Nazi hordes. Sheepishly they waited for a call from their
leaders, a spontaneous revolution being out of the question in
Germany. Whereas Austrian Socialists and Spanish Anarchists
can take up arms to fight against the Dollfusses and Francos
without waiting for orders, the Germans are incapable of direct action. Formidable fighters in war under competent command, they are without civic courage to fight against tyranny.
Leadership which they needed was not forthcoming.

The mechanistic universe of Karl Marx, with automatic and
inevitable developments which exercised such a powerful influence upon every immature brain everywhere in the
world, naturally found its stanchest disciples in Germany.
The German Communist leaders had great faith in the doctrine
of historic necessity which would catapult them into power by
the weight of Nazi mismanagement. They believed that they
would be able to take over on their own, and refused to co-
operate with the Socialists and Democrats. The latter, on
the other hand, actually thought that Hitler would remain, as
he promised, within the framework of legality, and afraid to
provoke him, they urged their followers to go home and indulge in no rash action. They were more afraid of losing their
positions and their salaries as party delegates and trade-union

bosses than they were interested in the preservation of German democracy.

The most ludicrous of all incidents prior to the Hindenburg decision to call Hitler, was the ousting of the Prussian government by the Federal Police under orders from von Papen, then Chancellor of the Reich. Throughout the reign of the Weimar Republic, the government of Prussia, one of the Federal states, had been Socialist. Von Papen found this inconvenient, and so he had its members physically ejected from their offices. It was a strong government, as democratic governments go. The entire police force of Prussia had been recruited from Socialist ranks; it was the only service which had been changed for the better by the Social Democratic administration. Besides, Prussia was the largest of all the federal states and had enjoyed a hegemony under the Kaiser. The Socialist government of Prussia could therefore have called upon its police force, devoted to its cause, for aid against the arbitrary action of the federal government. Instead, however, the Prussian government lodged a protest with the supreme court at Leipzig, one of the most reactionary institutions of the Reich. Before this court had an opportunity to decide the issue in favor of von Papen, Hitler was in power and proceeded to abolish the entire federal structure with such separate powers as the federal states possessed under the constitution. At the same time he herded into concentration camps Democrats, Socialists, and Communists—in fact, all those who had urged their followers not to let the Nazis provoke them to direct action.

Fascism versus Communism

The internal appeasement policy of the Liberals, Socialists and Communists, the political consequences of the defeat, the currency inflation, the brief period of prosperity, and the economic crises alienated the Nationalists and reactionaries, the middle classes, and finally the working class from the Weimar Republic. The very idea of democracy, always a feeble force in German national life, became distasteful to all. Both wings, the extreme left and the extreme right, gained the votes which the center parties were losing. They fed upon each other. A success of the Nazis drove decent people to vote for the Communists, who, by their propaganda, claimed to be the only ones possessing a formula which would defeat the Nazis, while on the other hand people who believed that the Communists were to be feared more than the Nazis, were driven to vote for the Nazis, although they did not necessarily agree with the entire Nazi program. In the end, the moderate government, unable to gain a majority in Parliament, governed by decrees which had to be countersigned by the Presidency. In this way, political power passed out of parliamentary control. It was exercised by President Hindenburg, who by that time had relapsed into second childhood, so that it was his secretary Meissner (now secretary to Hitler), who really ruled Germany. The story is told that when the Nazis triumphantly marched past the palace of the President of the Reich celebrating the nomination of Hitler as chancellor, Hindenburg, watching them from the balcony, remarked to his family: "Look, children, my Russian prisoners."

The Weimar Republic died in its infancy. It was born of defeat, and the German people never possessed the faculty of creative thinking and the courage to freedom which might have nursed it through its growing pains. In the end they had but the choice of the undertaker who would bury the corpse. The choice was a narrow one. Between the two authoritarian doctrines which competed for the job, it was a foregone conclusion that native-born National Socialism would carry the day against Moscow-inspired Communism.

Although the Communists had some five million voters behind them, they could not evolve an independent leadership. Moscow kept a strict discipline and insisted upon a policy largely dictated by the interests of the Russian state, interests which did not necessarily coincide with the interests of the Communist Party in Germany. In the feeblest democracy established institutions are entrenched firmly enough to require the utmost resourcefulness and maneuverability of the revolutionary leader to effect an overthrow. But only tenth-rate personalities could rise to the leadership of the Communist Party, since only such men will accept a subordinate position in a hierarchy, and the leadership of any Communist Party abroad is necessarily a secondary post. Subject to the will of Moscow, all Communist Parties, everywhere, are the executive organs of the government in Moscow whence come the inspirations and directives, the so-called party line. Such an organization by its very nature is not revolutionary: at best it is subversive, inspiring enough native opposition to prepare the way for some one else to take over after it has done its share in the undermining of existing institutions.

Nazi leadership was not thus handicapped. Hitler was his own master, indebted only in the monetary support which he received from the industrialists and which he accepted without the slightest inner obligation to repay at any time in either currency or a share in the power.

Furthermore, Communist Parties by the nature of their doctrine suffer from a severe handicap in the art of political oratory. Communism holds out a promise of power only to the proletariat, treating the other classes in society as so much dead wood which must be physically exterminated. The Nazis, on the other hand, could promise all things to all men, and were most convincing, since they had not yet been discredited by the exercise of power. The capitalist ruling class was promised absolute dominion over labor, and labor was promised Socialism, freedom from the rule of the plutocrats, and full employment. The middle class was promised elimination of the Jews from the professions and abolition of the chain and department stores with which the individual shopkeeper could not compete. The peasants were promised the land belonging to the Junkers, and the Junkers were promised the enactment of a law which would prohibit not only the division of the land among the peasants, but even the breaking up of the estates among their children: the eldest son would inherit the estate, and the others could find employment in the expand-

ing army. To the doctrine of Socialism the Nazis added nationalism and revenge for the defeat of 1918. The spirit of
nationalism to date has proved a stronger drawing card everywhere than the internationalism of the Second, the Third, and
the Fourth International, even among the so-called proletariat.
It offers an ideal which can be of equal inspiration to all
classes within the nation, and what it lacks in universality of
human appeal it makes up in nationalistic intensity.

The glaring contradictions in the economic program of the
Nazis in no way harmed their cause. In the general atmosphere
of despair, born of defeat and the economic crisis, each class
and profession believed that that part of the economic and
political platform of the Nazis addressed to it would be kept
at the expense of the others. Thus the task of burying the
Weimar Republic, with its liberal institutions, freedom of
speech and press, freedom of assembly, rule of law, and the
capitalistic freedom of liberal economy, fell to the Nazis.

3

The Army and Hitler

♦

WHILE the Nazi Party was gaining in strength, the German militarists, both professional and amateur, diligently sought to find the true causes of their defeat. At no time were they themselves deceived by their own propaganda—by the legend of the stab-in-the-back and the injustices of Versailles. The defeated have this advantage over the victors, that the lesson of defeat is deeply engraved upon their minds while the victors easily forget the method by which they won through. The menace which they have conquered no longer works as a stimulant upon the victors' imaginations, while the losers, smarting under their defeat, never forget. No one who refuses to accept defeat is ultimately defeated, and unfortunately this is as true of those who fight for an evil cause as of those who fight for liberty.

The principal lesson which Germany drew from her temporary defeat was that she would have won if she had avoided a two-front war and if she had provided against the contingency of a British blockade. The post-war German army consequently urged upon the Weimar Republic the necessity of establishing friendly relations with Russia. At the Conference of Rapallo in 1921, Walter Rathenau, then Foreign Minister of the Reich, succeeded in concluding a commercial treaty with the Soviet representatives. A military agreement was secretly concluded at the same time, and friendly economic relations between the two countries continued to evolve—from then until the Germans attacked on June 22, 1941—with only one interruption. In 1935, Russia and France signed a mutual-assistance pact which induced Hitler to add the adjective Bolshevist to his arsenal of hyphenated invectives.

The signing of the Rapallo Agreement was a great political triumph for the young Weimar Republic and for the German army. But a triumph for the Weimar Republic was also a setback for the reactionaries, and shortly afterward Walter Rathenau was assassinated by the Ehrhardt gang, which later merged into the Nazi movement.

The British blockade was the principal factor in proving the two-front war fatal for German arms. Since such a contingency could arise again, German militarists argued that food and raw material must be stored in sufficient quantities to outlast any war.

The opponents in the First World War were so evenly matched as to demand a supreme effort on both sides before either could win through to victory. It was this effort which gradually transformed all warring powers into totalitarian states for the duration. Though this transformation came too late for Germany, it provided post-war German militarists with a blue-print for a future total development of the German war potential in time of peace, a course of action which in theory would enable Germany to pack sufficient punch into her first onslaught to make all resistance futile.

The wide gulf between officers and men in the German army, fostered by a caste system which with few exceptions permitted advancement to the highest rank only to Junkers, proved to be a severe handicap to army discipline as soon as things began to go badly. The individual German soldier is a formidable fighter when well directed, well fed, and well equipped. But the morale of the most submissive soldier is apt to suffer under the cumulative evidence that his officers are not willing to share and share alike. Resentment expressed itself finally in the slogan: "Equal measure and equal grub would have won the war long ago." The spirit of absolute obedience fostered in the German army by an over-rigid training system proved to be an equally great disadvantage to the individual soldier and small combat unit whenever the situation demanded a measure of individual initiative. In these two respects the democratic armies had the advantage over the German army. Ironically enough, the spirit of democracy which the Weimar Republic failed to awaken in German civil life was introduced in the Reichswehr because it had proved useful to the enemy in warfare, and the Nazis, when they came into power, eagerly encouraged a system of decentralized combat units each equipped with a full variety of weapons and trained in the coördinated use of each as the situation might require. In the training of the Storm Troopers, Captain Ernst Roehm, a former officer in the German army, had employed the same method for street fights with the Communists and for eventual conquest of the nerve centers of the state in case of civil war.

When the German Army attacked Poland and France, it combined the advantages of centralized command with the advantages of decentralization in actual combat. At the same time it was fighting armies which were not only without modern equipment but which, under the influence of French postwar military theory, had lost the flexibility which they possessed in 1914. The French have alternated in their military history between the doctrine of decentralization, when reliance is placed upon the ingenuity of the individual soldier, and the tendency peculiar to a logical people of working out in advance a fixed theory of warfare to which the army command is then inclined to adhere long after the premises upon which the conclusions were based have been altered by unforeseen circumstances. This has given rise to the popular saying that the French are always well prepared to fight the preceding war. But that is only partly true. If they had prepared to fight the last war, they would have followed the example of Germany and built tanks and planes in sufficient quantities, for it was these weapons which finally won the war in 1918. The truth is that the Germans were prepared to fight the last war all over again, trying to avoid the old mistakes, while the French, like all peaceful people, were "preparing" to avoid war at all cost.

In the final stages of the last war, the utilization of the tank, a British invention, and of the airplane enabled the combined armies of France, Britain, and the United States to break the German front. In any future war Germany resolved to appear in the field with whole fleets of tanks and war planes, bombers and fighters. As the war of 1914–18 extended over all continents, knowledge of geography and space became of vital importance to the general staff of any army which intended ultimately to conquer the entire planet. Accordingly, a school of military geography, styled the school of geopolitics, was established immediately after the war by a German officer, Karl Haushofer. He taught that in a constantly shrinking universe, nations with a will to conquer must learn to think in terms of shrinking space. (It is well to note that geopolitics is not a science but merely an attempt to harness all geographical, industrial, and psychological knowledge to the art of war.)

Geopolitics endeavored to develop a program of conquest based on the man-power, the industrial resources, and the geographical position of Germany. German rule was to be expanded over neighboring countries which produced the material necessary to Germany for further conquest. Henceforth, the foreign policy of Germany was to be determined primarily by military expediency. All traditional ties of friendship, common race and culture with other nations, as well as all traditional hatreds, were to be subordinated to the principle of first things first in the program of total conquest of a European-African-Asiatic world under total German domination.

The main contribution to the body of German military doctrine was made by those intellectual forces in Germany which naturally and voluntarily gravitate toward the ideology of total warfare. In the victorious countries, individual military writers here and there speculated with equal foresight upon the nature of a future world war, but in these countries modern military ideas necessarily remained on paper, whereas under the Weimar Republic they were gradually incorporated in the official Reichswehr, which found ways and means to evade the restrictions imposed upon it by the Treaty of Versailles. Besides the Reichswehr, voluntary para-military organizations such as the conservative Stahlhelm and the Nazi military organizations devoted themselves to the task of translating these new military ideas into reality. By the time the Weimar Republic had faded away there had grown up in Germany, in and out of the Reichswehr, a whole body of theoretical and practical knowledge which required merely to be given a free hand and full government support to produce the tanks, planes, guns, and motorized bodies of troops large enough and powerful enough to beat any single army in the world.

Hitler invented little that was new in the methods of modern warfare. The groundwork had been done by the German army when he came into power. He adopted from the United States the dive bomber and the conveyer belt in industry, from England the tank, from Russia the parachute, from foreign writers the theories of geopolitics, from Charles de Gaulle in France the method of mechanized warfare, from the Italian Duhet the theory of the Blitzkrieg. The stabilization of the German mark after the inflation through the intermediary process of the Rentenmark—a monetary expedient based upon the total value of real estate in Germany—had demonstrated that a country is never bankrupt like an individual capitalistic enterprise. The currency may be destroyed, a profound maladjustment in production and distribution may render the factories idle while millions of workers are unemployed, but the basic factors of production, land and labor, are always there.

With these basic materials a powerful totalitarian war machine can be constructed without gold as a medium of exchange. That, in fact, is the meaning of the Nazi contention that money is not important. It is not important when the state can take by force or persuasion what it can not command by giving something in exchange. The model for this state, as well as for the concentration camps and the secret police, Germany found in her own past, the Germany of 1918, and in the totalitarian states of Russia and Italy.

On these grounds many historians are inclined to deny the applicability of the term "genius" to Adolf Hitler. Yet genius in any field—in art, literature, the sciences—draws upon the accumulated knowledge and skills of the past. Its chief characteristic is the ability to combine known elements into a consistent whole of new and vital importance. The term military genius would fit Hitler badly only if it is conceived to be identical with greatness. His personality combines these two explosive elements: genius and infinite philistinism.* His genius consists in the efficient use of the best possible means for his political and military ends. Without any knowledge of foreign countries and their civilizations, he was able to perceive in them military and political weaknesses which were hidden to themselves. Thus, his main contribution to German politics was the conviction, upon which he acted, that Germany would be granted all the time she needed for building up a military machine: there would be no intervention from abroad. He knew that he could go to any length in his speeches and in his action as long as he refrained from a direct attack upon the territories of his future victims, and such an attack he would not make until the army was ready. More remarkable still was his conviction that he would find the democracies virtually unarmed when he was ready for the attack.

Yet there is no mystery attached to this insight. He and his admirers were fond of talking of the Fuehrer's intuition, his uncanny sense of timing, and so on, but there is, in fact, a more rational explanation. His discovery was as simple as the egg of Columbus.

The ideals of the American and French revolutions, which had given birth to democracy, were feeble or non-existent in Germany, but the economic system was built upon the same

* A philistine is one possessed of faith in the ultimate corruptibility of man.

principles of private property, laissez-faire in economics, the profit motive, free enterprise and competition. It was obvious that within the framework of German capitalism no total armament program could be realized. The execution of the plan for a future war developed by the geopoliticians of Germany, the German Army, and the Nazi Party required a radical return to the economic system of the Germany of 1918, where the control over production and distribution, over industry, finance, and agriculture was centralized in the hands of the state.

Hitler planned the resurrection of this totalitarian state and that involved the destruction of capitalism. He knew that no such plan was contemplated or likely to be carried out in the democratic countries. They would consequently remain militarily as weak as Germany was under the Weimar Republic. The government of that republic, as we have seen, put no obstacles in the way of the army or the Nazi Party. The army could exercise in the use of modern weapons to their hearts content and train a black Reichswehr besides the official Reichswehr. The Nazis, financed by the industrialists, could organize combat units. But as long as the economic system remained free from government tutelage it was bound to continue to produce goods in response to a consumers' demand instead of tanks, planes, and cannons. Hitler could consequently foresee six years in advance that once his plan had been executed the democracies would be defenseless.

Hitler's conviction that he would find the democracies unprepared when he was ready for the attack explains his impatience. To be certain of an easy victory and yet be forced to wait six years imposed a severe strain on his nervous system. It is therefore not surprising to read in Mr. Shirer's *Berlin Diary* that Hitler chewed carpets as once Nebuchadnezzar ate grass.

The British Ambassador to Germany, Mr. Neville Henderson, corroborates indirectly Mr. Shirer's story. In his book *Failure of a Mission* Henderson tells that he finally succeeded in convincing Hitler that England would declare war if he attacked Poland. Hitler's rejoinder was: "But I am fifty years old already, when should I make war?"

An Absurd Utopia

Full military use of the economic resources of a country, its raw materials, the mineral deposit in its soil, the developed skills and efficiency of its workingmen, its engineers, its managerial personnel, and its buying power abroad, can only be made by a totalitarian state. In a liberal national economy the supply of goods is determined by demand which in turn is dependent upon the purchasing power of the consumer.

Under the capitalistic system the consumer enjoys a liberty many times more precious than the vote: the freedom to spend his money on goods of his own choosing. It is he who determines what the capitalists must produce in their factories and on the land if they wish to make a profit. If the individual purchaser felt the need for tanks, planes, guns and warships as urgently as he wants a roof over his head, food and clothing for himself and his family, capitalist economy would provide democratic countries with a wealth of implements of war and trained men to use them, so that no force on earth however totalitarian could defeat any large democratic country.

For its absurdity it is worth while to examine what such a militaristic Utopia would look like if there were no natural civilian demands beyond a minimum to keep body and soul together. If man were by nature a militaristic animal the capitalistic system would not produce motor-cars, refrigerators and washing machines in vast quantities. In such a Utopia instead of riding in thirty million automobiles United States citizens would be riding in jeeps, small, medium, and heavy tanks, according to the purchasing power of the individual buyer. There would be at all times as many battleships, cruisers and destroyers at the disposal of the armed forces as there are skyscrapers, apartment houses and municipal housing schemes, as many planes ready for combat or for throwing bombs as

there are railroad locomotives and freight cars, as many air-
fields as there are playgrounds, and instead of sending our
children to school we would have them trained from the tender age of six in military camps. Every Boy Scout would be a
walking arsenal, equipped with tommy gun, revolver and
dagger, trained to put out incendiary bombs, operate a stir-
rup pump and drive an ambulance, while his elders are at the
front.

If individual men chose freely to be armed to the teeth,
industry would have to retool every year for ever-improved
tanks, planes, and warships. The desire to display one's wealth
and standing in the community would spur the Smiths to show
more efficient weapons in their private arsenals than are possessed by the Joneses, and the sportive spirit would inspire
them to acquire greater skill in using them. There would be
no need to transform democratic governments into totalitarian
governments in time of war. On the contrary, such a concentration of economic and political power into the hands of a
centralized government would be disastrous for the efficient
progress of the armament industry. No organization is as in-
efficient as a totalitarian bureaucracy, whether its powers are
usurped by a tyrant or freely granted to a democratically
elected government for the purpose of defeating a totalitarian
state. The centralization of power in the hands of the few and
the regimentation of industry necessitate the setting up of a
bureaucratic machinery which by its very nature is inimical to
efficiency in production.

But since individual men, when relatively free, wish to live
in peace with their neighbors, since all men are selfish enough
to desire food, clothing, shelter and luxuries before they indulge in spending their substance upon implements of war,
liberal economy is primarily a peace economy. The heavy industries, responding to demand, produce steel for merchant
ships, motor-cars, refrigerators and washing-machines. The
demand for these products is so great that even recurrent
economic crises only temporarily interrupt the expansion of
the productive capacity of capitalistic industry.

It is not difficult to outline the conditions for a better and a more equitable social order than that provided by the capitalistic system. In the world in which we live means are not distributed in proportion to needs. If they were, economic crises would be things of the past. There would never be underconsumption owing to lack of purchasing power, hence there would be no overproduction, no idle money, idle machines, and idle men. But if industry were producing goods in response to needs rather than trying to anticipate demand the democracies would not necessarily be better armed in time of peace than they are at present.

The need for implements of war would not be any more urgently felt than under the system of scarcity and unequal distribution of purchasing power. Perhaps a society based upon complete human liberty and economic equality would be even more defenseless than the present democratic state. In the absence of unemployment and idle factories no society would be tempted to create work by an ambitious armament program, and still less could it hope to obtain consent for such a waste of human energies. In the United States during the long economic crisis which preceded this war, the New Deal administration acquired control over the process of production and distribution such as no previous American government had been able to exercise, yet its frequent attempts to employ WPA workers in the production of armaments and to train the CCC youths for the army met with determined and effective congressional and public opposition. Much the same situation existed in all democracies, particularly in France, which was more directly and more immediately menaced.

The government of Great Britain could not have obtained consent for complete regimentation of the country and total war production even if it had seen the need for such all-out preparation for war. The people of the United States even now, long after the Japanese attack upon Pearl Harbor, are still without the sense of urgency which the bombs raining down upon the British Isles gave to the English.

But if it is difficult for nations under attack, with all the moral argument on their side and with the knowledge that they are fighting for their survival impressed upon them, to sacrifice their economic needs for the uneconomic purpose of war, it is impossible for any but a totalitarian government to force them into preparation for war when the world is at peace. As long as the individual citizen has a say in the conduct of his government, however slight, as long as the capitalist is free to produce goods which he hopes to sell at a profit, and the individual purchaser is free to determine by his demand what these goods shall be, no expanding armament program can be inaugurated by any government.

In all states, whether democratic or totalitarian, the government alone is charged with the defense of the country. Only the government appears as buyer on the armament market, and the armament industries consequently produce goods ordered and paid for by the government. From a purely commercial point of view, the government is an unsatisfactory purchaser. At all times it operates in a buyer's market. Enjoying a monopoly on the funds available for defense purchases, it can impose prices and limit the profits of the manufacturer by using its wide powers to establish manufacturing centers of its own, where it can keep a constant check on the costs of production. Moreover, the government itself is dependent upon the electorate for its funds. These funds, the product of taxation, are granted only very reluctantly. Unless the taxpayer can be shown a very good reason for sacrifice, he is not likely to vote Congressmen or Senators back into office if they have spent his money too lavishly and voted for higher taxation to balance the budget.

In time of peace the consumer-goods industries enjoy a better and a broader market than the armament industries. Steady profits from a faithful buying public provide a sound basis for the continued existence of well-organized companies and sustain their expansion during prosperity. When industry is dependent upon the good-will of its customers, honesty is indeed the best policy, and efficient service, high quality of goods delivered, and a competitive price are essential for survival.

By contrast, the armament industry can expand in time of war only. By comparison with the consumer-goods industry it remains essentially a fly-by-night business, in spite of frequent wars.

One may say, therefore, that if to-day the democratic nations have to fight for their lives, it is because free men do not prepare for war.

4

The Rule of Force

IN accordance with its catholic program of being all things
to all men, the Nazi Party had recruited its members and
disciples from all classes, castes, and professions. Princes of
the royal house, ne'er-do-wells of the middle classes and the
working class, engineers and University professors with their
students, Junkers and peasants, newspapermen, lawyers, doc-
tors, and government officials, all those with a thirst for unlimited power, joined the party which promised power to each and
every one, and redress for the shame of the defeat. They were
not bound to one another by any a priori economic interests but
by the spirit of authoritarianism. Such common economic interest as they now have they acquired after they came into power.

It has been argued that if the people as a whole were unanimous in supporting this new ruling class and its purpose, the
régime would need to use no force. It would not have to suppress all freedom of expression and action, employ a secret
police, institute concentration camps and secret trials, and torture its prisoners.

Yet the degree of violence practised by the totalitarian rulers is no true indication of the resistance which they have to
overcome. They operate on the principle of: "Who is not for
me is against me." Thus, even docile submission to their rule
is no certain protection against violence. Even the active sup-
porters of the dictator's aim, the professional bootlickers and
slaves who surround all dictators and make a point of anticipating every whim and impulse of their masters, are not safe
from the machine which they have helped to call into being.

Within the framework of the totalitarian state only the most ruthless and cunning have a chance to survive. The selection of the fittest, which goes on all the time in the apparently static régime, favors the dirtiest hitter, the most underhanded practitioner of the stab-in-the-back. Consequently, it throws to the top of the pyramid of violence the most unscrupulous of them all, the dictator. To maintain himself he has to continue the methods which helped him come into power. Success confirms his belief in the efficacy of naked force, and power for the sake of power becomes for him the ultimate good. A respecter of force only, he is circumspect and cautious in the extreme as long as he senses equal force barring his way.

During his struggle for power, Hitler had to become the leader of the disintegrated reactionary groups and organizations. In his *Mein Kampf* he tells them that they can achieve nothing unless they are all united under one leader, and he leaves little doubt that he himself must be that leader. Unity within the movement is achieved by purging the different groups of those of their local leaders who do not wish to submit to his rule, while the others must consent to secondary posts under Adolf Hitler.

Paradoxically, Hitler was successful precisely because among the rivals for the supreme leadership of the Nazi Party during its formation he was regarded as a zero, useful only because he could electrify audiences with his oratory, but destined to be eliminated as soon as the party had gained power. They saw only the littleness of the man and not his genius. It was this misjudgment of the man which induced the numerous candidates for leadership within the Nazi movement to postpone the issue among themselves and to agree tacitly to let Hitler run the show until an opportune moment for his elimination. The same misjudgment of the man induced the leaders of the other political parties to ally themselves with the Nazis whenever they needed their votes in Parliament or their support during a strike. The industrialists and army leaders in turn supported "that petty fellow" Hitler for the same reason. They felt certain that they would be able to dominate him once he had gained power and had eliminated all their opponents for them. Consequently, the Nationalist Party, representing the industrialists and Junkers, the Democratic, Socialist and Communist parties, found themselves allied at one time or another with the National Socialists on some minor issue. Every such alliance served Hitler as a stepping-stone to power, increasing his prestige among the rank and file of his followers and training him by a process of trial and error in the art of divide and rule. Thus the internal struggle for power in the German state served him as a laboratory for his later struggle for world power outside Germany.

Once power within the state is achieved, and the forces which have opposed or aided the dictator, as the case may be, have been disarmed each in its turn, the totalitarian government hits its stride. Only when all effective opposition has been cleared out of the way does the rule of terror begin in earnest. Throughout his rule the dictator must remain on guard against the treachery he has employed and fostered in all those who share in the exercise of power. Each one of his followers on the pyramid of violence and treachery occupies the same precarious position as his leader—a mere foothold which can be maintained only by constant vigilance. The rule of force, like liberty, demands that it be sustained and expanded every day if it is to last. A dictator and his staff can not afford to relax, nor can they rest at any one point on their road to absolute power. All achievements are their own and none those of the people whom they have subjugated. In the end, to maintain themselves at home the totalitarians must seek to use abroad the force which they have generated, so that they may offer loot and glory to their subjects in exchange for the liberty and the possibility of economic well-being of which they have deprived them.

In the spring of 1933, after Hitler had formed a coalition government of the Nazi Party and the Conservative Nationalist Party, the last controlled elections took place in Germany. In these elections, the Nazi Party obtained more than 40 per cent of the vote, an appalling record for the people of Germany particularly when it is borne in mind that this 40 per

cent constituted the dynamic element of the nation. The opposing 60 per cent was split up into innumerable parties, the
strongest of which was the authoritarian Communist Party,
all warring with each other and unable to unite against the
menace which threatened them all. Yet even with such a powerful minority supporting them, and with the country's industries working part time or standing idle, the Nazis could
not hope to carry through their war program in a minimum
of time and with the greatest possible efficiency. Even if they
had obtained a majority in Parliament, the Nazis feared that
they might be held to account for some of the generous promises they had made to all and sundry. Moreover, such a het-
erogeneous mass of seekers after power are not easily held
together except under fear of reprisal from within or from without.

The Bruening government, to be sure, already ruled by
decrees, but it held its power from Parliament, with limited
duration and for a limited purpose. It still had to give an
account of its action to the popularly elected Reichstag. Without a suspension of legality, the Nazi government would have
been forced to render a similar account. The elements of dis-
unity might in time have led to a split into Leftist Nazis, more
socialist than nationalist, and Rightists opposed to nationalization. The opposition parties, though hopelessly divided, could
have opposed a solid front to Nazi home and foreign policy
at any time later. In any future election the disappointed voters could have deserted the Nazi Party *en masse*. For all these
reasons it was imperative to abolish Parliament and suspend
the constitution. The Nazis consequently burned the Reichstag, then blamed the act on the opposition, though they themselves were the ones who benefited from it. The Reichstag fire
gave them the opportunity to disarm the opposition, and the
reign of terror began.

The Economics of Totalitarianism

The reign of terror united the Nazis among themselves under the leadership of Hitler, but it did not solve the economic

problem, nor did the Nazis, as we have seen, have any intention of offering an economic solution. Theoretically, there are as many solutions to an economic crisis as there are social and economic theories. But for all practical purposes the solution is determined by the character of the nation and the structure of the government to which it is subjected. All crises, evidently, are produced by a maladjustment in the price of raw materials, the cost of production, and purchasing power. In the long run, liberal economists of the laissez-faire school insist, all maladjustments readjust themselves. But in the long run, says John Maynard Keynes, we are all dead. This is the view taken by the great majority everywhere. If a crisis lasts long enough and is profound enough, people are likely to grow impatient and start a revolution, if they know what they want to accomplish by the overthrow of the institutions which have failed them. In the absence of a social ideal and the know-how of realizing their aspirations in practice, people turn to the government and demand that it do something to find work for the unemployed and put the economic machine in high gear.

The easiest way out, the line of least resistance for a totalitarian régime, is the adoption of an armament program on a "colossal" scale. Such a program is by no means an economic solution. It is purely political. It offers guns instead of butter. It imposes a degree of sacrifice upon the nation as a whole which deprives that nation of all economic satisfactions except the very minimum necessary to keep alive. Any economic benefits accruing to the nation from such a program are incidental. The unemployed may all find work in the war industries, but just as many men are pressed into the armed services, whereas under the capitalist system they were not asked to lay down their lives in exchange for the dole. Furthermore, whatever wages the individual working man is allowed to draw for his labor, whether high or low, he can not spend them for goods which are non-existent, and at the same time he is forced to give up the most precious of all economic advantages, formerly gained in a long and painful struggle against the employer—a few hours of leisure on his working day. Nor can the formerly privileged class, the employers, remain economically independent. Such increase in paper profits as the armament program permits them to pocket must remain illusory, with the ever-growing stringency of consumer goods and luxuries, upon which they might formerly have spent their money. They too are deprived of their most important privilege, the control, which they enjoyed under a liberal economy, over the means of production.

Any national economy is a complex machine in which innumerable and infinitely variable cogs are interdependent. It is not possible to change any part of it radically without adapting all the other parts as well to the new situation. The totalitarian economy consequently grows to be radically different from the liberal economy of the democracies. All along the line changes must be made to bring each factor in the economic process into harmony with all others, if the war economy is to function at all. The state can not control labor and freeze wages without controlling capital, finance, and agriculture as well. It can not deprive labor of free trade unions and confiscate their funds without, at the same time, compelling large- and small-scale industries and agriculture to invest their capital in non-profitable enterprises such as the production of expensive substitutes and synthetics. It can not control the import of raw materials without controlling all exports as well, nor can this control be effective without a monopoly on the import and export of capital and foreign exchange. To accomplish its political program, it must have the power to compel the shut-down of "superfluous" factories working for the consumers' market and must allocate the raw material and the labor power thus liberated to the war industries.

Those who maintain that Fascism and Nazism are essentially capitalistic overlook this fact: under the capitalistic system, total preparation for war is impossible. If no effective resistance to the concentration of all economic power into the hands of the state developed in Germany, if a great many capitalists supported the Nazi program, it does not prove that they remained in control of their industries, any more than the submission of the unemployed and the working class proves that these retained the liberties and economic advantages which they won under a liberal economy. The Nazi state has not found it necessary or profitable to slaughter the capitalists and industrial experts in order to establish its ascendancy over them.

Ruthless in its suppression of a docile political opposition, its intervention in the economic process was facilitated by the economic crisis and the incidental economic benefits which the war program conferred upon employer and working man. The Gestapo could refrain from hounding to death such known members of the Democratic and Socialist world before the Nazi seizure of power as were useful experts in industry and science and who refrained from active opposition to Nazi aspirations. How powerless the industrial lords were rendered by the Nazi state is shown by the fate of Thyssen, who changed his mind too late and now is either dead or in a concentration camp.

The Switch-over, or Gleichschaltung

The absence of capitalist resistance to the suspension of private industry is explained in part by the crisis which the capitalists could not overcome by their own efforts. Before the crisis, industrialists were wont to regard themselves as captains of industry steering the national economy toward the common good. But the economic crisis took the wind out of their sails, and whatever evil wind the totalitarian state brought them in loss of control at first blew them and the unemployed some good. It froze wages and created full employment, piled up paper profits and established high tariff rates.

Most large-scale industries were controlled by directors, employed as managers by the stockholders. The position and influence of these were not noticeably impaired by the shift of ultimate power from the stockholders to the state.

A vast armaments program is somewhat like a currency inflation. Instead of printing paper which is backed by no corresponding increase in goods and services, the state fabricates implements of war in ever-increasing quantities, just as valueless as paper currency; since these implements are being paid for in paper currency limited in quantity, the illusion of wealth is created, even though the implements can not generally be exchanged for consumable goods or used to produce consumer goods, like machine-tools. While the value of the mark inside Germany was kept fairly stable, the quality, variety, and quantity of consumer goods steadily decreased. The threat of a currency inflation was ever-present and had to be kept in check by constant reabsorption of the profits made by industry.

High taxes which no parliament would have voted willingly in time of peace were imposed upon corporations and individual incomes. The money that the working class earned but could not spend on non-existent consumer goods was reabsorbed by the state, which forced the savings banks and the insurance companies to invest in government loans whatever liquid funds were accumulated in deposits and savings accounts. Every week "voluntary" contributions for this or that party purpose were collected from house to house with most publicity centered upon the "winter aid," and the compulsory loans for the people's car, which was never delivered, as the funds went to swell the war chest of the state. Thus whatever ready cash was anywhere about and might have been used to bid prices up on scarce goods was absorbed like a sponge by the state. Finally, to make any inflation impossible, all consumer goods were rationed, and there remained only a few luxuries which the rich could still afford and which could be allowed to go up in price without endangering the financial structure of the totalitarian state. Full employment at first increased the total quantity of consumer goods available for distribution. The two main categories of production—guns and butter—met at a cross-roads and ran side by side for a short distance, but after that they parted company, the production of armaments pulling ahead, while the consumer articles remained far behind.

In the over-all picture presented to the outside world, the socialistic part of the National-Socialist program was concealed for a long time. Since labor lost all its hard-won rights, the world concluded that the system must be of absolute benefit to capitalism, particularly as industry was working to full capacity and "everybody" seemed to be making money. This illusion many capitalists and liberal economists outside Germany shared with the Socialists and the Communists. Both believed that capitalism had found its ultimate ideal and its fullest realization in Fascism.

But in the totalitarian state industrial management is subordinated in the hierarchy of values to the government official from whom the manager takes his orders and to whose will he has to cater, just as his engineers, foremen, and working men bow to his will. Unless they are members of the party and occupy high government posts, the Thyssens and Krupps, all powerful in their own domain under a liberal economy, sink to the position of office clerks in the state factory under totalitarianism. Above all else, the totalitarian state is *totally* devoid of the economic motive which governs industry under a liberal economy, in spite of the wastes involved in this latter system by the fact that demand and not economic need governs supply.

The National Armament Trust

The totalitarian state is an attempt, more or less successful in the different countries where it has imposed itself, to transform the entire country into a single nationalized factory, on the model of a vertical trust. The boss is not an able administrator chosen by the stockholders and governed by the profit motive and the law of the land, but a dictator who is bound by no law save of his own making and who is driven to produce as a steady diet for his subjects implements of war, the only goods which can be of service to him in maintaining his position against his employees within and his enemies abroad.

Under the dictator, the highest dignitaries of the party and the military experts serve as managers of the various branches of his factory. Under them again are the importers and exporters, the bankers and the brokers, the industrialists and the Junkers, who perform the function of clerks in the offices of the state. Still lower in the scale are the engineers and experts, who act as foremen over the working class and the peasantry, who as always are at the lowest point in the social scale. The land is as rigidly under state control as the factories are. It is the factory canteen, which feeds the laborers and the army in the service of the state.

The total control of production and distribution of all goods enables the state to dispense entirely with orthodox ideas of sound finance. The money in circulation, the loans floated by the state, the payments made with promissory notes which can be rediscounted by the central government bank, are but so much shifting of cash from the right to the left pocket of the state and back again.

In foreign trade the totalitarian state enjoys all the advantages of a vertically organized trust on a nation-wide scale, backed by diplomacy and armed force. It facilitates the action of its traders as a group in despoiling independent foreign exporters and importers who compete with one another. A totalitarian state can outbid any private company on the international market. It can offer to sell foreign goods and German goods below world market prices, but against foreign currency, and pay with this currency a higher price for raw materials than the exporters can obtain in competitive world markets. Apparently incurring a loss, the totalitarian state still makes a profit in terms of raw materials vital for the armament industry, raw materials which it could not obtain except by paying in gold currency.

Since the state can not be forced to honor its commercial obligations, the foreign businessman who deals with a totalitarian country is forced to demand protection from his own

government. Theoretically he might refrain from doing business with Hitler, but in a practically interdependent world
that is by no means an easy solution. Many business concerns
depend for their existence upon trade with the totalitarian
countries. Nor could they feel that in sacrificing themselves
they would be of service to their country, since there would
be certain to arise some one less scrupulous to take immediate
advantage of the opportunity. When German importers of
French products failed to honor their obligations, France established a clearing system which compelled the French importer of German goods to pay to the French exporters the
money he owed to the German exporters, while the German
importer of French goods paid his debt to the German exporter. Germany took immediate advantage of this bilateral
clearing system to obtain credit from France. Up to the establishment of the clearing system, France had imported more
goods from Germany than she exported to Germany. Afterwards, Germany reversed the situation. She imported more
goods from France and thus compelled the French exporter
to wait for his money until sufficient goods had arrived from
Germany to permit the Banque de France clearance department to pay him with the product of German sales in France.
Thus French exporters helped, in spite of themselves, to
finance the German rearmament program.

During the life of the Weimar Republic, vast credits were
granted to Germany under the Dawes and the Young plans.
The German default, before Hitler, blocked this credit in the
German banks, but the money was there. It was invested in
German industry, and it served the German government for
continuous financing of the armament program. The blocked
mark fell in value to 50 per cent and lower in the capital markets of the world. These blocked marks were bought by the
Russian government and deblocked by the German state bank
to permit the Russians to pay for their imports from Germany.
Thus, although England and the United States no longer
loaned any money to Germany after the fall of the Weimar
Republic, the credits granted to the Weimar Republic to aid

German democracy in its struggle against the reaction and to ensure the payment of reparations to France, served to finance the totalitarian state, the arming of Germany, and incidentally —as luck would have it—the arming of Russia as well.

Russia took advantage of the ease with which she obtained a deblocking of the German mark to pay for German supplies by issuing long-term promissory notes in French francs and British pounds which were discounted on the "black markets" in London, New York, and Paris at the average rate of 30 per cent per annum. It was no loss to Russia to grant such usurious interest rates for short- and long-term credits, since she bought the marks at a greater discount. It was no loss to Germany, since the value of the mark inside Germany was unaffected by these transactions. The loss was borne by the financial institutions of France, England, and the United States—above all by American investors, who had contributed most of the loans granted to the Weimar Republic.

The world-wide economic crisis hit the countries exporting raw material harder than it hit the countries whose industries depended for their existence upon imports of raw materials. The crisis brought a disastrous fall in prices of all raw materials, and access to them was thereby greatly facilitated. It was the exporters of raw materials who found it difficult to find a market for their goods, while countries like Japan and Germany complained bitterly about their lack of access to raw materials, from which they pretended to be suffering. The wool growers of South Africa and Australia, the cotton growers of Brazil and the United States, the exporters of coffee and leather and scrap-iron all found the markets of the democracies shrinking, since these countries were not spending their substance upon total rearmament. In contrast there was an insatiable demand for all raw materials by Germany and Japan. The totalitarian state found itself in the enviable position of the buyer in a buyer's market. It could demand and get from the individual exporter of South Africa, Australia, South America, and the Dutch East Indies the most favorable credit terms against its consent to take the goods of the market.

Even after Germany failed to pay for the goods by exports of her own and demanded constant extensions of credits, these were granted in the hope that some day she might be willing and able to pay.

Whereas Russian imports and exports were carried out by government agencies, the German state contented itself with a strict control over the trade, which was conducted as before by individual importers and exporters, who employed a large staff of traveling salesmen throughout the world.

This retention of capitalist organizations at home, in home industry, and abroad, in the export trade, was without doubt the most ingenious solution of the totalitarian problem. The temptation for the Nazi Party to dismiss, imprison, and execute all former capitalists in Germany, expropriating their property and filling their shoes with stalwarts of the Nazi Party, must have been great. That it was not done is certainly to the credit of the political genius of Hitler. By retaining the independent capitalists in his employ he availed himself of their commercial, financial, and technical ability and their knowledge of foreign trade which it would have taken the riffraff in the Nazi Party decades to acquire.

Hitler had the service of Germans abroad, of members of international cartels such as steel and chemical trusts, with all the friendly relations which this implied between the leading industrialists in all countries. The entire apparatus of importers and exporters, with their established contacts among the inhabitants of foreign countries and the German settlements, was at his disposal. He utilized them all not only economically but politically as well. All trading establishments, salesmen, and sales representatives abroad were pressed into the propaganda and spy service of the state. Many of them acted as an extension of the Gestapo and gave the state the machinery with which it could keep an eye on Germans abroad, and an ear to the ground for public opinion, public prejudices, and channels which were open or might be opened for the corruptive influence of German money, ideas, and offers of power.

This efficient commercial apparatus, which the totalitarian state found in being and took over without having to pay for it, would have been destroyed if the Nazi Party had refused to employ the individual merchants of Germany as quasi-executive organs of the state. As compensation for their loss of economic independence under government control, the Nazi state offered to capitalistic Germany the glory after which it had been hankering for so long. Now German merchants were members of a powerful state before which the world would soon tremble. Something of the shabbiness of belonging to the civilian world was taken out of their hides, and they could now walk about in the uniform of the state almost on a par with the military and the S.S. Although they were still wearing civilian clothes, that was a mere disguise necessitated by the secrecy of their function. It is no accident that the loftiest position attained by a member of this class was the ministry for foreign affairs, which went to a former champagne salesman.

The Milking of the Scapegoat

Higher-ups in the Nazi hierarchy, such as General Goering, of course, had to be compensated by having turned over to them vast properties belonging to German capitalists. An office clerk before the Nazis' seizure of power, Goering now controls a vast iron-ore and steel empire—the largest in Germany: truly a royal compensation for a feudal vassal. The smaller fry in the party, however, had to be content with increased employment opportunities provided by a top-heavy bureaucracy and with what could be taken away from the Jews. The existence of Jews in Germany was a boon to the Nazis in many ways. In fact, it is difficult to see what they would have done without them.

In the economy of the totalitarian state the scapegoat can be made to yield milk for years to satiate the thirst of party members. The total elimination of the Jews from the economic life of the nation was carefully timed. To have accomplished it at one stroke would have dislocated the economy of the country and the rearmament program. Most of the Nazi Party members and ne'er-do-wells who got the positions, businesses, and shops of the Jews first had to be instructed by the Jews who had built it up, in the conduct of the trade, or the practice of law or medicine, or be acquainted with the clientèle in the import and export trade or even the local trade of the traveling salesman and the shopkeeper. Jewish employees were dismissed at once. But the longer the elimination of the economically useful (*wirtschaftlich wertvolle*) Jews could be postponed, just so long did the party retain a reservoir of rewards to be handed out to loyal party members. A reward not yet given is more binding than a favor already received.

Vulgar men are rendered happy by comparing their own state with the miserable state of their neighbors. If all Jews had been bankers and capitalists, their fellow-bankers and capitalists alone would have benefited by their elimination. Fortunately, however, the German Jews were to be found in all income groups of the German nation in exact proportion to their numbers. And again happily, this fact was obscured by the economic structure of German Jewry. They were to be found in larger numbers in certain specialized professions. A large proportion of German Jews were physicians and lawyers —that was noted. But it was not noted that by way of compensation there were none to be found in similar income groups, such as absentee land-owners, managing directors of industrial concerns, in the steel and mining industries, in forestry, among the higher ranks of the army and navy, etc. In the lower income groups there were few Jews who worked as foremen in factories, but there was quite a number of independent skilled laborers and salesmen whose income was no greater than that of other skilled workers, though as salesmen they often had a small turnover capital needed in their trade. Among the lowest income group, again, there were few unskilled workmen but many office employees and salesmen in stores and shops.

In the pyramid of wealth the vast majority of the Jews

were as poor as the rest of the German population, but, belonging to the white-collar class, they gave an external impression of greater wealth, an impression reinforced by the
popular superstition that they are more intelligent in business
than non-Jews. Their gradual complete elimination from the
economic life of Germany therefore could give satisfaction to
popular prejudice and confer by comparison a sense of privilege on the non-Jews—even upon those who were not directly
and materially benefited. As the Jews constituted only one per
cent of the entire German population their elimination from
the professions and the expropriation of their property could
not materially improve the economic well-being of the German nation as a whole, but the Nazi Party did not count many
more members than the Jewish community, and some of these
could take the places of the eliminated Jews.

Great as was the hardship imposed upon the vast majority
of the German people by their new rulers—the long hours of
fatiguing labor in the factories, the rationing of all food and
clothing, and the constant fear of the Gestapo—there was always a margin of misery not yet imposed upon them, which
could be brought to their consciousness by imposing it upon
the Jews. The creation of a dehumanized caste of untouch-
ables was a cheap source of satisfaction which the state could
offer to its subjects, giving them at the same time solid proof
of their racial and national superiority over the Jews. By organizing a pogrom from time to time, with smashing of windows, public beatings, and a proclamation to the world that
these deeds were spontaneous expressions of the popular will,
the Nazi state associated the entire German people with the
responsibility for this savagery, and at the same time trained
its young in the spirit of looting, arson, bombing of foreign
cities, and shooting of hostages, which the German army intended to use as weapons abroad.

The persecution of the Jews had an additional advantage because they are to be found in small numbers in all the countries
which were destined to become victims of German aggression.

Thus their persecution could awaken sympathies for the

Reich among foreign anti-Semites and at the same time could deter those whose sense of justice was outraged from intervening in the "internal affairs" of the Reich by putting the onus upon them of trying to involve their country in war for the sake of the Jews. As the Jews abroad naturally felt the menace more directly, the impression was created that no one but the Jews suffered from Nazi persecution, or were likely to suffer from it in the future, an impression which Nazi propaganda did its best to encourage everywhere. No wonder Rauschnigg reports a long conversation with Hitler on anti-Semitism which the latter finally broke off by remarking: "It is an inexhaustible subject."

Storm Troopers and Junkers

The restraint which the Nazis showed, in spite of the pressure of the Socialist wing of the party, in retaining the established management of industry and trade (with the exception of the Jews), they also showed in retaining the Junkers' direction of the armed forces of Germany. Considerable pressure was brought to bear upon the party to admit the S.A. into the army under the leadership of Roehm, with the avowed intention of eliminating the Junkers. But Hitler could not afford as yet to do without them. An army command is not created overnight, and if the Junkers had resigned from the army and returned to their estates, the building up of the new army under Nazi leadership would have delayed, perhaps indefinitely, the day of revenge for the defeat of 1918 and the conquest of the world. Hitler could not even afford to eliminate from active service the officers of Jewish descent.

There were few or no Jews of pure blood in the army, but the German nobility had intermarried with well-to-do Jewish families in Germany, and quite a number of officers had either a Jewish mother or a father or grandmother. As even these were too valuable to be replaced by raw Nazis, trained only in the use of knife and revolver for fights with the Communists in beer halls and public meetings, the so-called Aryan laws were not applied to the army. In some instances the

Nazis resorted to ludicrous subterfuges. General Milch, of the air force, for instance, had a Jewish father, who had died before the advent of Hitler. As Milch occupied a very high position and was receiving a great deal of publicity, his origin could not be passed over in silence. The Nazis, therefore, induced his mother to go to court and swear a solemn oath, that he was not the son of her husband and consequently was an unadulterated Aryan. Goering bluntly declared all this pure foolishness: "It is I," said he, "who determines whether a man is or is not a Jew."

In the absence of a scapegoat inside the army, Hitler adopted the simple expedient of slaughtering the S.A. Among the prominent victims were Roehm, his friend and comrade, and General Schleicher, the only brain in the army, who at some later date might have rallied the army command against the Nazis. The "blood bath" of June, 1934, claimed thousands of victims in the rank and file of the Nazis. What was their guilt? They were, said the Fuehrer, Communists, and they practised homosexuality.

Apparently Hitler had sacrificed his own army, the Nazi storm troopers who had helped him into power, to the will of the Junkers. But: beware of Greeks bearing gifts! In point of fact the army command paid a high price for their victory. Henceforth they owed allegiance to Hitler as commander-in-chief, and a few years later Hitler was able to dismiss von Blomberg and von Fritsch like office boys and appoint to the high command Nazi generals—either commoners or Junkers who had seen where the power was and who were willing to submit. To-day, the purge among these has begun. Altogether too many generals and field marshals have met their death for any one to believe in the ill-health, apoplexy, and accidents of the official explanation.

The Two Heads of the Hydra

Once the totalitarian ruler has established his supremacy over the industry, agriculture, finance, foreign trade, and army of the nation, he has the technical instruments at hand with which to build the machinery for world conquest. But since such a plan violates the will and the interest of the individual not participating directly in its development or in its incidental economic benefits to those in command, it is imperative to pervert the spirit of the nation as well. Like Jehovah, the totalitarian state can tolerate no other gods. It can permit no divergent opinion and no independent action which might interfere with its set purpose. A minimum of willing coöperation and even of enthusiasm must be gained for the plan if the entire structure of the state is not to break down by the weight of its own violence. Where it fails to gain support it must at least obtain submission to its will and paralyze by preventive measures the spirit of revolt.

Gestapo and propaganda ministry share this spiritual work between them. Their duties are often interconnected and overlapping, which leads to a great deal of friction between the two heads of the hydra, but on the whole they work well and efficiently together. The Gestapo creates by terror the vacuum of thought which the propaganda barrage seeks to fill.

Revolutions, like the Blitzkrieg, are only apparently spontaneous. Every revolution is preceded by an evolution of thought, a change of ideas which finally crystallizes into a definite conception of the purpose for which the revolution is made. The conception of the new world to be created need not be more definite than that which can be expressed in slogans such as: "Liberty, Equality and Fraternity," "Give me liberty or give me death," "No taxation without representation," or the more elaborate one of the Russian Revolution, "The land to the peasants, the factory to the workers, all powers to the Soviets"—a slogan which can be paraphrased: "Free access to the means of production"—but it must be widespread enough and inspiring enough to move the people to spontaneous action. It must have penetrated the police and the army to ensure its success. An atmosphere must be created in which a general strike can take place, a descent upon the arsenal of the state organized, and in which the nerve centers of the government—the telephone, telegraph, broadcasting system, and communications—can be seized and operated without effective opposition from the organs of the state.

The slogans of the revolution must be fully supported by the popular will, determined to make room for the new order —at the price of one's life if need be—by the overthrow of all established institutions of the despotic state. Such a determination is never born of misery and oppression alone. If it were, the state would not endure long enough to permit an analysis of its nature. The will and the resolution to create a better and more equitable social order, the slogan of the revolution itself, can be born only of a friendly exchange of ideas. It presupposes the existence of some freedom of speech, unhampered means of self-education, at the very minimum the fearless discussion of events among neighbors. In addition, therefore, to the suppression of all public meetings and the freedom of the press, the Gestapo must seek to undermine the confidence which friends and neighbors have in each other. Since it is technically impossible to set a watch over every individual in the nation, rewards of money and power in the state are offered to all who will denounce their neighbors for any subversive utterance or deed.

Thus an atmosphere of mutual distrust and suspicion is created which prevents the spirit of solidarity from developing among the exploited and the oppressed. The greater the general poverty, the more attractive the bribe, however small, which is held out to the informer, so that at times the wave of denunciation grows to epidemic proportions, and the necessity of rewarding the traitors threatens to put a heavy burden upon the treasury of the state and upon the available government posts which it can offer to them. When this point of diminishing returns is reached, the chase is called off. Newspapers and the radio are instructed to flay the practice of denouncing one's neighbor; several false denunciations are discovered and the culprit punished with ostentatious showing of justice, and the threatened dislocation of industry and administration is averted. The purpose has been fulfilled. The vacuum of constructive thought, in which the outpourings of the propaganda ministry can gain credence, has been created.

In contrast with the terror on the crest of the wave, the let-up brings relief. It is then that the propaganda ministry denies the horrors of the concentration camps and assures the world that it has never so much as hurt a hair on the head of a Catholic priest, a Protestant parson, a pacifist, or a Jew. If it has instituted concentration camps it has done so only for humanitarian reasons, to prevent the righteous indignation of the citizen from taking a spontaneous revenge upon the enemies of Germany. Hence the term preventive arrest for kidnapping, torture, and assassination.

5

National and Racial Hypocrisy

BUT the negative program of terror, which effectively prevents the crystallization of a determined opposition, can not be depended upon to inspire willing coöperation with the plan of the state. If fear and distrust are not to paralyze all action, a maximum of enthusiasm must be generated to build the totalitarian war machine in the shortest possible time. The propaganda ministry therefore manufactures an ideology in harmony with the plan of world conquest. To it is entrusted the task of making the unpalatable fare of the state palatable, the lie plausible, and the truth inaccessible. For lack of a human ideal it manufactures an ideology made up of the shoddiest material of calico words woven into a tissue of ready-to-speak phraseology and brought to the consciousness of the nation via the conveyer belt of the air. The radio, the loudspeaker in the street, the mammoth meeting supported by fanfares and Wagnerian opera settings, a press staffed with rewrite men whose duty it is to furnish variations on the theme handed out by the propagandist-in-chief and his lieutenants—all serve to build morale at home, and to undermine the enemies' morale.

In 1928, D. H. Lawrence spent a vacation in Germany and wrote a remarkable letter about his experience. He felt that Germany was receding like a great tide into the primeval forest.

By 1930, three years before Hitler seized power, the division of Germany between Communist and Nazi authoritarians, and the course Germany was taking could be seen with the naked eye. In February of that year I had completed a course

of studies at Columbia University in New York, and decided
to try to work my way back to Europe.

The employees of the German steamship company advised
me to apply for a job on one of their boats at the docks. There
was a little hut near the berth of the Hamburg Amerika line,
where I waited all day with some twenty German sailors for
the foreman to come and hire us. He never did turn up and
I never came back for the job. But the experience proved to
be more instructive than many a day spent at the University.

The sailors talked politics and nothing else. The debate was
dominated by a big fellow who led them on with the consummate skill of the born propagandist. He was a better man than
Goebbels. It took me exactly eight hours to find out where he
stood and by that time he had swayed the entire audience to
his point of view. All day long the discussion turned about the
respective merits of Communism and Nazism. There was much
to be said in favor of both. Neither party had been in power
in Germany and neither was discredited. None of the other
parties, every one agreed, were worthy of consideration. All
had been in power or had participated in a coalition government and all had proved that they were no good. The first
part of the day every one, following the leadership of the big
fellow, agreed that the Communists were preferable to the
Nazis, but toward the end they had all swung over to the
Nazis. The Young plan was being debated and Nazi opposition to the plan clinched the argument in their favor. "We
will," said the big fellow, "be enslaved to the third generation
if the plan goes through." (He said he had this on the highest
authority.) "But it will not go through. If Hindenburg signs
it, the Nazis have two hundred thousand men well armed who
will march into France and rip the country apart." There was
much nodding of heads and general approval. Having kept
quiet all day I asked a naïve question: "Where were these
two hundred thousand men in 1918?" This question angered
the big fellow. Up to then he had spoken in the suave manner of a man of the world. The whole discussion was carried
on by all with the calm with which well-brought-up people

decide in which restaurant they are going to dine that night.
When the good points of the Communist Party were in the
forefront they were all agreed on tasting of that dish, but they
switched to the Nazis with the same ease. My question stamped
me as an outsider. A skeptical fellow, eh, a calf making off
on his own, away from the herd. I was told in no uncertain
terms to keep my trap shut.

"What do you know about 1918? You are not even dry behind the ears."

"Don't talk until you are spoken to!"

After the seizure of power I saw the effect of Nazi propaganda upon Germans elated with its promise in a middle-aged
country woman who got on our train at Hamm. She wore a
black satin dress, festive for her visit to town. Her face flushed
with suppressed excitement when she confided to us apropos
of nothing, and before finding a seat for herself, that they were
building underground barracks for the soldiers near her farm!

But this starry-eyed adoration of underground funeral par-
lors for the burial of a civilization is only the Sunday spirit
of Nazi Germany. For weekdays the fare which feeds Nazi
morale is prosaic, substantial, cooked in one pot, and suitable
for every palate. This is the flavor of the *pièce de résistance:*

A few days before the conference of Munich which delivered the Sudetens to the Nazis and rendered Czechoslovakia
defenseless I was in Kaunas, the capital of Lithuania, where
I stayed at the Metropol Hotel on the Liberty Boulevard. The
Lithuanian Army, celebrating Independence Day, was parad-
ing past the hotel. At the hotel I had met a colleague of my
schooldays in Frankfort-on-Main and was having breakfast
with him. We had not seen or heard from each other for fifteen years and were exchanging reminiscences. My ex-school
friend, however, was more interested in the parade than either
in our conversation or the food. He told me that he was married and I asked after the mother of the girl who had been
very kind to us when we came to fetch her daughter for an
excursion or to a dance. He explained that his mother-in-law
was living with him and his wife, and was possessed of a spirit

of contrariness which was a disturbing influence in his peaceable existence. In spite of all she had been told, she still persisted in asking: "What harm have the Jews ever done to anybody?"

My ex-friend was untroubled by any doubts on the subject. While we were at school he had boarded with a Jewish
family and had seen and heard plenty. For one thing they all
stuck together, conspired to induce him to buy his clothes in
a Jewish store, themselves bought the breakfast rolls from a
Jewish baker, and read the *Frankfurter Zeitung*. The most
disturbing element was that it was all done so cleverly that
it demanded a really keen mind to detect the sinister purpose
behind it all. They did not tell him frankly that they wanted
him to make his purchases at particular stores because these
were owned by Jews, but ostensibly because the goods were
well priced and under the circumstances there was hardly a
way for him to refuse. Worse yet, he could not help reading
the *Frankfurter Zeitung*. It was there to be had for the asking
and it was well written with news from all corners of the
globe. It was true, it was not owned by Jews, but it was a liberal paper. Undeniably there was something very attractive
about the viewpoint of the editors and that was the worst of
it. It required prodigious efforts in self-control, genuine forti-
tude of character, not to fall victim to its insinuations.

I asked him about conditions in the Reich and he assured
me that everybody was well taken care of. There was, for
instance, Heinz Schroeder who had been in our class. His father had bequeathed him a cement factory. The factory had
burned down and the ministry of warfare had refused him
the material necessary for reconstruction, but that was no
tragedy. He had been assigned as an engineer to the construction of the Siegfried Line where he earned an adequate
salary. So and so had risen high in the Nazi hierarchy. I was
asked to remember that he had shown great promise as a
leader even at school. My friend himself had no reason to
complain. He was in the coal business, exporting to the Baltic
countries and even to Poland. Besides he was a reserve officer

in the German Army attached to the intelligence service. He
saw his own future and that of Germany as quite secure. The
mark had kept its internal value and there was only red tape
connected with obtaining foreign exchange for business trips
abroad. Hitler had the political genius which the older Germany had lacked and for want of which she had lost the war.
As to Czechoslovakia, there would be no war. France and
England knew well the state of German armaments. They
were too weak to fight Germany and besides the Fuehrer did
not want war. Since the remilitarization of the Rhineland, Germany was secure from any French aggression and certainly
England could do nothing. She had no army and her navy was
made obsolete by the German air force.

I assured him that in the long run the military strength of
any nation is no greater than the justice of its cause. Germany
might be getting away for a long time with what he called
diplomacy, but in the end she could not win. "You have
trampled underfoot your own blood brothers, the Austrians,
now it is the turn of the Czechs, next it will be all your neighbors. You have earned the contempt and the hatred of the civilized world, and even if you should be victorious in war, you
will find it impossible to live in a world of your own making."

I was not at all as certain of my argument as I tried to appear, but in any case, it was impossible to shake his complacency. I was, he said, with a friendly smile, a born preacher.
But words would avail nothing. He pointed to the parade of
the Lithuanian Army, at once fascinated by its martial air and
contemptuous of the penury of its equipment. For a tiny peasant people, considering their lack of natural resources, he assured me, with unaffected objectivity, they had not done
badly. They were as well equipped as the Poles, relatively
speaking, but, of course, a single German battalion would
make mincemeat of all that Lithuanian horseflesh, and but
little more would be needed to deal with Poland.

Not all of Germany was moved to frenzied enthusiasm by
the harangues of the Fuehrer. In his speeches before he be-

came Chancellor of the Reich and after his line was to emphasize the fourteen years of untold misery which the Versailles
Treaty and the "Jewish" Weimar Republic had inflicted upon
the innocent German people in general and the hard-struggling
Nazis in particular. Never a discourse without the fourteen
years. During one of them I sat next to a German girl who
took advantage of a pause in the Fuehrer's flow of oratory to
say quietly to herself: "Now come the fourteen years." And
so they did, producing a titter all around.

I, Too, Belong to It

In the years before the war, the other Germany, submissive
but unmoved by Nazi blandishments, was more in evidence
than now, when it has been successfully maneuvered into a
fight to the bitter end. That Germany was made to suffer from
the philosophy which, as Heine predicted, has produced the
German totalitarian state. It consists of people too terrorized
to dare lift their voice in protest.

Traveling through Germany before the war, I met many
people who had remained immune to Nazi ideals. Once, having missed an express train in Tilsit, I took a local to Insterburg, traveling third class. Both cities are in East Prussia,
which has been, from time immemorial, even more reactionary
than the rest of Prussia. Riding with me were five railroad
workers in their work-clothes. They laughed good-naturedly
at my struggles with too much luggage, and I offered them
cigarettes, which they accepted with thanks, but for a while
there was no conversation. At one of the innumerable halts
two of them got up to leave, one wishing me good day while
the other said, "Heil Hitler." As soon as these two had gone,
one of the remaining men got up to investigate whether there
was anybody outside our small compartment, and on his return we all moved together like conspirators, plunging into
the subject of the Nazis without any preliminaries.

The totalitarian victims develop a sixth sense which tells
them to whom they can talk freely without fear of denuncia-

tion. There was never any effort on my part to elicit information about the state of mind of non-Nazi Germany. It revealed itself without my asking. Whenever I was confronted with a pair of eyes holding that look which the hunted have everywhere, it required no more than a gesture of encouragement to call forth a flood of words too long dammed up. They were as thirsty for knowledge of the truth about the outside world as a traveler in the desert is for water. "We," the railroad workers told me, "are kept in total ignorance of what is planned or what is going on abroad. None of us believes a word these bare-faced liars have to say, nor do we listen. They are preparing for war, that is certain, and yet we must say nothing. Already we can not afford to buy margarine, let alone butter. And it is getting worse. Formerly, we could go across the frontier and have a meal in Lithuania, and read an uncensored newspaper. Now they have closed the frontier."

"But why," I demanded, "do you stand for it? Are you not man enough to band yourselves together and throw these rascals out?"

They looked at me without resentment. "How can we? They have the arms; the peasants are with them, and no one can trust his neighbor. Don't you know how the Socialists let us down when we did want to fight, and the Communists, for that matter: they have all gone over to the Nazis and are now strutting about in brown. And you, the world outside, will you do nothing until they fall upon you?"

Some time later I had the confidence of a peasant who told me that the workers were all for Hitler and one could not count on them.

One porter in Insterburg couldn't bear to say good-by to me. He seemed to feel as if I were a long lost friend about to leave forever. Taking advantage of the momentary absence of the Pullman porter, he carried my luggage into the sleeping compartment for me.

That gave him an extra word or two until the Pullman porter, whose privilege it is to take care of the luggage, appeared. When he found this rule broken, he terrorized my porter into instant flight by demanding to know what business he had to get on the train.

My traveling companion on that express train turned out to be the German vice-consul in Memel, going back to report to Berlin. This was the year 1935. The vice-consul took advantage of the long journey to read Hitler's *Mein Kampf*. It had only then dawned on him that it might be useful to his career to read the "tripe." Being a Junker, he had been inclined to think that the Nazis would not last. Owing to my misfortune in Tilsit, there was something wrong with my ticket which I straightened out by paying the difference to the controller, but not before he had dramatized the incident into a life-and-death problem. Think what would have happened to him if he had not noticed! Deathly pale with excitement, he demanded: "How could you have jeopardized my life? Don't you know the kind of world I live in?" Apparently unreasonable, his tirade against me was intended for the ears of my companion, who understood perfectly well. The Junker looked up from his book to chide the controller: "Come, come now, it is not so bad as all that; after all, I too belong to it [this régime]."

But as the years went by, and conditions grew worse, and the world outside began to bow to the will of Hitler, the other Germany withdrew into itself. Silence settled on the land. It was that peculiar apathy which all travelers to the totalitarian lands have noticed. Even the fall of Paris produced no genuine enthusiasm. Mr. Shirer reported that of all the multitude on the beach of the Wansee near Berlin, only three people bought the extra edition announcing the victory. This in spite of the fact that even before the war of 1914, we learned to sing, in the German kindergarten which I attended: "Our captain mounts on horseback, leads us to battle. Victoriously we will beat France, yes France. . . ." Perhaps it is with long cherished hopes of conquest as it is with long cherished worthier ideals: their fulfilment is not nearly as grandiose as it seemed in anticipation.

Where There Is Smoke . . .

Where the uninterrupted bark of the Nazi propaganda machine fails to generate genuine enthusiasm, it succeeds well enough in planting the conviction in the minds of many that the Nazis are right. For so much smoke there must be a fire somewhere. It is not always easy to see that the fire has been laid by the Nazis themselves, and they have never failed to take this elementary precaution. To give their action against the political opposition an aspect of legality, they burned the Reichstag, spread the legend of the stab-in-the-back, invented the international Jew as a polluter of the "pure" Germanic race, encouraged homosexuality in the lower ranks of the S.A. and exterminated them for the same reason. They violated daily the concordat with Rome and justified this violation by accusing Catholic priests of sexual perversions and illegal dealings in foreign currency. Hostility to Nazism in the world was described as being due to hatred and envy of Germany.

To justify the occupation of Austria, Hitler inspired the assassination of Dollfuss and then represented to the German people the suppression of the Nazi Party in Austria as an act of provocation against the Reich. The Nazis inspired Sudeten opposition to the democratic rule of Czechoslovakia and denounced the feeble measures of defense taken by the government of Benes in terms which would have been appropriate only for the treatment which they themselves inflicted upon their victims in Germany. During the Spanish civil war they sent tanks and planes to Spain to combat the Loyalists, but told Germany that France and England were intervening on behalf of Spanish Communists. As an experiment in warfare they wiped out the little village of Guernica, center of Catholic democracy in the Basque region of Spain, and so effectively denounced the Loyalists for this crime that British newspaper editors began to doubt the veracity of their reporters who had witnessed the attack. The correspondent of the London *Daily Express* in Spain had to cable three confirmations of his original story: he finally threatened to commit an act of violence upon the next person imprudent enough to ask him what *really* happened.

Before Munich the German press campaign against Czechoslovakia induced Mr. Chamberlain to send Lord Runciman to that country to find out just how badly the Sudeten Germans were being treated, though the consular representatives of Great Britain and the Embassy in Prague constituted quite adequate eyes and ears of the British Empire. The trouble was that they found nothing to report, since there were no persecutions. Thus the Nazis succeeded in putting the burden of proof upon the accused, a practice so dangerous to the innocent that centuries of jurisprudence have been devoted to the development of safeguards against the natural tendency in a judge or a jury to regard the accused as guilty merely because he has been under suspicion.

To justify their invasion of Poland they employed against the Poles the method which had succeeded so well against Czechoslovakia. Daily the German press invented assassinations and tortures of German men, women, and children in Poland. Czechoslovak and Polish mobilization was described as an act of provocation and aggression, while the invasion of Poland was defined as a counter-attack with pursuit.

The Colossal Lie and the Lie Seasoned with Truth

In addition to the method of laying fires wherever smoke was needed, the Nazis employed a variety of other forms of lying, as the situation required. The most favored method, which appealed to the Fuehrer himself as the most effective, was the colossal lie—so great and all-embracing, so much at variance with the truth, that people who are fundamentally decent and employ lies only where they do not hurt too much and in order to escape minor unpleasantness—such as being late for dinner—must be impressed. Since people judge others by themselves, it is assumed that they will think even a propaganda ministry incapable of lying to the point of murder. A further requisite for the success of the colossal lie is a knowledge of the truth in the liar. Evidently, one can not state the opposite of the truth unless one knows what the truth is.

The source of this knowledge is one's self. Do we plan conquest of the world? Then we must find some one else to whom we can attribute this intention. For this purpose the Jews were handy as a small minority. Hence the plan of world conquest as worked out by the Nazis, complete with propaganda and fifth column, is attributed to Jews and can be found in the document entitled the "Wise Men of Zion." Written long before the war of 1914 in Russia, by the secret police of the Czar, it provided a veritable gold-mine of inspiration for the Nazi state. Great minds meet across the decades.

In order to undermine a country for invasion, military men and spies are sent out by the German government as tourists to prepare the ground, to bribe government employees in key positions, to study the lay of the land, and to occupy strategic posts, all of which facilitates the invasion. Before the occupation of Romania by the Germans the Nazi press reported the discovery of just such an invasion army of tourists in Romania. Who were these people? The answer was, "Englishmen."

After the occupation of Poland, military documents were discovered to show that England and the American Ambassador to France, Mr. William C. Bullitt, had planned to induce Poland to invade Germany. In Norway, a complete plan for British invasion was found, from which horrible fate Norway was preserved by the German invasion, carried out just in the nick of time. It was in the nick of time, too, that Holland and Belgium were preserved from the atrocity of a French-British invasion, once again inspired by Mr. Bullitt and President Roosevelt—whose name is really Rosenfeld, as every one knows. France, in turn, went to war at the instigation of the United States and perfidious Albion. Fortunately, there was always Germany, the knight in shining armor, miraculous reincarnation of Joan of Arc, who rescued the misguided French from the fate of dying for Danzig and England or the even worse fate of being enslaved by Great

Britain. If the United States sent armaments to England, Britain had to be warned that Roosevelt wanted Englishmen to die for the preservation of the United States, so that America could absorb the defunct British Empire. On the other hand, it was equally obvious that President Roosevelt was getting his country into war step by step in order to rescue the British Empire.

If the democracies are pretending to have gone to war for the establishment of President Roosevelt's Four Freedoms, the Nazi machine has a moral purpose of its own: "Germany fights to redress an injustice; the others fight for its preservation." The democracies are denounced for trying to encircle Germany, by establishing a world-wide conspiracy against her, and a profound understanding is declared to exist between plutocratic nations and the Bolshevists. The potential force of the colossal lie is not exhausted by total inversion of the truth. The opposite of the colossal lie is not necessarily the truth. Thus Germany could proclaim her undying hatred of Bolshevism at one time and as expediency demanded conclude an eternal friendship pact with Russia at another time, and reverse that again by going to war against her.

Clearly the various methods fuse into one another, but there is still a variation which deserves separate mention. That is the method of seasoning the lie with a generous sprinkling of the truth.

Evidently life in the democracies is no economic Utopia in the very best of circumstances. The democratic state is a class state, with a very defective economy. In periods of prosperity and full employment for all, hope of constant progress makes life bearable, but in times of crisis, despair grips men who are thrown out of work and who have to fall back upon charity, the dole, and occasional employment to keep their families alive.

Nor can it be said that the political representatives of the nation, democratically elected to Parliament or Congress, are always inspired by genuine love for the interests of the people whom they represent. Where they are thus inspired, they serve to illustrate Plato's dictum that it is necessary not only to will what is right but also to know what it is right to will. The rare idealist who combines both qualities, the will and knowledge of the means to serve the collective interest of the nation, finds that the weight of established institutions, the inertia of the masses, and the resistance of vested interests effectively block radical changes for the better.

The idea that the state in its relations with foreign countries can do no wrong is no monopoly of German state philosophy. Democratic countries have been guilty in the past of aggression against their neighbors and against small nations and peoples in distant lands. The treatment of colonial peoples has not always been inspired by a fair give-and-take to the mutual advantage of the white man and the black. The white man's burden, as one Englishman put it, has for the most part been borne by the black. In the "freest of all democracies," the Negro enjoys no more than a purely nominal equality before the law, while he is barred from the more desirable professions and positions in the economic and social life of his country.

It is not only in Nazi Germany that people are unable to convince themselves of their own worth except by denying the worth of those who belong to a different race, creed, or color.

These grave defects of an order which has failed in reaching the ideal for which it was created—complete human liberty and economic equality—are of course grist for the mills of the German propaganda ministry.

With such material at hand, it takes little talent to paint a somber picture of life in the democratic nations. Here the lie is fed by the best minds, the finest social idealists, and the most courageous rebels against an unjust world. Every Utopist of the nineteenth century can serve as a stick with which to beat the hapless democracies, because from the lofty viewpoint of Utopia there is no difference between the modern capitalist and the feudal robber baron, between the wage-earner and the slave, between the Catholic Church and the

Spanish Inquisition. Socialist and Communist literature in particular have provided the Nazis with a phraseology which Goebbels knows how to fit perfectly to the comfort of a people suffering from constant and chronic deprivation. When speaking to the German people of the democracies, Hitler and Goebbels ascend to the rarefied air of the Utopian mountain-peaks and tell a story of decadence, corruption, ruthless plutocratic exploitation, poverty and want. Nothing else is so comforting to the downtrodden and the oppressed as the knowledge that they have fellow-sufferers and nothing so discouraging as the picture of a world beyond the frontiers from which there is no hope of salvation.

Nevertheless, in the Nazi view the democracies are wealthy. They are the "Have Nations," rich in natural resources and possessed of industrial plants which provide their citizens with a wealth of superfluous luxuries. A visit to the local German cinema showing a Hollywood movie is proof conclusive that all Americans live in palaces, ride to work in automobiles as big as the barrel of Heidelberg, and take their midnight snacks from well-stocked refrigerators as large as a house.

If Germany, Italy, and Japan are "Have Not Nations" it is because these enemies have grabbed and monopolized the world. But under the influence of their wealth and comforts, unheard of in totalitarian states, they have grown soft. They no longer know how to live dangerously. These petty bourgeois have no higher ideal than peace. They deck themselves out in their Sunday best, carry umbrellas, and take their families out for Sunday picnics after church. It is only right that the young and vigorous nations who know how to live dangerously should fall upon them and deprive them of the wealth of which they have robbed Germany by the Treaty of Versailles, first tricking her into surrender and then betraying her good faith in the humanitarian promises of their rulers.

The lie tempered by fact has been most effective in Germany, and it has the additional advantage that it serves without modification for foreign consumption. At a distance the inferno of Germany might look to the unimaginative no worse than Purgatory. Those who have nothing to fear from a 2:00 A. M. visit of the Gestapo because they do not live under German rule might, if they were lacking in imagination, believe life under a dictatorship no worse than under a democracy. Everywhere life is rather a hard struggle, and at least the Nazis abolished unemployment, strikes, and lockouts. The choice might appear to be one between the insecurity of the capitalistic system and the security of totalitarianism, where the state takes care of all, assigns a job and a place to each, and provides them with all the spiritual food they need.

The Truth versus the Lie

Abroad Hitler promised peace to a war-weary world, at home he promised to resurrect the military might of Germany. This contradiction did no harm to his cause in world politics for the same reason which accounts for the success of his contradictory economic program in domestic politics. He was believed abroad because peace was most desirable to a war-weary world; he was believed in Germany because military power was the highest national ideal of Germany.

The effect of German propaganda abroad will be more fully discussed in a later chapter. Here I shall attempt a more detailed analysis of the psychology of the German people up to the outbreak of war. The growing resistance of the nations under attack by the German army came as somewhat of a surprise to the people of Germany, and a discussion of their present morale is reserved for the chapter dealing with American counter-propaganda after the German declaration of war upon the United States.

Before the Nazis were able to suppress the opposition, an excellent liberal press in Germany attempted to fight their lies with the truth. The archives of the German foreign office revealed that the Imperial German Government had been spoiling for war in 1914. This fact was constantly recalled, as were also the frantic telegrams of Ludendorff and Hindenburg begging for an armistice at all cost, because the German army could not hold against the allied offensive in the autumn of 1918.

Although the archives proved Germany's war guilt and the telegrams disproved the stab-in-the-back, it was of no avail. In combating the propaganda of the Nazi Party with the truth the liberals were pushing in an open door. They erred in thinking that German youth in particular and the German people in general were being misled by the systematic perversion of history apparent in all of Hitler's discourses. In reality every man, woman, and child in Germany knew that the Nazis were lying.

The railroad workers to whom I talked in East Prussia, for example, were by no means men of overwhelming and penetrating intelligence, yet they could see through the Nazi game; the disciples of Hitler, and his growing army of fellow travelers were just as clever as the opposition, but they gloried in the multicolored lying of their Fuehrer because of the single-minded purpose which dictated all his utterances. The end justifies the means. Since the end of Nazism was the resurrection of militarism the attack on the means was bound to fail. It was bound to fail because the truth can not prevail against a lie hallowed by a sacred cause. And lest some simpleton be misled by the Nazi propaganda line for foreign consumption; lest he fear that Hitler be sincere in demanding universal disarmament, Hitler's paper, the *Voelkischer Beobachter* took good care to reassure him:

"Do not worry; if all are disarmed, then we shall strangle the French with our bare hands."

Hence it would be unfair to charge the Nazis with having misled the people of Germany by their propaganda. In 1926, Hindenburg was elected with an overwhelming majority under the slogan: The Saviour. But he failed to deliver the goods. Hitler on the other hand did not fail. He kept his promise. Thus it is clear that the broad masses of Germany were the only ones not misled by the personality of Hitler; by his violent misuse of the German language; the jargon of the infantry drilling-grounds, and his wisdom gathered from the reactionary press. Every one else, including such able foreign observers as Dorothy Thompson who was among the first to understand the menace of fascism, saw only the little corporal who had failed to rise in any peaceful pursuit.

Only the people of Germany were not deceived. With unfailing instinct they saw in him the military leader, the political genius who could best not only the puny politicians of the Weimar Republic, but the statesmen of the great foreign democracies as well. Throughout his career Hitler took the existence of a German national will to world domination for granted. He was not its creator but merely its prophet. In 1933 as we have seen he had convinced some 40 per cent of Germans that he was the leader, and it must be presumed that by 1935 it was clear to at least 90 per cent that he was fulfilling his promise because, in that year, the territory of the Saar voted under international control for a return to the Reich and gave Hitlerism a majority of 90 per cent.

A Just Cause

The crime being premeditated the principal function of the propaganda barrage was to provide the people of Germany with an apologia, a vindication of the justice of their cause. The propagandist pleaded not guilty at the bar of history before the assault upon all peaceful people at home and abroad was committed.

The need to vindicate German aspirations by a moral cause made up of the whole cloth arises from the incontrovertible fact that the people of Germany belong to the human race. Members of that race can not contemplate evil deeds against their neighbors without representing themselves as peaceful and peace-loving, while decrying their designated victims as full of evil designs. The wolf in a state of nature needs no such justification. It devours the sheep because mutton is its natural dinner decreed by nature, but the wolf in the fable representing a human being is compelled to adopt a stratagem.

"You are dirtying my water," says he to the lamb—or, in Nazi parlance,—"you are interfering with my living space."

"How can I," asks the lamb, "when I am drinking below stream?"

"You are, nevertheless, besides you spoke ill of me last year."

"How could I have done that since I was not born—I still suckle my mother."

"Then it was your brother."

"I have none."

Thereupon the wolf gets impatient: "It was one of yours for you never spare me, you, your shepherds and your dogs. I know this because I have been told and vengeance is mine."

It is only after this vindication of his rights under interracial laws, as it were, that the wolf in the fable can fall upon and strangle Austria. Thus Nazi propaganda did for the people of Germany what the wolf did for himself. It gratified a deep-felt human need for a moral cause without which human beings can not war on their fellowmen with any degree of serenity.

Precisely the same hypocrisy is apparent in the superior-race theory. None who know the Germans can believe that they look upon their fellow Germans as members of a superior race. It would be truer to say that they distrust and despise each other, an attitude which is the invariable result of glaring inequalities in power. Hitler is God, but Goering is a fat windbag and Goebbels is despised as a vicious clubfoot. Well aware of this, Goebbels furnished an explanation for his most unGermanic appearance. He was, said he, of a type which, originally blond and giant in size, had subsequently shrunk and darkened. All of which can be expressed in German in two composite nouns of high comic effect: *Nachgedunkelter Schrumpfgermane*, literally: "late darkened shrunk German." An explanation which incidentally takes care of some 90 per cent more Germans not quite up to specification. The need for affirming membership in a superior race arises because only members of a superior race can violate the moral law which makes all men equal. Hence the Nazi proclamation that this law is not binding upon the people of Germany and hence the eagerness with which that doctrine was accepted.

If might made right, if the end justified the means, there would have been no need for this colossal hypocrisy, the sword alone would have sufficed. But as might does not make right anywhere in the world the sword must be given a propaganda edge. Thus it is demonstrated once again that evil causes are best served by the lie, while a noble end can be furthered only by the truth.

Goethe and Heine on Germany

The fact that the people of Germany belong to the human race is cold comfort. This easy generalization merely affirms that all nations have the same basic potentialities for good or evil. However, at this time the world is confronted with the German people as they are and not as they might be, with their developed potentialities and traits of character which appear in their mores, in their political and economic institutions, the instruments through which nations try to realize their aspirations. "Germany," said Goethe, "is nothing, but the individual German is a great deal, and yet Germans believe the exact opposite. The Germans should be scattered over the face of the earth like the Jews, so that all the good in them may develop and serve the common good of all nations."

If the Germans were scattered across the world no generalizations could be made about them. Of the German-Americans, for example, no general statements can be made that do not also apply to all other Americans. But of the Germans in the Reich and of the Germans abroad who identify themselves with the German state it is perfectly possible to make objective general statements. The generalizations which deprive all decent folks from influence in the state are in reality made by the Germans themselves. The observer can only record them. Through their political institutions the Germans act as if they were born for no other purpose but to conquer and destroy their neighbors, as if, indeed, they were a race of warriors and seafarers as they claim every member of the Nordic race to be. But if it were true as the Nazis maintain that the Nordic babe is born with an irresistible urge to wield the sword and to fire torpedoes, the Swiss would have died of frustration for want of a navy and the Danes for want of an army.

Other nations, other mores. The head-hunters of the Amazon also belong to the human race, but when a civilized administration forbade the head-hunt they grew apathetic. They gave up sowing and reaping and no longer built their cleverly constructed canoes. All these activities were traditionally connected with the head-hunt and it was not worth while to pursue them, since the hunt had to be given up. The force of national traditions is no less strong in the larger units of modern nations. Thus, when Germany was deprived of an army she destroyed her national economy by an uncontrolled inflation, biting off her nose to spite the Allies.

Nor can any comfort be drawn from the fact that Nazi doctrines were acceptable to the German people because the Nazis paid lip-service to the dictates of Justice. Hypocrisy on a scale large enough to embrace an entire nation constitutes almost as great an impasse, a dead-end of morals in evolution, as for the individual. The individual hypocrite is beyond salvation. No moral appeal can reach him because his own use of morality as a means to an unworthy end renders him immune to moral blandishment. Judging others by himself he is convinced that all moralists are hypocrites.

National characteristics are considerably more flexible and therefore more adaptable than the character of the individual. A nation may change for better or for worse in the course of several generations and the element which brings about this change is the rebellious spirit of the individual who can emancipate himself from the narrow prejudices of the class, the state, or the time to which he belongs, and who can inspire a movement toward universal liberation.

But prophets of social revolution in Germany have been few and they have been invariably without honor in their own country. Though every German is proud of Goethe, Schiller

and Beethoven few have cared to remember that, like Thomas
Paine, they considered themselves citizens of the world; still
fewer have walked in their footsteps in our time. Only the German writers of talent and character have consistently opposed
the Nazis. And every one of them was forced into exile when
Hitler burned their books because, in the totalitarian state,
there is no room for the individual capable of creative thinking.

In the nineteenth century there was only the one solitary
poet, Heinrich Heine, the only German of the stature of the
great revolutionaries of the West, the men of the American and
the French revolutions. Most of his life was appropriately spent
in exile, and in the Germany of his time his books were banned,
not only those he had already written but also, by way of precaution, all the books he was going to write.

While living in enforced exile in France, Heine drew inti-
mate portraits of his fellow revolutionaries of 1848. Up to the
revolution of 1918 his characterization of these men looked over-
drawn, painted by one made bitter by the long years spent "in
climbing the hard staircases of exile." But the leaders of the
1918 revolution, the Scheidemanns and Eberts proved to be exact copies of Heine's comrades, every one of whom deserted to
the enemy. In a poem entitled *Kobes I*, Heine described a plebe-
ian who fits Fritz Ebert, first President of the Weimar Republic,
like a glove. In this poem Heine urged the revolutionary convention of 1848, meeting at Frankfort-on-Main, to give the
crown of a unified Germany to this Kobes I. By way of recom-
mendation Heine wrote:

"A pregnant woman who heard him talk was delivered of an
ass."

In 1830 Heine published an essay on German religion and
philosophy for his French readers, warning them that that philosophy is not to be passed over lightly because it is expounded
only by a small élite group and is full of intended obscurity.
Philosophies have a way of filtering through to the masses.

"The German thunder may be slow like a German, but when
it comes, and come it will," the German people will return to
their Germanic gods of the primeval forest.

Christianity—and that is its finest achievement—has somewhat softened the brutal Germanic lust for battle, but it has failed to destroy it, and when once the taming symbol of the cross breaks, it will set free the savagery of the old warriors, the senseless berserk rage which the Nordic poets of old have glorified in their songs and prophecies. . . .

Do not smile at my warning, the warning of a dreamer, against Kantians, Fichtians, and nature philosophers. Do not dismiss as fantastic my contention that these revolutionary ideas will be translated into reality. Thought precedes the deed as lightning precedes thunder. Beware. I mean well, and I am telling you the bitter truth. You have to fear more from a *liberated Germany* than from the entire Holy Alliance and all its Croats and Cossacks.

Once in a beer-cellar in Goettingen a young Pan-Germanist proclaimed that revenge must be taken on the French because they beheaded Conradin von Staufen at Naples (anno 1268). Undoubtedly you have long since forgotten about that. We, however, forget nothing. You can see that we shall never be lacking an excellent pretext for going to war against you. No matter who rules in Germany the Crown Prince or Dr. Wirth always remain well armed. . . . I mean well by you and was genuinely frightened when I learned recently that your ministers intend to disarm you. . . .

Remember, among the nude gods and goddesses frolicking on Olympus, there is a goddess who in spite of joy and laughter which surround her, always wears a coat of mail, a helmet on her head, and a spear in her hand. She is the Goddess of Wisdom.

This passage of Heine was resurrected and reprinted in full in 1870 when Germany invaded France, in 1914 when she went to war against Europe, and again in 1933, when she prepared to go to war against the entire world, and each one of these dates seem to be but stages in the evolution of German morale.

I have quoted this passage not for its prophetic value but as evidence that the spirit of National Socialism was discernible a hundred years ago. Virtually unknown is the hope Heine set in the Communist movement, a hope which he expressed in 1855 in the preface to the French edition of his book *Lutetia*.

This preface reads as if it had been written only yesterday by some liberal contemporary:

I can think only with horror and féar of the epoch when these dark iconoclasts [the Marxists] will hold the power. With their uncouth hands they will break mercilessly all the marble statues of beauty so dear to my heart. . . . They will destroy the laurel woods and plant potatoes instead. . . . The nightingales, those useless singers, will be driven out, and alas, my book of songs will serve the grocer as wrapping paper for the coffee and the snuff of the old women of the future.

. . . Nevertheless, let justice be done. Be it destroyed that old world where the innocent perish and egoism prospers, where man is exploited by man. Be it destroyed from top to bottom, this graveyard, wherein flourish lies and iniquities. And blessed be the grocer who some day will use my poems as wrapping paper for the coffee and the tobacco of those good old women of the future who perhaps in this unjust world of ours have been deprived of these delicacies. *Fiat justicia pereat mundus.*

But there is an even more powerful, an infernal voice in me which speaks in favour of communism and that is the hatred which I have sworn to a party of which communism is the most terrible opponent and therefore my ally. I speak of the party of the so-called representatives of German nationalism, of these false patriots, whose love for the fatherland consists only in their idiotic hatred for everything foreign and for their neighboring peoples; the party which pours out its venom every day particularly against France. Yes, these debris or descendants of the Teutons of 1815 have only modernised their fools' costumes, ultra-teutonic, and have had their asses' ears shortened a little. I have detested and fought them all my life and now that the sword falls from my dying hand I am consoled by the thought, by the absolute conviction, that communism will find them the first to bar its route and will give them the death blow. Most certainly no great thundering blow will be needed. The giant communism will destroy them as one steps on a worm.

My hatred for the nationalists could almost inspire me with love for the communists. At least their fundamental dogma professes the most absolute cosmopolitism, a universal love for all nations, a cofraternity equalitarian between all men citizens of this globe. That at least makes them better Christians than our so-called Germanic patriots, these bigoted champions of an exclusive nationalism.

Thus even Heine failed to foresee the depth of degradation to which the German nation would sink: The venom of nationalism fused with five million Communist voters producing the synthesis, National-Socialism.

Not all generalizations now current about the people of Germany are true. It is not true that Germans are incapable of revolt, which was the opinion of Bismarck. "A revolution in Prussia," said he, "don't make me laugh." It is only a revolt in favor of an abstract ideal of justice and liberty of which they are incapable.

It is decidedly not true that they suffer from a split personality, a Jekyl and Hyde soul, as some have maintained. That is metaphysical nonsense. An individual who is afflicted with schizophrenia is a clinical case, fit for the insane asylum, but a nation can not suffer from a split soul because it has none. The mind is the exclusive possession of the individual, a nation has only the collective result, the sum total of individual thought processes, which is its culture and civilization and which is the common heritage of all individual members of a people. In spite of a venal and top-heavy bureaucracy Germany within six years achieved rearmament at a scale great enough to threaten with conquest the entire world. Such a feat can not be accomplished unless there is practical unanimity as to the ultimate goal, the essential aim of the Nazis, though there might be at the same time widespread opposition to isolated features of the régime. If that opposition is evidence of a split personality then every institutional hypocrisy in history was due to schizophrenia. The princes of the Church, for example, turned over the heretic to the secular arm to be burned because the Church must not shed blood.

Germany, Japan, and Others

Other nations reacted differently to the event of totalitarianism. The Austrian socialists, unlike the Germans, did not submit to Dollfuss without a fight. And the Spanish people for two and a half years stood alone in defense of liberty against the combined armies of Franco, Mussolini, and Hitler.

The Italians have lived long under Fascism without revolt but at least they saw no reason to die for the glory of Mussolini. They had just enough "morale" to conquer unarmed Ethiopians, but they bolted before the Greeks, almost as ill-armed, and the not-too-well equipped British in Libya. By their lack of combativity in an unholy cause they have earned the contempt of the Nazis, and by the same token they deserve more of the sympathy of the civilized world. Outside Mussolini's domain the Italian communities in the New World have fought untiringly for the liberation of their homeland. Many Italians in the United States have risked deportation to Italy and certain death at a time when the official fiction maintained that the Italian Government was a friendly government. Whereas there is not a single newspaper published by German settlements in the New World against Nazi tyranny, except by refugees, the Italians abroad have maintained numerous dailies of anti-Fascist tendencies.

For more than twenty years, until the invasion of the Nazi armies united government, army, and civilians, the Russian people have waged a stubborn underground civil war against the Communist dictatorship to the near despair of the party. Totalitarianism in Russia came as a reaction to a revolution which failed, but the spirit of that revolution lived on in the hearts of the people. Though the people of Russia were no longer master of their fate, they still prevented the state from becoming master over them. In spite of three five-year plans, the totalitarian war-machine of Russia remained incomplete. Whole series of finished engines of war joined the junk-piles, having grown obsolete. From the vast resources of Russia the state had to draw ever more material for the fulfilment of newer plans and the mass-production of newer models. It lavished its whole energy and all its wealth upon the war industries, it paid the armies well and made skilled labor and trained engineers the privileged class—to little avail. Workingmen and peasantry re-

mained obdurate. The peasant's resistance to the collectivization of the land cost Russia a famine in 1932 which wiped out
millions of peasants, but the state won only a Pyrrhic victory.
The collective farms proved as difficult to manage and the collective farmer proved to be as unruly as the individual peasant
who had been liquidated.

Only the Japanese have manifested the same adoration for
the state, the Emperor, as the Germans have for their Fuehrer.
Japan is astonishingly like Hitler Germany in her economic
structure, in her military might, and the moral depravity of
her rulers.

Indeed, the example of Japan throws further doubt on the
supposition that the defeat of 1918 accounts fully for the rise of
National-Socialism in Germany. The Japanese have reached
totalitarianism, like the Germans, without civil war, but as a result of an unbroken string of victories.

To be sure if there had been no German defeat in 1918, Hitler would not now rule Germany, but it is by no means certain
that there would have been no totalitarian state. It is in fact
difficult to conceive that the Imperial ruler of Germany and his
staff would have willingly abandoned—like the democratic governments of the West—the totalitarian powers which government acquired everywhere during the First World War.

After the defeat of 1871, France lost two of her richest provinces and had to endure German occupation until the last franc
of the crushing reparations imposed upon her had been paid.
That defeat gave rise to the movement of General Boulanger,
who, supported by radicals and nationalists, aimed at the establishment of a military dictatorship for revenge upon Germany.
But the French populace preferred to forego recovery of the
lost provinces if it could be had only at the price of despotism
at home, and the movement came to naught. In France, too,
there was a tendency to search for a scapegoat upon whom responsibility for the defeat could be settled, a tendency which
inspired the condemnation of Captain Dreyfus as a traitor. But
that act brought the country to the brink of civil war, with the
nation up in arms because of a point of justice—a piece of

paper, the famous bordereau which was alleged to contain the evidence of this officer's guilt, was not produced in court. The general staff pleaded in vain that to make this important military document public would endanger the security of the father-land. In vain they said that it was criminal to cast doubt upon the honor of a French military court, undermining the morale of the army and its faith in its leadership. No one in France doubted that there was more at stake than the fate of one man. Justice itself was at stake. An injustice to one threatened to be-come an injustice to all. To let it pass would invite the establish-ment of a military dictatorship and the abolition of all civil liberties. The investigation forced upon the government not only cleared Dreyfus but revealed such corruption and incompetence in the army that a general housecleaning was imperative to save the honor of the army and the security of the country.

A defeated and a devastated France after 1871 resisted the temptation of succumbing to a military dictatorship and by a moral effort recovered her sanity. France retained the elementary liberties, social and economic, for which she had been fighting her internal enemies for a century and more, and thereby regained her prosperity, while the light shed by her civilization won her the love and respect of the world. Neither the victory in 1918 nor the defeat of 1940 has changed the spirit of her people.

Finally there is the example of the United States and England, who suffered an unprecedented economic crisis only a decade ago, a crisis as profound as the German depression which gave the death blow to the Weimar Republic. Did it occur to the governments of these nations or to their people to blame some racial, national, or religious minority for a defective economic system? Did they conceive of a well-organized armament program, intending to fall upon their neighbors to the north and south or beyond the seas, to solve their domestic difficulties? They tried to cultivate their own vineyards, well-knowing that their economic treasure was hidden there and not in the land of other peoples and their living spaces.

6

The Western World

THE Treaty of Westphalia, concluded after thirty years of war, outlined the political map of Europe. All subsequent wars fought by kings and feudal lords served to sharpen the contours of the European states, but failed to alter their political frontiers in any radical and decisive manner. Throughout European history wars were more frequent than peace. Yet until the Napoleonic wars the vast majority of Europeans took little part in the struggle which their rulers carried on against each other, except as victims of the thirst for power which animated those who ruled over them. The great mass of mankind lived from day to day engaged in a constant struggle against poverty and want, pestilence and famine, and that worst affliction of all, man's rule over man.

Paralleling the wars of kings there was an uninterrupted struggle of the submerged masses to free themselves from their masters. The once free peasantry of Europe, reduced to slavery by conquest, attained serfdom, and freed itself from serfdom by winning charters from the kings, who needed the support of free men to curtail the power of the nobles. Magna Charta and the free cities of medieval Europe were victories of the spirit of liberty over the spirit of oppression and prepared the soil for the Protestant revolutions against the secular power of the church. Protestantism, by freeing the individual from the tyranny of the church and proclaiming his right to communicate directly with God in accordance with his own conscience, inspired the secular revolutions of the seventeenth and eighteenth centuries against the power of the state over the individual.

But this revolution failed in Germany. There the leaders of Protestantism made common cause with the innumerable ruling princes of the German states, against the people in revolt. The betrayal of the people's cause by Luther and Melanchthon rankled for centuries, and such liberation as later came to Germany was confined in the main to the southern regions, and to the Rhineland, which had remained faithful to Rome, and which had been receptive to the ideals of the French Revolution.

In the wars which the French Revolution fought against the reactionary and absolutist powers of Europe, foreign war and the struggle for liberty became one. The soldiers of' the Revolution, clothed in rags and inadequately armed, won their battles because the ideal of liberty and equality which inspired their action transcended political boundaries and struck a responsive note in the hearts of all oppressed peoples everywhere. This war of France was the first people's war, and it was as yet untainted by the narrow spirit of nationalism. Because it was universal in its appeal the gates were opened to it from within the fortresses of reaction by men aspiring to the same ideal of freedom. For the first time in the history of mankind a nation united by the spirit of liberty carried the fight beyond its own frontiers in the clear knowledge that its own liberties could not survive if its neighbors remained enslaved.

The victorious armies of the French Revolution recognized no division of mankind into nationalities, creeds or colors, and no right of the rulers over the ruled. In 1792 the National Convention pledged itself to *"accord fraternity and aid to all people who may desire to recover their liberty."* And by a later decree of the same year: *"The French nation declares that it will treat as enemies every people who, refusing liberty and equality or renouncing them, may wish to maintain, recall, or treat with a prince and the privileged classes. On the other hand it engages not to lay down its arms until the sovereignty and independence of the peoples whose territory the troops of the republic have entered shall be established, and until the people shall have adopted the principles of liberty and equality and founded a free democratic government."*

Had such a policy inspired the action of the democracies of our own time, had the United States, Great Britain, and France possessed the same clarity of vision, at the latest, when the Nazis seized power in Germany, the civilized world would not now be engaged in a struggle for survival.

Indeed, the honeymoon of the French Revolution with the spirit of universal liberation was short-lived. The reaction against the Revolution produced the figure of Napoleon, the man on horseback, who grew great by conquest and by conquest had to maintain himself. At the beginning of his career, still a son of the Revolution, he observed that in warfare morale carries thrice as much weight as equipment, and this remained true as long as his conquests brought to the conquered liberation from the yoke of their rulers. But at the end of his career he came to the cynical conclusion that God is on the side of the heaviest battalions. Having lost the theme of the Revolution he put his trust in force alone. And as all force is eventually defeated by a greater force which it engenders, he united all Europe and the people of France against himself, thus spelling his doom. On his return from Elba he knew the cause of his failure. Advised to call for a levee en masse, as the Revolution had done in the past, he told his adviser that he could no longer count upon the Revolution, whose spirit he had betrayed.

7

The Nucleus of Resistance

EVERY European conqueror sooner or later finds the British Isles the nucleus around which all continental nations resisting aggression group themselves. For the unity of Europe like that of the world can only be of the spirit; a unity imposed by one European conqueror upon the continental nations can not last as long as Britain remains unconquered. The rule of force can not stop short of the conquest of the world. In Napoleon's time that world was, for all practical purposes, the European continent and the British Empire. In our own time, the political world and the globe are one. As long as the British Isles and the United States are unconquered, the spirit of revolt on the continent continues to feed on the hope of liberation, while the compulsion which drives the tyrant to extend his conquests works with equal force upon the remaining free peoples, who, in order to survive, must abandon their isolation and come forth to the rescue of the subjugated.

Britain in the time of Napoleon as in our own time played for long the rôle of the passive onlooker. In the end she found herself under attack, and by resisting the threatened invasion she became the ally of all Europe against the man on horseback. Against Napoleon she stood her ground alone until the tide turned. In 1914 she was more fortunate. The idea of the national sovereign state had reached clarity of definition and was under attack by an enemy of rare political stupidity. On the principle that the strong are strongest when they stand alone, William II united the world against himself before his armies had crossed a single frontier. Without a league of na-

100

tions, a concert of powers, a European federation or an international police force, the sovereign powers of 1914 manifested
a spirit of solidarity they were not able to recapture after victory was won. In 1914, when Serbia was threatened by Austria-
Hungary with what must appear in the light of recent history
as a minute infringement of her sovereign rights, it was clear
to the governments of Europe that a threat to one was a threat
to all. Regardless of the internal structure of each, they put
up a solid front against the aggressor.

As always, Great Britain was the last to recognize the enemy.
Secure in her "splendid isolation," she might have claimed
that she knew nothing about distant Serbia, as Chamberlain
was to say later about Czechoslovakia, but she could not ignore the violation of Belgian neutrality which brought the
war to her doorstep. Later, Imperial Germany forced the hand
of the even more distant United States by the declaration of
unrestricted submarine warfare.

The Imponderables of War

Those who can not justify their own actions by any moral
principle of universal validity must seek to discredit their victims in the eyes of the world. Nazi geopolitics is a program
devoid of all moral purpose. It seeks merely to define the conditions, material and psychological, which permit the full military exploitation of the geographical position of the German
Reich on the European continent—a position which gives her
the advantage of interior lines for a war of aggression, permitting her to shift her forces at will for an attack in any direction. Britain, at war with Germany on the other hand, suf-
fers under the loss of time involved in transporting her troops
and supplies around the periphery of the circle of aggression,
and as the enemy extends the war her difficulties increase.
The enemy's gain in space is Britain's loss in time, over ever-
lengthening communication lines.

England's geographical position has advantages of its own,
however, and these the Nazis have tried to represent as proof

of moral turpitude on the part of the British. England, so runs the accusation, always gets other people to fight her battles. This propaganda line belongs to the category of exact inversion of the truth, the beloved colossal lie of the Fuehrer. In reality, provided Britain refrains from any aggressive action against any continental nation, it is the continental aggressor who supplies her invariably with a whole crop of allies.

To conquer the obstacle of the English Channel the continental aggressor must establish bases on the coast facing the British Isles. To establish these bases he must first attack and conquer the nations lying athwart his path to the sea, and in this process he makes enemies for himself and allies for Britain. For centuries Britain fought Spain, Austria, and France, to prevent these powers from dominating the Low Countries, and even the Low Countries themselves, whenever they were allied with the enemy or challenged Britain's sea power. This has been Britain's Monroe Doctrine, or in Nazi parlance her geopolitics. But this policy could be used to full advantage only after England had given up her ambition of retaining a foothold on the continent, only after she had withdrawn into "splendid isolation."

The experience of the United States has been similar. Like Britain she has followed a policy of isolation whenever practicable. The Monroe Doctrine by itself could hardly have gained for her the friendship of the South American states. To make that doctrine effective the United States had to abandon aggressive diplomacy and adopt the good neighbor policy in its place. With the growing interdependence of the world and the shrinkage of space, the position of the United States has become to-day what England's position has been for centuries. She has refrained from aggressive action in Europe or on the Asiatic mainland, gaining allies in both continents through the action of the aggressor. The United States has done little in the years of the Chinese ordeal to gain China's friendship. If to-day the United States has allies in Europe and Asia, Germany and Japan have made these allies for her.

Since no direct surprise attack upon the British Isles was possible, England could afford the luxury of a wait-and-see policy. It is a policy which does not avoid wars, since lack of provocation does not restrain the aggressor, but it is of inestimable value as a method of finding out how to fight the enemy effectively.

The basic principles of warfare, tactics and strategy in the field, are eternally the same, but every war presents an entirely new problem to the offense as well as to the defense. The enemy may always appear in the field with new weapons or with methods hitherto untried. The number of variables is infinite, and it is often the imponderables of war which decide the issue of victory or defeat. Every war, however well prepared, is a gamble for defense and offense alike. The greatest military genius can not foresee with any exactitude what his armies or the enemy's will do on the battlefield: he can not estimate the reliability or staying power of his own allies, or count the friends which the enemy is liable to gain for his cause. War has been compared to a chess game, but the analogy is not a happy one. The opponents in chess always start as equals, and the property and strength of each piece on the board are known in advance, so that the outcome depends solely upon the skill of the player. War, on the other hand, is played blindfolded. It is only a slight exaggeration to say that battles are won not so much by the ability of the generals as by the strategical errors committed by the enemy. Seen in this light the battle of the Marne in 1914 was not won by a miracle: given the action of the German armies, it would have been a miracle if the French had lost it.

In *War and Peace* Tolstoy denies all military genius to Napoleon. He chose to see in him only the petty vanity of the man, a characteristic which all conquerors seem to share. One need not go that far to admit Tolstoy's contention that it was materially impossible for Napoleon to have directed any of his battles while they were going on. The battlefield presents a constantly shifting scene, and in the absence of two-way radios, field-telephones, and highly developed signal systems, the time required for any accurate information to reach Napoleon, and for his instructions to be carried back to the officers in the thick of the fight, was too long as to assure any of his orders a faithful execution. Tolstoy, like the early Napoleon, therefore concluded that the morale and the ingenuity of each individual soldier and the quality of the leadership on the spot were the decisive elements. However, if the enemy appears on the battlefield with an overwhelming superiority in men and engines of war, using a superior grand strategy, the morale of the defense may count for naught.

Perhaps a better analogy for war than the chess game is provided by contract bridge. In that game the player can not know the strength either of his opponents or of his partner, nor can he know the exact distribution of the trump cards, although the players all give each other some indication by the bidding which precedes the play. In war, likewise, the intelligence service can gain valuable information as to the power of the enemy, the number of his reserves, the nature of his weapons, and possible weak points in his armor. All these factors, however, can not become fully known except as they are revealed in the heat of battle. No parades or maneuvers witnessed by military attachés, and no intelligence service however efficient, can be an adequate substitute for the trial by fire. The Germans never made a great secret of their growing military might, but before this war few military observers, wedded as they were to the proposition that the defense is invariably superior to the offense, took the parachute troops, the massed tanks and planes seriously. It would be wrong to blame this lack of foresight wholly on incompetence on the part of the military. The task which their governments had set for them was purely defensive, and it colored their thinking just as the spirit of aggression inspired the thought of German army men. Moreover, it is with militarism as it is with other branches of human endeavor—in the arts and sciences, for instance: the new is decried by those who have mastered the craftsmanship of the old.

Among England's most important military assets must be counted the fact that she can never be taken wholly by surprise. The building of an invasion fleet can not be kept a dark secret, no matter how ingenious the enemy is in material and diplomatic camouflage. Not the battleship nor even the submarine can be built in quantities remotely comparable to the prodigious mass of weapons at the disposal of a land army. Men-of-war are elaborate machines or rather constellations of machinery, swimming factories of destruction, too bulky to be hidden from the watchful eye of the enemy. England warned in time could always outbuild any potential aggressor on the sea.

No enemy land army unsupported by sea power could stage a direct attack upon the British Isles. The invention of the bomber plane has not, to date, materially altered the problem set to the would-be conqueror of Britain. To be effective, the bombing armada must be based as near as possible to the target, where it can be accompanied by fighter planes for protection. To establish these bases consumes time. And to protect his flanks Hitler had to conquer not only the Low Countries but Poland, France, Denmark, and Norway as well, just as Napoleon had to conquer Spain and Portugal. Time has therefore always been on the side of Britain's defense, and the enemy on the continent is forced to try to make up in the conquest of space what he loses in time to the English Channel and the British Navy.

In the process of conquering the small and the large powers on the continent to get at Britain, the armies of the conqueror, regardless of the speed of their advance, reveal the full measure of their power, and no surprise can be kept in store for an attack upon the British Isles. For the aggressor, swift conquest of the obstacles barring his route to the sea is of the essence. Haste in preventing Britain from gathering her forces by far outweighs any advantage which may accrue to the attacker if he pull his punches. In the end it would avail him little if he sacrificed time to secrecy by withholding some of his weapons from demonstration under combat conditions, particularly as his greatest advantage consists in the coördinated use of all his weapons.

The Nazis gave much thought and study to this problem. The doctrine of surprise attack, their chief stock in trade, was sacrificed only very reluctantly. The desire to make full use of it against England was a contributory cause of their efforts to obtain submission of all continental nations to their will without war. And in this strategy they succeeded almost well enough.

The Nazis obtained non-interference with their plans in Spain, submission of Austria, abandonment of Czechoslovakia by England, France and Russia, and finally as a crowning achievement a non-aggression pact with Russia. Had all Europe submitted without a fight, they could have turned the full fury of their surprise attack upon the British Isles. The full impact of their preparation would then have hit England alone and might have conquered her. But the cleverest diplomacy can not obtain such submission without the backing of armed force as a threat, and to be able to threaten the continental powers Germany had to build an army designed primarily for conquest on land with incredible speed and force. Only the possession of such an army obviated the necessity of fighting.

In the end, however, Germany did have to fight and thus was forced to lay all her cards on the table. Apparently even in a game where there are no rules it is impossible to hold more than a limited number of trump cards in one hand. Having played these, Germany, it appeared, had neglected to build an air force independent of the army and powerful enough to conquer the British sky. The battle of time was lost to the handful of R.A.F. fighters, but not to these alone. Poland, Denmark, Norway, Holland, Belgium, Luxembourg, and France, the topography of the continent and of the English Channel, the necessity of building a series of airdromes as bases for the Nazi air force before the all-out attack could be launched, all contributed their share. Without them the

tenacity and courage of the few might have been expended in
vain.

Nelson's victorious attack on his fleet compelled Napoleon
to turn on Russia, and the victory of the R.A.F. turned Germany in the same direction. While Germany was trying to
make good her defeat by the conquest of space Britain, apply-
ing to herself the lesson which the enemy had taught her,
gained the time necessary to build an army and an air force.

Britain's Geopolitics

Britain's wait-and-see policy is not determined solely by
her geographical position. Japan has the same geographical
advantages as the British Isles but has used her island home
as a spring-board for a program of unlimited conquest. In her
will to power—as in Germany's—the accent is placed not upon
geography but upon politics. The difference between British
and Japanese geopolitics is determined by differences in the
internal structure of the two states and in the character of
the people.

The British have taken advantage of their comparative security from foreign invasion to win for themselves a measure
of individual liberty, which has provided the basis for the
growth of their Empire and of England's supremacy in international trade and finance. For centuries her yeomen, squires,
and merchants fought the absolute rule of kings, until in the
protracted struggle Parliament emerged victorious. Political
power passed from king and feudal lords to the chosen representatives of landowners, merchants and industrialists.
Through a process of decentralization of power older even
than Parliament the individual gradually freed himself from
the worst tyranny of state and church, while the king became
a mere symbol of national unity, inviting the derision of
George Bernard Shaw in his *Saint Joan:* "What is the good of
sitting on the throne when the other fellows give all the orders?"

The ruling classes of England made an art of yielding to im-

perative change though yielding no more than seemed un-
avoidable. Britain consequently advanced on the road to
democracy—toward the goal that is never attained—as fast
as France, without endangering her national unity and with
less violence. The French ruling classes were easily tempted
to seek support for their privileges abroad, since such support
could reach them, but thereby they also provided more work
for the guillotine.

To wrest power from the king, Parliament consistently opposed the creation of a standing army in the service of the
monarchy. Generous in providing funds for a navy and a
merchant marine, both vital to the security of the islands, the
Empire, and the trade, Parliament refused to open the purse-
strings for a standing land army which might be used by a
tyrannical king to deprive Englishmen of their religious and
civil rights, and Parliament of its prerogatives. Control of public funds by Parliament and opposition to conscript armies are
the two traditional principles of British democracy which the
settlers of the thirteen colonies brought with them to the New
World as a sort of portable fatherland. These principles thrived
well in the new soil—isolated from the rest of the world by
the wide expanse of the oceans as England was isolated from
the continent by the Channel and the white cliffs. To this day
England and the United States have been reluctant to follow
the example of the continental European powers since the
Napoleonic conquests in establishing conscript armies during
peace.

The slogan of the American Revolution, "No taxation without representation," likewise was a branch of the old tree, and
the American Revolution consequently found support in England by King George III's opposition. The warning of the
founding fathers of the American republic against entangling
alliances might have been spoken by Walpole and a host of
other British statesmen. It was a thought born of the British
past rather than a clear anticipation of what the future would
hold in store for the United States and for the world.

In the absence of a permanent army ever ready for instantaneous attack upon a potential aggressor, there is little that a country can do besides try to gain time: time to study the nature of the enemy; time to build up an army patterned upon the enemy's army but improving on it, an army which, in conjunction with sea power and with the aid of allies generously furnished by the enemy, can defeat him decisively. Meanwhile, the enemy can hope at best to arrive on Britain's doorstep with much of his power spent and in bad need of a pause permitting him to get his second wind.

A good player starting with bad cards must continue to play in the hope that the law of averages will favor him in the end, permitting him to make full use of his skill. For a consistent adherence to such a policy in a life-and-death struggle, a steady nerve and a stubborn will to endure to the bitter end are indispensable. The English possess both, reinforced by a certain lack of imagination and a wisdom born of experience which tells them that the aggressor must lose in the end and which permits them to remain calm in the face of disaster.

The Growth of Empire

Like Rome, the British Empire was not built in a day, but unlike Rome it did not develop as a result of purposeful conquests by a warlike people. The British are fond of saying that they stumbled into the possession of an Empire. The insignificant peacetime armies of Britain could never have conquered it for her. The work was done by individual merchants and seafarers—part trader, part pirate—in India and in the middle east, while British emigrants colonized the sparsely inhabited regions of the New World. In Britain's expanding Empire, conquest played a rôle subordinated to trade, which thrives best without the use of force. Even where naked force was used, as in the war against the Boers, the object was not conquest for its own sake but the establishment of rights for British merchants and industrialists to participate in the development and exploitation of the rich regions of the Transvaal.

As soon as that point was gained, England renounced the maintenance of her ascendancy by force and granted to the conquered the same degree of individual liberty as her population enjoyed at home, with the result that both the Boers and the British prospered and that the Dominion of South Africa—like the other dominions virtually a self-governing state—is solidly with her erstwhile conqueror in this war as she was in the last.

In view of this achievement, the elements of liberty and equality in so far as they are parts of a liberal economy, must be adjudged superior to the naked sword as a cohesive force. Where Great Britain has tried to rule by force alone she has found as Napoleon did that one can do everything with bayonets except sit on them. England tried to sit on the bayonet in all the wars she fought in medieval times, when she strove to retain a foothold on the continent and lost, as she lost the American colonies and Ireland, incurring the lasting ill-will of the Irish.

The case of India is far more complex. Undoubtedly the offer of self-government was too long delayed, but for that delay the internal divisions of India are in part responsible. No one who knows Europe can be sanguine on the subject of what Indian unity might have been without British rule. Religious fanaticism is no less fatal to Moslem and Hindu than it is to Protestant and Catholic: it requires no inspiration from the outside to degenerate into religious and civil wars. The present opposition on the part of the Indian nationalists to a decentralization of political power must be disheartening to all who have seen elsewhere in the world the spirit of narrow nationalism in the raw.

This is not to suggest that the morality of capitalistic democracy, however liberal, contains more than a faint echo of the ideals of the French or the American Revolution. The trader and industrialist turned diplomat can drive hard and inhuman bargains. Many of the heroes of the revolutions in which modern democracies had their origin might have hesitated to give their lives had they known that they were to achieve no more than this. A Clive and a Cecil Rhodes hardly deserve the monuments which Imperialists have set up to them: few will quarrel with the opinion of Mark Twain, who thought that a rope would have been more appropriate. But a world which is rapidly falling victim to a worse tyranny than the rule of the industrial lords, the tyranny of the centralized state, must remember that the saving grace of nineteenth-century economy was the element of liberty which it did contain and without which it could not have functioned. It is to that element of liberty alone that progress in technology and in social thought is due. All the evils of that world and the seed of its decline spring from the elements of feudalism and inequality which it contains, inherited from the past. Either a new and better world will be built upon a more generous human liberty than the old, or its road, albeit paved with good intentions, will lead once again to the gates of hell.

Under the system of capitalistic liberty, the worst commercial skulduggery and cut-throat competition are not wholly devoid of an element of coöperation, a recognition of equal rights as between buyer and seller, consumer and producer. Even where the seller had nothing to offer but his labor he was able by a persistent and relentless struggle to obtain the right to bargain collectively and thus oppose to the power of management the power of his massed strength, ensuring that an agreement, when reached, should not be wholly devoid of benefit to him.

In a world where the parties to a deal enjoy equal freedom of choice to take it or leave it, conditions approach nearest to the ideal. Where no force can be used to obtain strict adherence to the letter and the spirit of an agreement, rules and regulations are developed spontaneously which correspond to the interest of all and are therefore faithfully adhered to. In a liberal world economy commercial transactions are carried on for the most part on faith in contracts signed and on the given word. Industry and trade would be paralyzed if the breaking of contracts were the rule rather than the exception. When differences do arise, the businessman hesitates to invoke the law. It is better to compromise or arbitrate than to appeal to force. Procedure of the courts is slow and costly, and both sides stand to lose more than they can hope to gain in the end.

Translated into the language of politics, this commercial spirit has accepted compromise and peaceable adjustment of differences between political parties and economic classes as preferable to civil war and mutual destruction. This same principle applied to imperialistic expansion has made Britain's ruling class the partner of the ruling classes in the colonies.

British colonization refrained from dispossessing native chieftains, ruling princes and Maharajas of their wealth and power. England elected to become their economic and military ally and to share in their rule, while respecting the religion and the traditions of the ruled. To do more, to liberate the "backward" people from their native exploiters, Britain would have had to be a revolutionary force, on the model of the great French Revolution, rather than a conservative one. A program such as the National Convention adopted (immediate universal liberation) can remain alive only as long as the people proclaiming it are themselves dedicated to revolutionary ideals. England could not hope to inspire a swifter progress abroad on the road to liberty than that which her people were traveling at home.

This pedestrian spirit lacks the glamour associated with barricades in the streets and glorious revolution, but it is also free from the brutality and bloodshed of civil war and violent reaction. In creative ideas and in revolutionary thought England has often led the world. In the world of reality, in the practical application of these ideas, she has shown an inventive capacity in the creation of social institutions that is far more important than the invention of industrial technics. In the decentralized Empire the advanced ideas of her creative minds have found a measure of realization unique in the history of Imperialism, and in colonization her methods have been second only to American treatment of the Philippines.

The History of Appeasement

That this spirit of adjustment and accommodation presupposes willingness in an opponent to meet the other side half-
way is a platitude. But it is a platitude which a pacifist world
in the period between the wars was inclined to forget. It was
thought that peace could be maintained unilaterally by one
nation disarming and thus setting the example to the world,
morally compelling the others to follow. Unfortunately, war
can be started by one nation, but peace and understanding
require the coöperation of all.

In a treatise published at the end of the nineteenth century,
Jean de Bloc argued in six volumes on war that the advent
of the Industrial Revolution throughout the western world and
the consequent growing interdependence of all great powers
had made war impossible. He predicted that if a war were to
occur, in spite of the impossibility which he had demonstrated,
its consequences in a world united by the development of
international trade and communication, would be such that
neither victor nor vanquished could survive. Such a war would
end in a stalemate, exhausting the resources of the world, and
would prompt its victims to rise against the governments responsible for the carnage and destruction. It is not surprising that the Czar of all the Russias was profoundly stirred by
these arguments, since his absolute rule was tempered by
dynamite even in time of peace. He was moved to call an
international conference for the limitation of armaments which
duly took place and accomplished as much as did all subsequent conferences of this kind—precisely nothing.

Jean de Bloc, himself a banker and industrialist, looked upon
war from the practical viewpoint of the merchant whose trade
would be disrupted by war and revolution. His was the ra-
tionality of nineteenth-century liberalism, which inspired the
economic theories of the Manchester school, a school of
thought which in turn exercised a considerable influence on
the conduct of government in all democratic countries and

particularly in Great Britain. It is under its influence that England adopted nearly a century ago the principle of free trade, abolishing all tariff barriers in the vain hope that her example would be followed by other nations, because of its manifest economic advantages, and because it would bring about peaceful international relations to boot.

The intellectual labor expended by Jean de Bloc notwithstanding, the war of 1914 occurred. Before the outbreak of war in 1939, Bloc found an echo in the arguments of a leftist writer, Willi Schlamm, who tried to account for the peace-at-any-price attitude of the capitalistic world. Willi Schlamm argued that this predilection for peace on the part of capitalists so astonishing to the Marxist world could be accounted for materialistically by the invention of the bomber. According to this line of reasoning, the capitalistic world of 1914 risked little destruction to their source of power, the means of production which they owned. But any future war would threaten to destroy not only the life of soldiers at the front but through airpower the very possessions of capitalists as well. Schlamm argued, that on the principle of a bookkeeper's balance sheet the capitalists had concluded that it was cheaper to grant Germany all she demanded in colonies and territorial aggrandizement than to risk losing all through aerial bombardment.

Both Jean de Bloc and Willi Schlamm attributed rational calculations to absolute rulers and exaggerated the influence of cold figures upon the conduct of man. Moreover, though the material destruction caused by such a war as the present total war is great indeed, the life of machinery and factory buildings is short even in time of peace, and they are not as vital a source of wealth as the "know-how" of industrial management, skilled labor, and the good-will which established enterprises secure for themselves in home and world markets. As long as the accumulated technical knowledge is not destroyed and men remain free to reconstruct a devastated world the material destruction of war can be made good in a very few years.

Liberal economists of the nineteenth century, in search of economic laws, sometimes facilitated their studies by creating a hypothetical character: the economic man. This abstract personage always bought goods at their lowest competitive price and sold them at the highest price. He bought in a buyer's market and sold in a seller's market. From his rational commercial behavior one could deduce the laws of supply and demand. One would assume that any one who has been in business would readily understand that this ideal personage does not exist. Nevertheless, what was a workable hypothesis to the social theorist became body and flesh to Liberals and Marxists alike. They assumed that the action of men is dictated exclusively by his economic interests and also that in the aggregate he possesses sufficient discernment to act always in accordance with these interests.

It is true that those who possessed business acumen in the liberal economy which preceded the totalitarian state were favored in the struggle for survival. In the totalitarian state, however, the race is no longer to the swift in figures but to the "political man" who is quick in denouncing his neighbor and who is as ready to settle by the gun an argument of his own making as the gangster of the Prohibition era.

In the growing economic interdependence of the world, survival demanded coöperation in the farthest corners of the earth. But coöperation is possible only between free men, and freedom excludes dictatorship at home and abroad, thus cramping the style of individuals and groups mad with the thirst for power. These are in revolt against the imperative demands of international economy and against such submissions and restrictions as the liberties of others would impose upon them.

This revolt has realized its purpose in the totalitarian state, cutting off its citizens from the free markets of the world by monopolizing all imports and exports and depriving the individual of all safeguards to his freedom. This revolt spread to the democratic nations as well. A neo-mercantilism with high tariff walls, contingents and currency manipulations replaced the liberalism of the nineteenth century. In part these measures were defensive measures against the totalitarian methods of economic warfare. But the best defense would have been close coöperation among the democracies. That it was not forthcoming was due to the growing spirit of narrow nationalism in the democratic countries themselves.

There is bitter irony in the fact that the economic isolationism of totalitarians, deliberately adopted for the purpose of building the machine with which to destroy all the forces of coöperation in the world, was answered by the future victims with an isolationism of their own. The totalitarian rulers were well aware of the fact that they would not reap any economic benefits for the nations which they rule by waging war against the economic interdependence of the world, but they were not interested in economics, in wealth and well-being for their slaves, but in power to themselves alone. They were well aware too of the fact that those who exercise power never go hungry.

They knew how to estimate the full force of the growing interdependence of the world. They have harnessed it to their chariot. They knew also, long before their victims discovered it, that their power could not survive as long as there was anywhere in the world a nucleus of economic liberty. If all wars were fought to gain economic benefits for the nation as a whole or even for a ruling class which is dependent for its power upon economic forces, Jean de Bloc's impossible war would have become indeed impossible long ago.

A century before Jean de Bloc, Napoleon, exasperated by the influence of what he called "Pitt's gold" on the European continent, spoke of the English as a nation of shopkeepers. He was giving vent to his feelings because clandestine trade with the British threatened to nullify completely his continental blockade. His rules were constantly violated by smugglers who did not share Napoleon's grandiose schemes for a united Europe dominated by himself. All democratic nations in this sense are nations of shopkeepers, who can see the economic advantages of peace more clearly and immediately than feudal lords, emperors, and dictators. The influence which the best interests of the shopkeepers exercise upon the conduct of government in democratic countries has tended more often toward the preservation of peace than was admitted by the post-war radical world.

In a century and more, serious differences between the great democratic powers have been settled as between equals and by treaty agreements faithfully adhered to. Since the War of 1812 and the Napoleonic wars, peace has been maintained amongst England, France, and the United States, not to mention the small democracies of Europe. Even in their dealings with smaller nations and empires, such as Portugal, Holland, and Belgium, all three democratic powers have consistently negotiated on a basis of equality. Recognition by Great Britain of the Monroe Doctrine permitted tacit coöperation between the United States naval power and the British and produced the novelty of an undefended frontier between Canada and the United States. The independence of Belgium from French rule likewise led to a reconciliation between the British and the French Empire and permitted the settlement by peaceful negotiation of serious differences such as the Fachoda incident.

There is a century-old treaty between Switzerland and France where France is pledged not to fortify a strip of her frontier with Switzerland, a treaty to which France adhered even when the growing German menace threatened to turn her defenses in the south in 1914 and again in 1939. In the north, Belgian objections to the extension of the Maginot Line sufficed to stop the execution of the plan until the outbreak of war. The world has never heard that France found it humiliating to a Great Power that she was pledged not to fortify part of her frontiers, but it never ceased hearing about the frightful humiliation caused to Germany by the Treaty of Locarno in which she consented not to fortify the Rhineland.

This is an aspect of history which the socialist school of thought has chosen to ignore. It does not confirm the theory that all wars are determined by economic considerations and that rivalry in foreign trade and the need of expansion inherent in capitalist economy are at the bottom of all conflicts.

If this were so, Germany should never have invaded France, for the two countries have long possessed a complementary economic structure. In their eagerness to prove economic determinism "scientific," the Marxists are apt to select the facts which suit their theory, a failing which they share with a great many other schools of thought that, in the words of William James, treat all facts as if they were born free and equal.

Confronted with the spirit of the totalitarian states, the will to accommodate and adjust differences is powerless. In the face of a foe bent upon aggression there is no longer any give and take, and one-sided concessions become appeasement, on which the aggressor waxes fat. "He who negotiates is lost" says Adolf Hitler, and so he is, when negotiating with Hitler and his like.

In the pattern of British foreign policy, appeasement of the enemy fits in at times as a sort of extended wait-and-see policy; at other times it is woven into its fabric. The enemy, having failed to break his neck by reckless warfare upon all and sundry, can perhaps be satiated with concessions. Provided that he pursues limited objectives, it does not seem beyond the realm of the possible that he will settle down and not risk losing all in an effort to gain more.

But appeasement is not necessarily a reasoned principle adopted with malice aforethought. It may be in part a product of national temperament. The British historian David Hume, a contemporary of Pitt and Napoleon, narrates that the ancient Britons tried to appease Caesar when they first heard of his intention to invade their island. "But," adds Hume gravely, "their submissions [concessions] in no way retarded the execution of this design."

A satirical English journal during the premiership of Gladstone gives an account of the procedure of the appeasement policy, or the "rage to negotiate," as it was called in the time of Walpole. Gladstone was an advocate of a little England and violently opposed to Disraeli's imperialism. The satire assumed that Russia would take a fancy to Scotland, demanding that England cede that country to her on the ground that possession of Scotland was vital to the defense of Russia. Upon receipt of the Russian note, Gladstone would ask for further details of Russian intentions. An unsatisfactory or dilatory reply by Russia would cause him to recall the British Ambassador to the court of St. Petersburg for a more detailed report, and he would send him back with an offer to negotiate in a round table conference. Refusal of the Russian Government to participate in such a conference would by no means exhaust the resources of a British statesman. Gladstone would suggest that the controversy be arbitrated by a third and disinterested power. Should a Russian expeditionary force set out to take Scotland by force, Gladstone would propose that peace negotiations be started before things went too far.

Britain has treated every potential aggressor to a dose of appeasement: Philip II of Spain, Louis XIV, Napoleon, the Kaiser, Mussolini, and Hitler. Always late to wake up to danger and never in possession of an adequate army, temperamentally slow to anger, the British hope that, given rope enough, the enemy will hang himself. As British diplomacy yields the enemy may betray himself by his own ambitions and, growing overconfident, may overplay his hand, thus laying himself open to counter-attack. It is true, he may gain allies for himself as his successes add to his growing prestige, or he may obtain them by domination, but such allies are more often a burden than a help. The coördination of allied armies and navies is difficult enough when they are under attack and fight for a common cause, but devoid of a good cause alliances are as brittle as glass. When the Armada of Philip of Spain arrived in the English Channel to join the Dutch Navy the latter were not ready, and during the wait at Calais, the British attacked and burned some of the Spanish ships while the rest fled to the sea. Commanded by an inexperienced seaman, the Armada ran into storms off Scotland and foundered. The period of appeasement had permitted the British to provide their ships with guns of a longer range than the Armada's, and also to construct ships smaller and faster than the ships of Spain.

Louis XIV, though successful in nearly all his military campaigns, accumulated too many enemies on the continent. For that reason he never gave serious thought to a concentration of all his power against the British Isles. He did put his fleet at the disposal of James I whom the British had chased off the throne, but the British attacked and destroyed that fleet before it was ready to sail. Unable to invade England for want of an adequate navy, Napoleon tried to cut Britain's communication lines with the Empire by the conquest of Egypt. He lost his army there, while Nelson destroyed his fleet. He then tried the continental blockade and made an enemy of Russia, though the Czar was by no means a friend of England. What the Channel is to England her vast space is to Russia, and in his retreat Napoleon lost not only the grand army but his allies as well.

In spite of the kinship which the Germans claim with their "British cousins," it would be difficult to imagine a wider gulf between two national mentalities. The British, given to understatement, believe that boastful men have a bark worse than their bite, and gather confidence as the enemy pounds imaginary tables with figuratively mailed fists. The Germans, on the other hand, when they boast of their ferocity are honest to a fault. They mean what they say and never fail to prepare carefully the faithful execution of their threats, while they are convinced that people who indulge in understatement mean less than they say.

Thus the Kaiser and his staff were misled by the British refusal to say beforehand what they would do in case of a German attack upon France, Belgium, and Russia, and as the British Army was small it was also contemptible in German eyes. Since the British constantly urged a naval holiday upon Germany and even yielded the fortress of Helgoland, which commands the northern coast of Germany, in exchange for some useless colony, the Germans were convinced that Britain was easily intimidated. (France was not a little alarmed at the British offer to accept a naval holiday. It was feared in France that the money which such a holiday would liberate in Germany would be used to increase the power of the German land army. Fortunately for France the Kaiser literally thought the world of his navy and refused the British offer. "Germany's future" said he, "is on the water.")

Every conciliatory note sent to Germany by President Wilson before the American entry into the war was similarly regarded in Germany as proof that America was too proud to fight, and this phrase, in German translation, became "afraid to fight." After the German declaration of unrestricted submarine warfare, the foreign office in Berlin assured the American Ambassador Gerard that America would not go to war or even break off diplomatic relations. This in spite of the warnings sent by Count Bernsdorff, German Ambassador to the United States. When the declaration of war came, Germany was outraged because by a curious twist in psychology she interpreted the American action as a breach of faith, since Wilson's notes seemed to contain a promise that he would back down.

Few people in Germany have ever understood American and British diplomacy or the internal politics of democratic countries. Germans have often recognized their lack of comprehension, saying that they have no talent for politics, but the difficulty is more profound. What holds the British Empire together is a mystery to them unless they explain to themselves that it is done by force. Consequently, Germans were always inclined to believe hopefully that Canada, Australia, New Zealand, and South Africa were anxious to break away, while India and the other colonies groaned under the British yoke.

To the United States, nationhood is blandly denied. The first shock must cause her to break apart into innumerable fragments of nationalities, races, and religions. In the last analysis the German attitude proves to be a congenital inability to understand how liberty can be a unifying force and lead to willing and even enthusiastic coöperation. It is significant that the *Déclaration des droits de l'homme* (the Bill of Rights) of the French Revolution has found no translator in Germany in a period of 150 years, though many philosophical Germans have quoted whole passages to prove its basic conception wrong.

A 1929 exchange student from Germany at Columbia University invited my sympathy as a fellow student about the plight of the German-Americans. He could not understand why all the important posts in the Federal and local government were held by Americans of Anglo-Saxon stock. This at any rate was the impression he had gained—although, according to him, there was a majority of German-Americans from which to choose. I drew his attention to the fact that there was universal suffrage. He admitted that, but doubtfully gave me to understand that he suspected some sinister conspiracy against people of his race. I suggested that perhaps the Anglo-Saxon politicians had mastered the business of compromise and mutual forbearance which leads easily to coöperation, and told him the fable of the traveler and the bet between the sun and the wind as to which could induce him to shed his coat. Even the obvious malice of the analogy left him unconvinced. Other national and racial minorities struggle for equality, a German feels discriminated against when he cannot dominate others.

The Necessity for Appeasement

Democratic nations can not go to war spontaneously, nor can they, like the totalitarian states, prepare for total war methodically, unhampered or even aided by public opinion. Even when, as is rare, a few farsighted members of the government or parliament become convinced that war is inevitable, they must first gain the consent of the governed before they can take the offensive or prepare for total defense. At times that consent is given readily enough, as in 1914, and it appears then as if a press campaign, flag-waving, and a few patriotic speeches are sufficient to arouse war fervor. But this is a delusion under which the world between wars has lived for twenty years. Governments can not make public opinion at will, particularly since they are as often as not themselves a product of the electoral mood. What made the task of government easy in the democracies of 1914 was the action of the enemy, which at the time hit a world that was not war weary and understood easily enough the meaning of the action.

Even then Germany failed to provoke France into an attack upon her frontiers. Poincaré asserted in France that mobilization was not yet war, and ordered the withdrawal of the troops from the frontiers. To justify her invasion of France and Belgium, Germany, anticipating Hitler, had to invent a French airplane attack upon Nuremberg and a Franco-Belgian agreement to let French troops march through Belgium. Thus the internal unity of the democracies in 1914 and the unity among the Allies was produced by German action—the German armies attacking almost simultaneously in all directions.

In the absence of a clear-cut case of aggression, the problem of winning the enthusiastic support of democratic nations for war is by no means easy to solve. Yet without such enthusiastic support neither a well-timed offensive nor total preparation for defense is possible. The problem presents greater difficulties to such a far-flung empire as the British Empire than it does to France or the United States. A British government must win not only the united support of its people living on the British Isles but also of the self-governing dominions far from the probable theater of war, who are naturally inclined to measure their safety by the distance which separates them from the potential aggressor. Moreover, as the preservation of her life-line to the Empire is vital for a successful conduct of war, England must be certain of the neutrality or eventual support of the nations and continents which border or lie across the routes her troops and supplies must travel.

It is difficult to see how in the absence of a clear-cut case of aggression such world-wide unity and moral support can be obtained except by a long period of appeasing the enemy: granting him concessions and offering him immense loans in the hope that he will reorient his economy toward peace production and agree to peaceful coöperation. In a world divided into sovereign states lacking the spirit of solidarity, appeasement is imperative. It is the only means by which a peaceful nation can prove its devotion to peace and at the same time make clear to world opinion that the aggressor is insatiable, and his ambitions a threat not only to that nation but to the world at large. The determined aggressor, having provided himself with a total war economy in time of peace, may disregard the opinion of the world. But the defense, yielding to him in advance all the advantages of the offense, must lean heavily upon the imponderables of international morality.

In the absence of a clear case of aggression in a world of hostile powers including not only one but many possible aggressors, all must be appeased in the hope of winning over one or more of them, while the main enemy emerges as the enemy of all.

If, therefore, appeasement is not wholly devoid of advantages to the appeaser, it turns into a boomerang when it is practised too long and too lavishly. There is a point of diminishing returns at which its advantages begin to evaporate. That point reached, the continued practice of appeasement no longer tends to unite the nation. On the contrary, it divides the nation against itself and separates it from its friends and allies abroad. On the home front it creates dissension among political parties on the subject of foreign policy—the one subject on which they are normally united, since the public takes little interest in foreign policy in times of peace. The government or party in power then falls under the suspicion of acting against the best interests of the country for the sake of a certain class or faction. An atmosphere of distrust is created in which tales of connivance with the enemy gain widespread credence. All the dissatisfied and antisocial elements, all born traitors and seekers after power in every class, awake to the idea that there may be advantages for themselves in practising what they suspect the government is doing for the established and privileged class.

The effect of prolonged appeasement upon potential allies

is even more disastrous. All governments, however unpopular, still exercise greater authority at home than they do abroad, and faith in the integrity of those in power is not easily undermined. For some reason unfathomable to the rational mind nations usually prefer to be ruled by a rogue of their own language and what is erroneously conceived to be their own flesh and blood than by a foreigner of the same stamp. The exceptions, Napoleon and Hitler, merely confirm the rule, since the French made the Little Corsican one of their own, as the Germans have made Hitler a German. (I have heard it argued by people who are interested in such distinctions that he could not even be reckoned an Austrian, since the inhabitants of Braunau are Slovaks and therefore Slavs.)

Baudelaire once explained that if he were offered a choice between a louse and a bedbug he would refuse to choose. This is a notion foreign to the spirit of nationalism. Be this as it may, if a government can fall subject to suspicion at home of conniving with the enemy, it is even more likely to be suspected of such treason abroad—and suspected very much sooner.

England, destined by her geographical position and also by her internal state structure to be the last citadel of European freedom in jeopardy of attack by an aggressor, can still afford to wait and see, to appease the enemy long after continental nations living close to the potential enemy have been placed in deadly peril. Britain's margin of safety is greater than that of any other European power with the exception of Russia. As her margin is reduced, the margin of the others evaporates completely. But her action is determined like that of all sovereign states primarily by what she considers to be her own interests. Thus as long as Britain appeases the enemy she does so not only at her own expense but even more at the expense of her potential allies. Only Russia, having vast space at her disposal, can wait as long as Britain, but the space at the disposal of the other Europeans is negligible. In the last war the space into which France could retreat before the onslaught was just great enough, and even then it required the combined efforts of Russia and Britain to enable her to deliver the Battle of the Marne.

Before appeasement has given the enemy too many bases and yielded to him the full strategical advantage of time and space, the European nations can still, singly or in combined effort, deal with him without the support of Britain's sea power, but as they wait for Britain, too little and too late arrives for them much sooner, and they are then inclined to pray God to deliver them from the friend who has delayed too long.

But they too must have the clear moral argument on their side before they can take the offensive, and as each is on a different time-table, determined by its own geographical position in relation to the enemy, the unity which might have saved them at first is destroyed. Demoralization, such as begins to set in inside the nations which practise appeasement too long, also appears among the allies. Each withdraws into isolation, seeking safety in its proclaimed neutrality and leaving the larger powers to settle the differences among themselves. Some, attracted by the growing power of the enemy and the declining prestige of Britain, connive with him economically for the sake of immediate gain and thus facilitate the task of the aggressor, enabling him to practise the method of divide and rule. "Farsighted," they take advantage of the fact that they have nothing to fear from Britain. Thus they conclude that they can not lose. If Britain wins, well and good; if she loses they will have picked the winner.

Throughout her history Britain has time and again laid herself open to the charge of being false to her friends and friendly to the enemy, whenever she has practised appeasement, a policy which has earned her the epithet of Perfidious Albion. Time and again this policy, based upon the hope that the enemy will hang himself if given rope enough, has caused her the loss of her allies and brought the fortress set in a silver sea to the brink of irretrievable disaster. But it has also enabled her to fight in the eleventh hour, when all seemed lost, with right and justice on her side and with a courage and devotion which never acknowledges itself beaten and which, bringing victory in the end and liberation to the continent, has created the legend that she loses every battle except the last.

In this war as in the war against Napoleon she faced the enemy alone until she regained all her allies on the continent by the action of the aggressor and by the example of her courage. England took it for a whole year, seeing her cities destroyed and her civilian population mercilessly bombed. In the field of battle at Tobruk (in 1941), Malta, and even Dunkirk, she stood her ground as well as the Americans in the fox-holes of Bataan. Meanwhile, the internal structure of the island has been undergoing a profound change, approaching the appearance of a city under siege. Social distinctions and caste differences tend to disappear, and the realization of the common fate brings out the finest quality in men—the moment in the soul of man when he is nearest to the full realization of the meaning of liberty, equality, and fraternity.

In the life of nations these moments correspond to the days of genuine happiness in the life of the individual. If such moments could be held to and remembered in spontaneously created institutions after the danger is passed, life would become worth living for all.

England to-day is still true to the words spoken a century ago by Ralph Waldo Emerson: "I see her not dispirited, not weak, but well remembering that she has seen dark days before:—indeed with a kind of instinct that she sees a little better in a cloudy day, and that in storm of battle and calamity she has a secret vigor and a pulse like a cannon!"

8

The Birth of Modern Appeasement

APPEASEMENT of post-war Germany originated in the fourteen points proclaimed by President Woodrow Wilson during World War I. Like the conciliatory notes sent by President Wilson before the American entry into the war, his declared peace aims were read in Germany in Germany's own way; a way of which, in the French phrase, she holds the secret. The fourteen points were interpreted as meaning that if Germany but consented to stop shooting she would not have to support any of the consequences of the war.

This interpretation, however, was put upon the fourteen points only after defeat had become a certainty. When first published they were by no means hailed with delight. The liberal *Berliner Tageblatt* called them the fourteen mousetraps. A poster illustrated graphically in a series of pictures what peace without a clear German victory would mean. It would leave Germany with a huge internal war debt, the size of which was symbolized by a man staggering under the weight of an immense sack of money, and trying to subsist on a mutilated map of Germany, minus Belgium, "vital to Germany's existence" and minus a large slice in the east which had gone to make up the new Polish state. On the opposite side of the ledger, the poster revealed the desirability of a German victory: The sackful of debt had shrunk to insignificant proportion carried in the hollow of a hand; while the European continent was shown to be hardly big enough to contain the map of Germany. Short of a German victory,

128

Germany was not interested. But when that victory evaporated, then suddenly the fourteen points were conceived to be of Messianic import and Wilson acquired the stature of a savior.

In the aftermath of the war much was written on the difference between the reality of Versailles and the spirit of the fourteen points. But at the outbreak of the war of 1914 the Allies offered no promise of a "fair peace." Such an offer would have been adjudged an absurdity, encouraging the invader to persevere in his effort to conquer the world by promising him that if he lost he would but have lost that which never did belong to him. Such a promise puts a premium on aggression, unless the assumption is justified that the armies of the conqueror are unwilling tools in the hands of their rulers. It was in fact upon such an assumption that Wilson based his offer of a just peace, proclaiming at the same time that the American people were not fighting the German people but only their government.

The effect of Wilson's fourteen points upon the German people may be measured by the German offensive in the spring and summer of 1918. The German Army had lost none of its drive. Once again they advanced to the Marne, until they were stopped by the Americans at Chemin-des-Dames. At Arras they succeeded in separating the British and French armies and might have won victory if they had been able to exploit the gap. What prevented such exploitation was the fortuitous circumstance that Arras was stocked to overflowing with food. Not the Wilsonian peace offer but hunger broke down the morale of the German Army for one day. For twenty-four hours the German soldiers at Arras dispersed and ate their fill. No commands were obeyed until they had had enough. But by that time the French and English had succeeded in closing the gap between their armies and after that they held. To the new generation of Nazis swaggering with insolence, contemptuous of the older generation which had lost the First World War, Captain Marx told this story in the *Militärische Wochenzeitschrift* admonishing the young militarists not to believe that their elders had lacked in leadership or fighting spirit.

France and England were in no position to repudiate the American thesis. When the United States entered the war, the Allies were near exhaustion. The Russian front was about to collapse, threatening to liberate millions of fresh German troops for a renewed assault upon the western front. There had been mutiny in France, British losses had been heavy. And war weariness threatened to make the German unrestricted submarine warfare effective in knocking Britain out of the war.

Clemenceau in France rallied the people by his war cry: "*Je fais la guerre,*" while Lloyd George promised to make England a country fit for heroes. The allied nations, nevertheless, stood in grave need of material and spiritual aid to endure the ordeal as there was no end in sight. The United States provided both man power and an ideal reaching beyond victory. She gave generously of her vast resources, promising to make of this war an end to all wars, and to aid in the construction of a world in which democracies could live in security.

Actions speak louder than words. In 1914 the people of the countries invaded by Germany needed no more eloquent plea for their cause than the action of the German armies. But the people of United States were separated from the theater of war by thousands of miles of ocean, and stood in no danger of immediate invasion. The American people were divided in their sympathies and traditionally opposed to entangling alliances. To win their united support to the cause of the Allies required more than the German threat to the freedom of the seas.

Though there can be little doubt now that Germany would not have been content with the conquest of Europe and the destruction of the British Empire, had she been victorious, the people of the United States remained skeptical in 1917. Wilson's fourteen points consequently acted both as a stimulus to the flagging morale of the tired armies of the Allies, and at the same time appealed to the native idealism of the American people. To all it set a goal well worth the sacrifice, but it also contained the seeds of failure. The goal it set itself could only be attained if its fundamental thesis were correct. It risked all on the assumption that the German people had been misled by their militaristic rulers and that they had gone to war only because they believed that they were fighting to protect their country and their homes. It was assumed that once they were liberated from their masters they would willingly coöperate in the reconstruction of a devastated world and that, given a fair treaty, the people of Germany would be reconciled to the defeat of their armies.

The government of the United States could more easily act upon such an optimistic interpretation of the causes of German aggression, because, if the thesis were proved wrong, the consequences would be borne at once, not by the United States, but by the immediate geographical neighbors of Germany, and by France in particular. In the view of the French Government the magnitude of the risk was too great for them to feel secure in the creation of a League of Nations, even though the United States promised to become a member. Thus the war aims announced by Wilson also planted the seeds of dissension among the Allies.

At the Peace Conference, Great Britain supported President Wilson in his opposition to Clemenceau's demand for annexation of the Rhineland by France. Though there were profound differences of viewpoint and temperament between Lloyd George and Wilson they were more nearly in accord with each other than either was with Clemenceau. Germany had lost her fleet. Neither the United States nor Great Britain thought that they stood in any danger from renewed German aggression. At Versailles, the narrow channel which separates England from the mainland of Europe loomed as large in the British mind as the expanse of the Atlantic Ocean which divides America from Europe. Both powers consequently thought that they could afford to be generous to the vanquished.

On the night of the eleventh of November, 1918, while the people of France, England, and the United States rejoiced at the deliverance, a conference took place between Lloyd George and Winston Churchill. They discussed ways and means of putting Germany back on her feet. In 1815, after her victory over Napoleon, England sided with France against the Holy Alliance which was formed by the victorious powers for the express purpose of destroying the spirit of the French Revolution. After 1918, it seemed equally wise to appease Germany since she presented a picture, albeit deceptive, of embracing the ideals of democracy. France had emerged from the war the dominating military power on the European continent. Germany had not only lost her fleet, but she was also going to be disarmed and would have to bear the cost of the war to boot. Under the circumstances it appeared as if France stood in no further need of continuous British support. It is true that Germany had been the greatest commercial and industrial rival of England in the markets of the world, but to men brought up on the economic theories of the Manchester school such rivalry holds no terror. They were even inclined to welcome it, as they welcomed competition at home. Something of the spirit of fair play prevalent on the cricket fields, demanded that a helping hand be stretched out to the beaten enemy, or perhaps more accurately, it was a case of extending accommodations to a debtor who, although meriting bankruptcy, must yet be supported for the sake of one's own best interests.

Balance of Power

The main reason, however, for the British support of the American thesis remained the principle of the balance of power. In the absence of permanent bonds between nations— as long as sovereign states place the interest of their sovereignty above the moral law, in a world in which the military might of nations wanes and waxes like the moon—the maintenance of a balance of power between nations presents the only usable, though often useless, instrument for the safeguard of peace. It is a principle which reads like a formula by Euclid. When the power of all potential allies is equal, or nearly equal, to the combined military might of all potential enemies, peace will be maintained by all, since none can hope to gain any lasting or decisive victory. But the mathematical presentation of the theory is a deception. The balance is in fact arbitrarily determined by each power in its own way, and in estimating the power of the enemy there is a wide margin for error. That margin is all the greater when the estimate concerns the comparative strength of the ally in relation to the enemy. Free from anxiety for themselves the United States and Great Britain felt none for France. It was feared that if she were allowed to exercise sovereignty over the industrial regions of Germany a new cause for war would be created, similar to the problem of Alsace-Lorraine.

That mechanical application of the balance-of-power principle took no account of the difference in the national aspirations of France and Germany. The two countries were put on a common denominator, leaving out of account the fact that not France, who had lost Alsace-Lorraine in 1871, but Germany, who had gained these provinces, became the aggressor in 1914. It further failed to take account of the fact that although Germany was disarmed, she still had all or nearly all the industrial and agricultural resources which she possessed in 1914, and that she could rebuild her armies at any time unless constant vigilance were exercised by all. In 1914, Germany was strong enough to defy the whole world, and very nearly to defeat the whole world. Without the support of Russia and Great Britain, France could not have won the battle of the Marne, in spite of the military error committed by the German High Command. Without the aid of the United States, France would have lost the second battle of the Marne. How, then, could the French be expected to believe that the series of miracles originating in German stupidity which had saved them and the rest of the civilized world, would be repeated?

Clemenceau saw well enough that France would never be

able to withstand a German assault alone, unless she were in control of the industrial regions of the Rhine. Nor could any German pretense to democracy and protestations of innocence convince the old tiger that the leopard had changed its spots. With Gallic wit he referred to the Wilsonian peace aims: "He has fourteen points, has he? God, mercifully, only had ten."

The story of what took place behind the closed doors of the Peace Conference differs, as each reporter has told it, in accordance with his own bias. On the assumption that there would have been no Hitler if the Wilsonian viewpoint had prevailed entirely at Versailles and if the United States had joined the League of Nations, Wilson was presented as the tragic hero of the drama, and Clemenceau as the villain. Unfortunately the historian is deprived of the means so simple in the laboratory, of repeating his experiments in order to test all possible variables, which would permit him to demonstrate beyond question the accuracy of his thesis. Clemenceau, certain of his case, fought as valiantly for France as he had fought the war against Germany and against the internal reaction in France throughout his life.

In retirement he remained bitter against Wilson, whom he described to Konrad Bercovici and other American correspondents and visitors as that great humanitarian who had been a humanitarian to the wolf and not to the lamb. "Ah, there is a good man who loses our country for us. . . . Wilson was so good, he was worse than the Germans who are so very bad."

In comparing the Germans to wolves, Clemenceau referred to a fable by La Fontaine, *The Wolves and the Lambs*. It so well describes our epoch that it is worth recounting:

After a thousand years and more of declared war, the wolves concluded peace with the lambs. Evidently it served the common good, for although the wolves had gorged on many a lost sheep, the shepherds wore many fine coats made from the skins of the wolves. Thus none could enjoy life, without trembling. Freedom from fear neither for the pastures nor for the blood-bath.

Hence PEACE was concluded and hostages exchanged. The wolves gave their cubs; and the lambs their watch-dogs. The exchange, it must be noted, was made in accordance with established forms of procedure and supervised by a commission.

Time passed. The master cubs grew to be perfect wolves, thirsting for blood. They kept on the lookout until the shepherds were gone. Then they tore half of the fattest lambs, took them between their teeth and made off to the forest. Secret messages had reached their people. The dogs, relying upon the good faith of the wolves, were surprised in their sleep and strangled. All this was well planned, the dogs hardly felt any pain as each was torn to bits; none escaped.

Moral: We may conclude thereby that war must be waged constantly on the wicked.

Peace is a great good, I do concur; But of what use is it with enemies devoid of honor?

The only truly effective fifth column anywhere were the Germans, who had basked in the hospitality of their neighbors. It was their secret messages rather than native treason which reached their folks in the forest.

After the last war, undernourished German children had found a home in Norway. By 1940, they had grown into perfect Nazis, returning with their people to the land of the lambs. Surpassing the imagination of Æsop or La Fontaine, among the several thousand grown Nazis who had benefited as children by the love of their foster parents in Norway none was found to betray his country by warning his benefactors. Thus the analogy between the fable and the German attack upon Norway is not a perfect one: there had never been a war between Norway and Germany, no hostages exchanged, and no eternal peace concluded.

The League of Nations

It was only by threatening to continue the war alone that Clemenceau obtained a promise of a permanent alliance between France, England, and the United States. In the League of Nations he had no faith at all. On this point he was immediately vindicated, since the United States Senate repudiated the Treaty of Versailles and the alliance with France and refused to let the United States join the League. The isolationist Senators feared that the League would be powerful enough to endanger the sovereignty of the United States Congress. But Clemenceau knew better, he anticipated that it would have no power at all.

It is difficult to speak of the League of Nations with reverence. During one of the sessions of the League the Lithuanian dictator Valdemaras orated on the injustice suffered by his country at the hands of the Polish Government. Early in the life of the Lithuanian Republic, Poland had taken possession of Vilna, the capital of Lithuania, and no power on earth short of war could make her give it up.

Valdemaras dictated in Lithuania until an army revolt put him behind bars. He deserved it, if for no other reason than for having talked at the League with deadly dullness for three hours. The entire galaxy of European statesmen were assembled to hear his speech and at the end every one of them was sound asleep. Only Zaleski, foreign minister of Poland could get no rest. He had to have every word of the Lithuanian discourse translated for him. Though his country held Vilna it was important to him to defeat his opponent in debate. Restlessly he shifted in his seat, looked at his watch, chewed a fountain-pen, stared at the ceiling and frowned at his colleagues who were sleeping the sleep of the well-fed just. Finally and inadvertently, while throwing his legs about, he kicked Aristide Briand. Briand woke up long enough to sympathize with Zaleski's plight: "My poor friend, suffering from insomnia, aren't you?"

In the balance of the League's achievements the constructive work was incidental while the harm done finally swept away whatever good it accomplished. The representatives of the member nations at the League used the building as a club, a permanent meeting place for diplomats; but by no means an exclusive meeting place. Something of the spirit in which the League of Nations was conceived lingered on and made it inconvenient to wash all the dirty linen on the premises.

By its very existence the League created the illusion that something vital might be done through its agency for the establishment of permanent peace. But behind its façade of magnificent oratory there stood the reality of separate sovereign states whose action and inaction were not determined by words but by their geographical position, the nature of their institutions, and the character of their people. As an instrument for restraining the action of the totalitarian state the League proved as effective as the sleeping dogs in La Fontaine's fable. It was not only their faith in the honor of the enemy which rendered the dogs helpless. By the time the wolf cubs had grown up the dogs had become old and toothless. While the League debated total or partial disarmament Europe was in fact disarmed as measured by the potential of its industries. The League was marking time, waiting for the cubs to grow up.

War Guilt and France

The psychological error committed at Versailles and resented so hotly in Germany was not the guilt clause written into the Treaty. But once written there, the United States and England proceeded to act as if all had shared equally in the responsibility for the war. Lloyd George gave it as his considered opinion, which was also the opinion of the post-war world, that "none of the statesmen of Europe had wanted war, but that they had stumbled or glided into it." It would be difficult to overestimate the extent to which this idea colored the thinking and influenced the action of the western world in the aftermath of the war.

The reaction to the horrors of the war, and the disillusionment born of the post-war economic crisis made this comfortable view acceptable. Since no one wanted the post-war world, people also assumed that they had not wanted the war, and in the democracies this was true enough. It was even true of the democratic governments who made every effort to solve by peaceful negotiations the controversy which led to the war and which was deliberately engineered by Austria and supported by Germany. Not having wanted the war themselves it seemed inconceivable to the democratic peoples that the German people *had* wanted it as well as the glory of conquest which they had been promised by their government. Germany had not wanted the defeat, and not having wanted the defeat people in Germany also believed that they had not wanted the war, which brought them the defeat. The flood of pacifist literature consequently reached Germany as it swept the world. Hardly a novel or a treatise was written which did not illustrate, and emphasize by human and convincing examples, the viewpoint that the war had just happened and that nobody really at any time had ever wanted it. It followed logically that the way to prevent the recurrence of war was to prevent the government of one's own country—the only one over whom public opinion can exercise some control—from stumbling or gliding into war.

In truth, however, there is no collective enterprise of which man can conceive which requires more purposeful activity than the preparation and conduct of war, except it be an aggressive war. Love and hate between individuals may strike like lightning for unaccountable reasons; people are known to have stumbled or glided into marriage and divorce, suicide and murder. But "busy as the devil is," how can Hans Schmidt of Hinter-Pommern get at Jean Martin from Marseilles in no man's land, between barbed wires, except that he has been ordered to go there, to kill people he has never heard of or seen, and to go there in company with millions of others all equipped with implements of death they are well trained to use to evil account. And who else but the men of his government, to whom he thinks he owes allegiance, could have organized—years in advance—so vast an army of fanatical men, supplied them with arms, and conditioned them psychologically to march on Paris at the risk of their lives, when in peacetime they could have traveled there in comfort for the price of a railway ticket? A street brawl may develop spontaneously, but no disciplined army moves across the frontier to wage a war of aggression without orders from its government and its generals. Did the German Panzer division rumble into Poland without orders, or did the Japanese army, navy, and air force just glide and stumble into the attack upon Pearl Harbor? It is sufficient to-day to ask this question to have the answer. But the world between the wars was engaged in a metaphysical investigation of the ultimate causes of war, and found the wrong answer.

If all nations had been equally guilty of the war then, indeed, the Versailles Treaty imposed unjustified hardships on the people of Germany, and the guilt clause was an uncalled-for humiliation of a great people. The Weimar Republic knew well how to take advantage of this change in world opinion. If the Nazis knew how to be grateful they would have set a monument to the republic they killed for the yeoman service which it did for them in the field of propaganda. Long after the world at large had conceded the point, Germany refused to allow herself to forget the clause which proclaimed her responsibility. It is the one and only signature which she has set to a treaty that she was unwilling to forget. It did not suit her purpose to forget, because events have a logic of their own which men can not escape. If Germany was not guilty, then who was? France, of course, since she had a motive; never a criminal without a motive, is the cardinal rule of every detective story. But for France and Alsace-Lorraine, of which she had been robbed, there would have been no war. But for her the war would have been long forgotten. It was the intransigeance of France which made of the Versailles Treaty an unjust treaty, and it was she again who was responsible for the post-war crisis, since she refused to see the treaty abrogated.

Supported by public opinion in England and in the United States, the theory was evolved that concessions must be granted to Germany so that her democracy might survive the attack to which it was being subjected for having "capitulated to the dictates of Versailles." The whole weight of world opinion was thrown into the balance to force France to yield one concession after another in favor of Germany. Up to the Treaty of Locarno, France resisted this policy which she saw well enough was losing her the peace. Poincaré, who succeeded Clemenceau, tried to compensate France for the failure to obtain control over the Rhineland, and for the loss of the British and American alliance, by insisting upon strict fulfilment of the letter and the spirit of the treaty and by concluding alliances with the Balkan countries and Poland. In Germany he was denounced as the instigator of the war. Newspaper columnists throughout the world indulged in learned comparisons between the legalistic and narrow mind of provincial France, symbolized by the lawyer Poincaré—unable to escape the strait-jacket of juristic formulas in the broad expanse of world diplomacy—and broad-minded England, fair to the enemy of yesterday, stretching out a helping hand to the man who is down instead of kicking him in the groin.

The Munich of the Pre-Hitler Era

Until the conclusion of the Treaty of Locarno, France resisted stubbornly the policy of appeasement forced upon her, pointing out that every concession granted merely called forth a new demand from Germany. In the end, however, she was unable to withstand the weight of world-wide disapproval of her action. Liberal and socialist France, afraid of the isolation into which she was being forced, made a cardinal issue of the foreign policy of Poincaré. He was nicknamed by the leftist press: Poincaré-la-guerre, an epithet which became a slogan of the Cartel. The pacifist and antimilitarist forces of France triumphed in the elections of 1924. Poincaré was replaced by Edouard Herriot. At the same time Great Britain gave herself a labor government supported by the Liberals. Ramsay MacDonald, leader of the Labor Party, and the greatest misfortune in British politics next to Neville Chamberlain, became Prime Minister. He and Herriot prepared the ground for the Treaty of Locarno which was concluded by Austen Chamberlain for England, Aristide Briand for France, and Gustav Stresemann for Germany.

The Locarno Treaty (1925) was a German suggestion, and Stresemann had every reason to be proud of his achievement. It was the Munich of the pre-Hitler era. By that treaty England assumed the rôle of holding the balance while Germany and France were placed in the two scales. Britain promised to both that she would throw her whole weight into the balance on the side of Germany if Germany were attacked by France and on the side of France and Belgium if these were attacked by Germany. The treaty was hailed throughout the world as an eminently fair arrangement, holding out hope that henceforth peace and coöperation between the European powers might prevail. But the fairest treaty is worth no more than the spirit in which it is concluded.

It contained a vital clause forbidding Germany to fortify the Rhineland after the withdrawal of the French troops. Violation of this clause was to be regarded as a *casus belli*, but Britain, reluctant as always to bind her action in advance, left a door open for retreat. In case of German violation of the clause, there were to be consultations between France and England.

On the part of Germany the pen which freely signed the treaty was filled with a blend of several poisonous reservations and interpretations. It was regarded as an open admission that an attack by France upon Germany was at least as likely to happen as an attack by Germany upon France. The German reactionary press resented that France should have received any guarantee at all, seeing that she was still armed while Germany was disarmed. Since the treaty was not supplemented by an equal guarantee to Poland against German aggression it was concluded in Germany and Poland that it tacitly gave Germany a free hand to alter the eastern frontiers of the Reich at the expense of Poland. Thus it loosened the bonds of alliance between Poland and France. If Poland were attacked by Germany, France could not count upon England, and thus the likelihood of French failure to come to the aid of her eastern ally was measurably increased. Anxiety on this point weakened the bargaining strength of Poland in the field of diplomacy which, according to Clausewitz, merely prepares the settlement of differences by arms. But this achievement by no means satisfied reactionary Germany. The Treaty of Locarno was under attack for failure to give her a free hand explicitly to deal with Poland as she saw fit. Furthermore, if an attack by France upon Germany was as likely to happen as the other way round, it followed that she had been as guilty of the war in 1914 as Germany. Thus Germany was vindicated, but by no means content. Stresemann was under attack for having eaten breakfast with Briand in some quiet and peaceful inn. There was grave danger that he had been sincere, that a real spirit of peace might prevail in the end and thus rob Germany of all hope of revenge.

Among the former allies, however, Briand became an apostle of peace. In thundering speeches at the League of Nations he announced that as long as he lived there would be no war. He was an old man, and before he died Japan had attacked Manchuria, testing the League of Nations and the Briand-Kellogg Pact and finding them both wanting. But Briand did not mean that he was going to prevent the outbreak of war anywhere in the world singlehanded. He spoke for France, driven into the defensive against the Weimar Republic, England, and the United States. It was a declaration of appeasement. France, accused of disturbing the peace of the world by retaining her arms, proclaimed that she would do all in her power to reconcile and appease Germany.

Henceforth the Locarno Treaty, concluded outside of the League of Nations, set a precedent and developed a practice. Diplomatic negotiations were no longer conducted between the governments of the Great Powers exclusively through their ambassadors and foreign offices. These had to be supplemented by the League of Nations and by personal contacts

between foreign ministers and prime ministers, turned traveling salesmen for the commodity of peace. They journeyed to
each other's capitals or met in some quiet bathing resort, disturbing the peace of the old and the infirm. International conferences outside of the League of Nations met and appointed
committees. The instruments of peace negotiations were multiplied and with them multiplied the number of treaties and
agreements signed. Each conference was accompanied by the
prayers of a war-weary world hoping against hope that some
good might come of it. But as the treaties multiplied they lost
value, as all goods do when the market is flooded with them.

One of the last products of this era was the sheet of paper
—a non-aggression pact signed by Hitler—with which Chamberlain returned from Munich. Waving it in the air, he claimed
that he had brought back peace with honor. He also quoted
Shakespeare: "Out of this nettle, danger, we pluck this flower,
safety."

The quotation was looked up, and it was found that Hot-
spur, after making this statement, went on to read from a letter as follows: "The purpose you undertake is dangerous; the
friends you have named uncertain; the time itself unsorted;
and your whole plot too light for the counterpoise of so great
an opposition."

Years before Adolf Hitler had outlined to Rauschnigg the
advantages of signing agreements. The aggressor can always
break them at will, meanwhile he lulls the defense into the
belief that they are safe. Unable and unwilling to take the
offense, militarily weak nations must needs make a virtue of
necessity and believe in the sanctity of treaties, while the aggressor can choose the time and place for the attack, certain
that he will find the defense asleep.

Bon gré, Mal gré

From the Treaty of Locarno to the fade-out of the Weimar
Republic the stream of appeasement fed by the tributaries of
Pacifism and fear of Bolshevism, flowed on, corroding slowly

the order created at Versailles. After Hitler came into power it changed into a torrential stream until it shed itself into the lethal sea. The feeble action of international conferences seeking to regulate its course towards peace and coöperation proved too light for "the counterpoise of so great an opposition."

The symptoms of its failure appeared at every turn. Neither the universal admission that all had been equally guilty of the war; nor the early evacuation of the Rhineland; nor the immense loans floated for German economy on the financial markets of the world; nor the moratorium on all German debts proclaimed by President Hoover to help Germany over the economic crisis; nor the subsequent annulment of all reparation payments consented to by France, succeeded in preventing the growth of the Nazi Party and of the war spirit in Germany.

By the time Hitler seized power in Germany nothing was left of the Versailles Treaty except its territorial clauses and the limitations to German armaments. Up to that day the policy of granting concessions could still be justified. As long as there is life there is hope. Léon Blum, a better man than he has been a prophet, assured France that German socialists would never capitulate before Hitler. The English, less inclined to prophecy, were resigned in advance. If the Germans have never understood the English neither have the English, with few exceptions, shown any ability to fathom the German spirit. Judging others by one's self is no monopoly of the individual; nations likewise are liable to lapse into this error. It was argued in England that Hitler would prove to be more reasonable once he had gained power. It was all very well to act the wild man while in the opposition, but the responsibility of power had made many a fire-eater feed on humble-pie ere this.

The dilemma with which Nazism triumphant confronted the world was brought out in a debate in the French Chambre des Députés, after Germany had left the League of Nations, following the example of Japan. Léon Blum argued that Ger-

many must be integrated *bon gré, mal gré* into a system of
collective security. Flandin, then Prime Minister, demanded
further elucidation of the cryptic phrase. What did M. Blum
mean by *bon gré, mal gré?* If it proved impossible to do so
bon gré by peaceful persuasion, would M. Blum suggest that
it be done *mal gré* by war? There was no reply. The question
was unanswerable in a world which would have regarded intervention in Germany as an act of aggression.

There was at that time still sufficient solidarity left among
the members of the League of Nations to decree sanctions
short of war when the Italians attacked Ethiopia, but a preventive war, a war waged upon the aggressor before he had
decided upon the time and place most suitable for the waging
of a Blitzkrieg could not even have been proposed openly,
either in Parliament or at the League of Nations. It was rumored that Pilsudski, dictator of Poland, had proposed such
a course of action in 1933. He had offered to go it alone, provided Britain mobilized the fleet to blockade Germany and
France manned the Maginot Line as a demonstration of solidarity. A dictator himself, Pilsudski had no need to ask for
public support in Poland for his plan, and it was even more
important for him to act than for his western allies. Hemmed
in by Russia and Germany, Poland could expect that she
would have to fight on two fronts unless she took the initiative. Failing to obtain the support of England and France,
the alternative for Poland was an alliance with either of her
two neighbors, Germany or Russia. Poland could, in fact,
choose only between trusting the word of Hitler or trusting
the word of Stalin. Herself a Fascist state, it was a foregone
conclusion that she would side with Germany. Hence the ten
year non-aggression pact between Nazi Germany and Poland
which constituted the first official break in the solidarity of the
allied powers.

The point of diminishing returns in the usefulness of the
appeasement policy had been reached. But in 1933 it passed
unperceived. War with Germany had become inevitable, but
the world-wide opposition to war prompted every official

spokesman in and out of the League of Nations to repudiate that idea as too dreadful to contemplate.

Perhaps at no time in the history of mankind, and certainly at no time in the modern era, has opposition to war been as universal and unconditional as in the years between the wars. Paradoxically it was precisely this opposition which made it inevitable that the peaceful nations would have to accept war under the most unfavorable conditions for themselves. It left the aggressor free to chart his course and load his guns unperturbed, while his intended victims imposed rules and regulations upon themselves and upon their friends, unwittingly designed to deliver the prey bound hand and foot to the predatory power which would emerge the strongest in the totalitarian constellation. In retrospect it is easy to see that Germany was the chief enemy, but the pre-war years seemed to offer a wider choice.

Collective Security

After the fall of France Mr. Churchill expressed the opinion that the catastrophe could have been avoided if all the democracies had stood together. It is still thought that strict adherence to the doctrine of collective security would have prevented the aggressor from picking out his victims one by one and hanging them separately. But that is too easy an assumption. The principle of collective security could not become operative until the enemy was fully prepared to launch his attack, and by that time any measure short of war is doomed to failure. While the enemy makes his preparations, the doctrine of national sovereignty prevents his intended victims from intervening in what is regarded to be his internal affairs. National sovereignty, which was guarded jealously by all the members and non-members of the League of Nations, is meaningless unless it is based upon reciprocity. It says in effect: "I shall not meddle with your business unless you meddle with mine, or with the business of my allies."

Under modern industrial conditions, however, when the

enemy starts meddling with the business of another nation, he is well prepared for all contingencies. The time of grace which he has been granted permits him to concentrate his forces against the point of attack which he has chosen in advance. He can take advantage of the business as usual practices of a world with which he is still at peace, import all the material he can not manufacture, and stock up in raw material and foodstuffs against a possible blockade. Furthermore, under modern industrial conditions, only a totalitarian government can gather the forces necessary for the offense, and thereby acquire at the same time sufficient strength for the defense as well. Once such a government has given the order to its armies to advance, its prestige is engaged to the hilt. The die cast, it can retreat only at the price of losing face abroad and at the risk of revolution within.

Sanctions, even with teeth in them, are powerless to stop the aggressor. Moreover, even to institute sanctions a democratic government must first have the consent of parliament and public opinion. Where sanctions are automatically decreed by a League of Nations for all its members, it is still imperative that consultations take place between the member governments; organizations set up to administrate the blockade; provisions made to meet the contingency of war. All this consumes time, which the aggressor uses to full advantage, generally carrying off the price before the sanctions can be put into effect, and invariably before they can hurt him. While the totalitarian aggressor can not retreat, however, the democracies can. The price they have to pay for such a retreat does not appear to be fatal at once. The secretary of the foreign office can be made the scapegoat and sacked. At the worst a vote of censure overthrows the whole cabinet, in which case it is reshuffled. Thus the road of least resistance beckons the democracies with irresistible lure to retreat, while the alternative appears to be war for a lost cause.

In the case of Japan and Italy before this war, a clear-cut case of aggression was provided. They tested the doctrine of collective security and found it wanting. It was rumored after the attack upon Manchuria by Japan, in 1931, that Secretary of State Stimson had approached the government of Great Britain with an offer of collective action against Japan. Sir John Simon, then secretary of the British foreign office, had seen fit to put the proposal into the "Don't give it a second thought" department.

The facts of the case are still buried in the archives, but it is by no means certain that even a Winston Churchill could have done much better at the time. Under the democratic form of government neither war nor sanctions can be decreed by the sole will of a minister of state or even by the President and Prime Minister respectively. In the United States an alliance with a foreign power must be voted by a three-quarters majority in Congress. In England a simple majority in Parliament is theoretically sufficient, but for all practical purposes there must be unanimity. If there was an American plan for action against Japan it is not likely that anything more than the use of sanctions was being contemplated. But sanctions are useless unless they are backed by the determination to wage war if the enemy fails to retreat. Such a threat must be backed by loaded guns, and in sufficient quantities, to give him any pause at all. A long-range blockade of Japan from Singapore, Pearl Harbor, and Vladivostok would not have stopped her from conquering Manchuria. She had collected all the necessary material for that conquest before she began the march. The conquest consummated, the blockaders would have been confronted with a *fait accompli.* Not having gone to war in the first place, it would have been even more difficult to go to war in order to liberate an already conquered Manchuria, and so in all likelihood the blockaders would have called the whole thing off.

The mere public airing of the plan to stop the Japanese aggression by concerted action with the United States was certain to have earned the two powers the everlasting enmity of Japan. They got that in the end anyway, but in 1931 it was not wholly unreasonable to hope that Japan was following a limited objective. For the British, the thought of a possible future alliance with Japan in case of war with Russia was not excluded. Perhaps the most important cause of failure, however, was the distance of Manchuria from both the people of the United States and the inhabitants of the British Isles. Manchuria could, in the imagination of the many, not have been farther away if it had been situated on the North Pole, and our sympathies fail where our imagination does not reach.

The City of London, on the other hand, arguing from the viewpoint of a liberal economy, assumed that Japan would not be able to exploit its newly conquered territory for lack of capital, and that therefore sooner or later she would have to come to the chief capital market of the world for loans. In that case terms could be dictated to her. As late as 1938, Neville Chamberlain defended this point of view in Parliament, and in the United States, Japan was appeased to the day of her occupation of Indo-China after the capitulation of Vichy, France. The State Department was counting upon the business interests in Japan to restrain the militarists. It looked for the maintenance of peace to the right source, but it underestimated the power which the state had already acquired over the business world in Japan.

In the case of Italy's attack upon Ethiopia the victim was as far removed from the sympathy of the western world as Manchuria, but the enemy was close, and indignation ran high. This Italian war upon Ethiopia provided the last opportunity for the League of Nations. There is no reason to assume that if Italy had been stopped German totalitarianism would have been seriously hurt. That was another illusion of the time, but a defeated Italy would have greatly facilitated the task of the Allies in dealing with Germany.

In Great Britain the League of Nations Union organized a peace ballot which was signed by eleven million Englishmen. It declared in favor of collective security and sanctions with teeth in them. It was this overwhelming unanimity of British public opinion which forced a reluctant conservative government to take a strong stand in favor of sanctions at the League of Nations. But in the course of the debate, and due to obstructive tactics applied by Laval, Prime Minister of France at the time, the sanctions were voted with the ammunition carefully removed from all the guns. The toothless mouth was provided with a set of artificial teeth. The British home fleet sailed into the *mare nostrum* of Mussolini and provokingly paraded its guns. But it was rumored that disarmament had progressed to the point where the home fleet disposed of only one round of ammunition in its magazines. However this may have been, Italy had had the time to transport sufficient troops to Eritrea and Somaliland for her assault upon Ethiopia. Even the closing of the Suez Canal would not have crippled her offensive any more than the stopping of all oil supply. Neither of these measures were taken.

Harold Laski is fond of saying that the trouble with public opinion is the difficulty of deciding when is it public and when is it an opinion. The British Government decided that the peace ballot wanted strong sanctions against Italy, but that there was no support for a declaration of war. The wish was father to the thought. Whatever the state of the British Navy may have been, it was certain that Britain was badly prepared for war. Besides, the Baldwin government felt no hostility to Mussolini. Fascism in those days was still regarded as the lesser evil. It was felt that a revolution in Italy would have led to the establishment of a Communist régime.

Before the attack on Ethiopia, moreover, Italy was a potential ally of France and England, in case of war with Germany. Hitler's 1934 attack on the life of Dollfuss, Chancellor of Austria, had caused Mussolini to send his troops to the Brenner Pass as a warning to Hitler that he would not tolerate an *Anschluss*. When Germany decreed the reintroduction of universal military service (1935), in violation of the Treaty of Versailles, Mussolini had participated at the Conference of Stresa where Italy, France, and England agreed to consult with one another in case Hitler dared violate any more clauses of the Versailles Treaty. At Stresa a ridiculous version of collective security emerged: The-next-thing-you-do-out-you-go-policy.

All these considerations played their part in the decision of the Baldwin government to postpone the issue until after the elections in England. The Conservative Party, taking its cue from the peace ballot, adopted a pacifist platform and was overwhelmingly victorious. The Labor Party had little that it could offer after the treason of its leader MacDonald in 1931. While it was in office it had itself been on the friendliest terms with Mussolini's Italy. Having received a clear mandate the Baldwin government proceeded to act on its own interpretation of the peace ballot. It offered Italy and Ethiopia a compromise, or in other words it retreated.

The situation in France was more complicated. Laval had tried to form an Italian-French bloc, supported by a Franco-Russian alliance, to counteract the influence of British diplomacy on the European continent. He hated England, even then, with a personal hatred. The support he found in France for this anti-British course was due in the main to the appeasement-of-Germany policy which Britain and the United States had forced upon France, at and after Versailles. Reactionary France resented particularly the support which liberal France had given to the British policy and which in fact had lost France the victory of 1918 as it had lost it for the rest of the world.

Under Laval's premiership, inspired articles appeared in the French rightist press wherein a new theory of the balance of power on the European continent was advanced.

Britain it was claimed now needed France more than France needed Britain, in defense against Germany. The Maginot Line had provided France with a barrier against German aggression as effective as the British channel. But while France can not be blockaded, having a well-balanced economy, able to live off her soil, and in possession of a powerful fleet of her own, England was vulnerable to a blockade of her coast by the German air force and such a blockade was likely to prove more effective than the submarine war of 1914–18. Without the aid of the French Army and Russia, England could not strike back, nor could she, without them, institute an effective blockade of the German Reich. Thus France under Laval confirmed the British thesis that France was wielding too much power on the European continent.

Laval obtained his mutual-aid pact with Russia. Upon its conclusion Premier Joseph Stalin urged the Communist Party in France to vote the French war budget and to support the military forces. For the French Communist Party which had voted with clocklike regularity against every war budget and had carried on intensive anti-militarist propaganda, this change of the party line came as a blow. There was at first profound consternation, to be compared only with the discomfiture of the *Daily Worker* in New York when Russia concluded the non-aggression pact with Germany in 1939. Soon, however, the patient and defenseless walls in Paris were covered with posters which bore the legend "Stalin is right."

This constituted a radical departure in the foreign policy of Russia. Hitherto the enemy had been the capitalist world, and Moscow had refused its consent to the Communist Party in Germany to join with the German Socialists and Democrats in a common block against the Nazi Party. It had acted on the theory that the destruction of the Weimar Republic and the capitalist system would automatically prepare the ground for a Communist dictatorship in Germany. Failure of the Communist Party in Germany led to a change in method. Moscow now advocated a popular front, a union of Socialists, Radical Socialists (Liberals), and Communists in France.

Following his plan of an alliance with Fascist Italy Laval had gone to see Mussolini in Rome. He returned very satisfied with his accomplishments. The rumor was bruited about on all the café tables in Paris that he had told a few friends of his promise to Mussolini to give him, in addition to a few strips of desert in Africa, Ethiopia as well. One of the deputies had thereupon drawn Laval's attention to the fact that Ethiopia was a member of the League of Nations. Laval had sat up in amazement: "You don't say."

Laval began his political career as a Socialist sympathizing with the Communists and all Frenchmen knew that his name read as well from left to right as from right to left.

All French politicians were of the left. They had to be to get elected. The memory of the feudal régime was astonishingly fresh in France, particularly in the country. The peasantry of France still had no use for the nobles, even though they were impoverished and shorn of their power. A politician who stood for reëlection in the rural district invariably wound up his speech with a warning to the electorate against the deputy of the right. "Do any of you want the nobles to return, and reclaim the land? Then vote for my opponent." That would bring the house down.

Consequently there was only one political party, the extreme right, which had to try to get along without the adjective leftists. The party led by Louis Marin held that unenviable position. It called itself the Republican Party and was correspondingly small. The party to its immediate left in the semi-circle, just as reactionary, called itself Republican of the left, which was logical, since in Parliament they were seated to the left of Louis Marin. That is how it happened that the Radical Socialist Party, led by Herriot and later by Daladier, was neither radical nor socialist, but just plain middle class.

The Radical Socialist Deputy Seitz once asked the Corsican poet Vincent Muselli to what party he belonged. Muselli thought this over very carefully, and then explained that he regarded the Communists at the extreme left as the ranking reactionaries in French politics; he, Muselli, was consequently so radically to the left that there was no room for him in the semicircle of the Parliament. Seitz generously offered to provide him with a bench in the garden on the left wing of the building.

France never had any illusions about the qualities of Laval. Seated with a few friends, one of them English, at Fouquet's on the Champs Elysée, I pointed out a personage walking down the Avenue, and said to our English visitor: "There goes Laval." Our English friend was amazed. He could not understand why no one tipped his hat to the Prime Minister of France, adding: "In England we always do that." The sculptor Violet explained simply: *"Ici on ne salut pas les voleurs."* (Here we pay no homage to thieves.)

Frenchmen have never been consumed with any overwhelming respect for their government. Of all the parliamentarians during the epoch between the wars, only Léon Blum enjoyed any genuine popularity due to his evident devotion to the cause of the common man. Jean de Pierrefeu whom we had nicknamed *"fier de peu"* (proud of little) because he had written all the official bulletins during the First World War, once returned from the Chambres des Députés to greet us at the Café des Deux Magots. He was in ecstasy. He had just heard a speech by Léon Blum in which Blum had tried to justify his non-intervention policy in the civil war of Spain. Jean de Pierrefeu was opposed to this policy, but that in no way interfered with his appreciation of the man. What a triumph of the spirit, he exclaimed, every phrase a prose poem, what a man!

Generally, however, Frenchmen shrug their shoulders, exclaiming *"l'administration,"* pronounced in quotation marks as it were and with a sigh of long suffering resignation. When the government was headed by such an inveterate grafter and potential traitor as Laval the café tables of the capital had their field days. A decade had passed since the death of Rudolf Valentino, but the film magazines in the United States had not yet forgotten. At the anniversary of his death one of them, commenting on his early demise, concluded that he had died so young because he was too beautiful to live. Accordingly French wits claimed at least one immortal for France: Pierre Laval. Those who defended him maintained that at least his character did not belie his appearance. He looked like a horse thief and he was one.

As long as the checks and balances of the democratic system of government are operative, such men as Laval can do great harm, but the damage can still be repaired. They can be thrown out of office. The limits set to their power explains adequately the hatred of the Lavals and Quislings for the democratic form of government.

France feared the isolation into which she was maneuvered. Laval's unsavory attempt to secure Italian support was therefore not opposed by liberal France while the rightists refrained from opposing the alliance with Soviet Russia. As a matter of fact if Russia had seen fit to honor the Czarist debts, they would have hailed the Russian dictatorship as a great experiment with the same enthusiasm as certain sections of the liberals throughout the world. Their genuine sympathies, however, went out to Mussolini. Rightist professors and writers, a minority in France whose work was little known abroad, signed a document supporting Italian claims on Ethiopia. Italy was hailed as the *sœur latine* (the sister nation of Latin blood and culture), unjustly calumniated by Liberals and Socialists for the sake of a race of savages. In vigorous thought, however, the France known to the world for the splendor of her civilization surpassed by far her internal enemies. The *sœur latine* slogan was instantly killed by a happy pun: *L'agresseur latine*, and that was that.

After the elections in England, which had given the Conservative Party an overwhelming majority in the British parliament, Stanley Baldwin admitted that he had determined upon a rearmament program before the elections, but, said he: "I kept my lips sealed." Indignation ran high in England. The confession that the Pacifist platform was a deliberate deception moved even the stately *Times* to join in the chorus of condemnation. The Labor press compared the lie to the manufactured Zinovieff letter which had helped to drive the Labor Party from office in an earlier election. Yet at that time British engineers had been working for two years to perfect the first model of the Spitfire which later saved Britain from a German invasion.

Evidently the Pacifist world wanted both to eat the cake of peace and have it, too. In a speech on Britain's foreign policy, Stanley Baldwin had the merit of recognizing that the world was getting smaller. He extended the age-old British Monroe

Doctrine by stating that England's frontier was on the Rhine. Only two years later the White House in Washington tentatively gave out the same statement, regarding the position of the United States in a European conflict.

The hope of gaining Italy as an ally in the coming struggle with Germany, or at least to keep her neutral, must be regarded as the principal reason which decided the Baldwin government to retreat from the earlier position which it had taken at the League of Nations. It was also the principal cause which moved the French foreign office to agree with the British view. The Hoare-Laval pact offered Italy half of Ethiopia as a compromise solution. It was a compromise which put England and France squarely between two chairs, and in both countries it was recognized as disastrous. The half-hearted sanction had driven Italy into the German camp, the compromise did not bring her back. Hoare resigned and shortly afterwards the Laval cabinet received a vote of censure. The cause of Laval's fall was not exclusively due to his foreign policy; there were domestic reasons as well. But his horse trade with Mussolini finished his political career until the defeat of the French armies gave him his opportunity for revenge. It was he who persuaded the French generals to ask for an armistice, pointing out that if they went to Africa, Parliament would go with them. They would thus forego a golden opportunity to finish once and for all with a hated institution which was constantly cramping their style.

The Pact of 1935 and Perfidious Albion

The Hoare-Laval Pact gave the final blow to the League of Nations. It disillusioned the smaller countries which had hoped to find protection in the League against encroachment upon their sovereign rights by an aggressor nation. After the failure of sanctions they knew that, either alone or in combination, they could not hope to stand against Germany. Henceforth they could depend only upon a declaration of neutrality in case of war. Neutrality, however, works to the advantage of the determined aggressor and does so even better than treaties signed with him. Nations who respect the neutrality of their neighbors yield them in advance as bases for the aggressor.

Though the small democracies of Europe put the heavy burden of respect for neutrality upon the large powers friendly to them, they nevertheless looked forward with confidence to protection by France and England in case the aggressor should violate their neutrality. When the test came, the armies of the Allies, seeking to fulfil a moral obligation and to regain their lost prestige, were lured out of the defensive positions which they had occupied along the Belgian frontiers, and thus became easy prey to the mechanized armies of the conqueror.

The Hoare-Laval Pact lost for France and England nearly all their natural allies on the periphery of German aggression and nullified in advance whatever merit the theory of defense as expounded by Liddel Hart might have had. Germany, on the other hand, was given the assurance that Belgium, Holland, Denmark, and Norway could not be used by the Allies as advance bases from which to attack her when she would be ready to invade Austria and Czechoslovakia. At the same time the half-hearted sanctions had pushed Italy into her camp and the Allies had locked to themselves the back door to Germany in the south. Long before the German armies were ready for the attack the diplomacy of the peaceful nations was preparing the ground for them.

In 1935, France was still powerful enough to have come to the defense of her allies in the Balkans, of Czechoslovakia, and of Poland, singlehanded, without making use of Belgian or Dutch territory. As long as the Rhineland remained demobilized, the direct assault upon the western frontiers of the Reich was still possible. Germany consequently remained cautious.

In 1914 England had sought to obtain a naval agreement with the Kaiser and had failed. Hitler proved to be more amenable to reason. He regarded the entire British Navy as so much scrap-iron in any case. "There are no islands any more," was one of the tenets in his military creed. It sounded well as a catchword and could be used indifferently for a popular song or a serious poem. Edna St. Vincent Millay used it after the fall of France as a refrain to warn America against pinning her faith on the protection of the oceans. As a military theory it was not wholly erroneous. General William Mitchell had demonstrated that a battleship could be sunk by aërial bombs, and Germany was planning and building vast air fleets. Moreover, Hitler knew when his land army would be ready and that there was no time for the construction of a surface fleet powerful enough to rival the British Navy. Coördinated action against England on sea and land was therefore impossible in any case, and without such coördinated weapons the only hope for a direct attack upon Great Britain remained the air force.

Moreover, Hitler had no intention of keeping the treaty. In the meantime a German naval agreement with Britain, successfully concluded, would drive a wedge between France and England and thus prepare the ground for the remilitarization of the Rhineland.

What intentions moved the British Government to conclude a naval agreement with Nazi Germany must remain conjecture. If that naval pact had provided a strict limitation on the number of submarines Germany would be allowed to construct, it would have made some sense. But as the pact was written, it implicitly gave Germany a free hand to construct as many submarines as she wished. The only weapon which had proved nearly disastrous to Britain in the last war was thus granted to her without any hesitation for a future war. The pact, consequently, could not serve to put Germany in the wrong by tempting her to break one more agreement freely arrived at. Neville Chamberlain as Prime Minister of England, persisted to the very end in speaking of this naval pact in glowing terms. Under his premiership the horse of appeasement was finally ridden to death, throwing its rider as it fell.

Chamberlain brought to the job of governing the British Empire the qualifications of a mayor of Birmingham, an industrial city where he had acquired great experience in dealing with solid burghers of the British manufacturer and merchant type, and in arbitrating disputes between them and the well-organized British Trade Unions. These qualities proved useful for the solution of internal economic problems. Under his premiership a sort of conservative socialism was instituted which took the wind out of the sails of the Labor Party. A vast building program of private houses mitigated the curse of permanent unemployment in the British Isles, and the rearmament program was pushed ahead as far as this was possible under a business-as-usual economy.

It is generally conceded that the British are distinguished by perseverance. Unfortunately, when they follow the wrong course they do so with the same characteristic, unbending will which nothing can deflect except a merciless Blitz. After Germany had violated the Munich agreement and occupied all of Czechoslovakia, Neville Chamberlain spoke at a banquet in Birmingham, comparing himself to the younger Pitt. Pitt had appeased Napoleon as long as this was at all possible. In the end, however, he had accepted the challenge, and Britain fought Napoleon for fifteen years, emerging victorious. Perhaps in this speech Chamberlain revealed the inner workings of his mind. Perhaps there was some malice aforethought in the course he was following; on the other hand, it is equally possible that it was only in retrospect that he saw himself in the rôle of Pitt. From 1935 to Munich there were only three years. In the life of nations three years are like eternity in the eyes of God—which, according to the Psalm, is but a moment. Yet that moment lost a civilization.

For the friendship between the people of France and England the Naval Pact proved disastrous. In the spring of that year (1935), Germany had announced the reintroduction of conscription and had thus broken one more clause in the Treaty of Versailles, but she had done so without obtaining the consent of the Allies. A year earlier Hitler had asked for "equality of treatment" for Germany, permission to build up an army of some 250,000 to 350,000 men. Barthou, then Foreign Minister of France and the last of the old guard of French statesmen, had put his foot down. Sir John Simon, at the League of Nations, had taken Germany's part, but Barthou subjected him to a piece of his mind in the Gallic tongue which left him speechless. A few months later, Barthou and King Alexander of Yugoslavia were assassinated in Marseilles by Croatian Nationalists.

After Barthou's death, England sanctioned by her signature the breaking of the naval clause in the Treaty of Versailles, granting Germany naval parity with France in surface ships. Moreover, by setting her signature to the naval pact, England at the same time sanctioned in retrospect the violation by Germany of the military limitation clause. What made matters worse was that she concluded the treaty without consulting France. Presented with a new German *fait accompli,* France was in uproar. For the first time since the war, the epithet "perfidious Albion" was on everybody's lips. Strangers in Paris stopped to talk to each other at the news-stands.

"Go," said one of them to me as I was buying a paper, "go and ask the Normans what they think of the English—their next-door neighbors. They know the canaille."

During the Italian war on Ethiopia, while sanctions were still in force against Italy, I had gone to England to visit friends. At that time, Mussolini was popularly regarded in England as the main enemy, while Hitler looked more like a windbag. Throughout these pre-war years world opinion fluctuated. Hostility to one or the other of the potential aggressors shifted in accordance with the rules of a ball-game. The "enemy number one" was always the one who was running with the ball. While the other enemies were quiescent they even acquired a degree of credit for being so well behaved. Like musical virtuosos, the peaceful people could stand no distraction. Their dislikes had to be concentrated.

While we were riding on the train to their country home, my friends asked what people in France were thinking about the stand England had taken against Italian aggression. The degree of hostility which Mussolini had engendered against himself in England may be measured by the fact that in the conversation which ensued our traveling companions on the train took part without hesitation. Even during the general strike of 1926 I had witnessed no such revolutionary departure from customary reticence on the part of the English. I reported that the French did not believe that the British Government was in earnest. Britain, so it was thought in France, would fight Mussolini in the end, but she was going to give him all the rope he wanted. It was certain that his navy would go to Mussolini's head, since he was easy prey to *"crise de grandeur"* and he would then try to dislodge the British from his *"mare nostrum."* In the meantime the task of conquering the inaccessible regions of Ethiopia could be left to Mussolini. He would either break his neck, which would be just as well, or he would conquer Ethiopia. In the latter case Ethiopia would fall under British influence as soon as the British Navy had sunk Mussolini's fleet.

The English take well such Machiavellian expositions of the cunning of British statesmanship. The public was delighted. Did I think good old Baldwin was as brilliant as all that? Perfidious Albion, eh?

The Hoare-Laval Pact had lost for France and England the solidarity of the small nations: the Anglo-German Naval Pact drove a wedge between France and Great Britain. Thus the isolation of France, begun on the eleventh of November, 1918, had advanced in 1936 to the point where Germany could complete it by remilitarizing the Rhineland and by constructing the Siegfried Line.

Strategically Germany secured herself against a direct assault on her western frontier by France. Henceforth it would be beyond the strength of the French armies and of England to come to the aid of Austria, Czechoslovakia, Poland, and the Balkan countries. The Rhine barred the direct route into Germany via Coblenz, while principles of international law barred the route through Belgium, Holland, and Luxembourg, leaving this road open to Germany. At the same time, the task of dealing with Germany fell exclusively to the British. France was deprived of the means of developing any foreign policy of her own since she was no longer able to sustain it by force of arms. By their naval pact, Britain and Germany had out-maneuvered Laval and his Latin bloc supported by Soviet Russia.

And the Franco-Russian Mutual Aid Pact concluded by Laval had given Hitler the inspiration of adding one more piece of invective to his string of abuses: bolshevik. Up to that day all his references to Russia had been nicely couched in diplomatic language, composed and written by the staff of the Wilhelmstrasse. Germany, Hitler had explained in all his speeches from 1933 to 1935, was on friendly terms with Russia both politically and economically. The internal régime of Russia was none of his concern, nor was there any reason why differences in ideological conception should stand in the way of close collaboration. From the Franco-Russian pact onward, however, his tone changed radically. From then on, all passages referring to Russia were written, by himself, without restraint. But while he fulminated against Russia he meant France, a fact unperceived by the foreign office in London, or rather by Mr. Chamberlain. England remained complacent when Hitler tore up the Locarno Treaty because he pleaded that he could not resist Communism as long as France was able to come to the assistance of her Russian ally. Moreover, how could he be certain that France would remain a democracy? If she should go Communist he would be under attack from two fronts, and the non-militarized Rhine would spell the doom of the only bulwark against Communism, Nazi Germany, a veritable lamb between two ferocious beasts.

Germany had gained a diplomatic victory. For Britain, however, the elimination of France as a power on the continent proved a Pyrrhic victory. She had not put her whole weight on the side of France as promised in the Locarno Treaty. The balance of power had shifted radically to Germany, while France was thrown up in the air. Appeasement had advanced to the point where the principal trump cards were being dealt out to Germany. Every one of the players now sought to withdraw from the game as best he could, leaving England to hold the depleted bank while Germany, under the able leadership of Hitler, continued to deal back marked cards.

9

The Fruits of Appeasement

THOUGH 1936 reduced France to a secondary power in world politics, she was not yet defenseless. Beyond metropolitan France lay a vast empire in Africa and the far east. From this empire France not only could draw raw materials and commodities for the conduct of war, but could also draw on its immense reservoir of fighting men, nearly all faithful to France. For, knowing no racial prejudices, France had treated the natives in her Empire as equals. The geopoliticians of the Reich overlooked nothing. Hitler was determined to play his game absolutely safe. The time still needed to complete his armament machine he could therefore put to good account by depriving France of secure communication lines with her Empire. Here the signal for a Fascist revolt in Spain, long prepared with the assistance of Mussolini, was flashed to Franco.

The entire epoch of appeasement has nothing to compare in cowardice with the non-intervention policy adopted by the democracies in the Spanish civil war. The fiction of non-intervention was maintained through a maze of lies perpetrated by the entire press from the extreme right to the extreme left. From the frequent meetings of the non-intervention committee there emanated a stench of moral corruption which made breathing difficult. With few exceptions there was not a newspaper which cared to tell the story honestly. It seemed at times as if the world would never see an honest press again or hear a statement without subterfuge from a democratic politician.

Anarchism in Spain

Spain was the last nation on the European continent to be touched by the cycle of the great French and the American revolutions. All the evils of medieval Europe had found their last refuge in Spain and clung to the Iberian peninsula with the tenacity of an inquisition. In fact, as late as 1909, rebellious working-men in Barcelona had been tortured by a revived inquisition. A group of several hundred victims fled to London in that year. There was a mass meeting on Trafalgar Square during which they tore open their shirts and showed the marks of torture on their flesh. In that year, too, the founder of modern secular schools in Spain, Francisco Ferrer, was turned over to the secular arm and executed for his known sympathies with the Insurgents.

The revolutionary movement in Spain consequently bore all the characteristics of violence now made familiar to the world by the resistance to the Nazi régime in the conquered countries of Europe.

What European countries under the Nazi heel are enduring to-day, Spain endured for centuries from the princes of the church, the nobility, and the military caste. The vast majority of the Spanish people were as indomitably opposed to Communist dictatorship as they were to the rule of church and feudal lords. They drew their inspiration from the ideals of the French Revolution, which had given birth to modern democracy. To most of them the liberal government established in 1931 after the abdication of Alfonso XIII was only a poor substitute for the society of which they had dreamed. Nevertheless, when the Franco Putsch started they ranged themselves on the side of the government. While the government itself was taken by surprise, the people descended into the streets spontaneously, and, armed with kitchen knives and pistols, successfully resisted the Phalangists and those few soldiers who obeyed their officers. In Barcelona and elsewhere the Fascists were installed in the churches, ideally suited to serve as fortresses, machine-gun nests, and arsenals. Those churches were burned in order to smoke the aggressors out. In most parts of the country the uprising was put down by the people within twenty-four hours after it had started. But the putschists had succeeded in taking possession of a few strategic harbors and bases where they could bring in Moroccan troops from the Spanish colonies, while arms, ammunition, and soldiers would be supplied by Germany and Italy. In those first days a few planes and tanks from France and England would have saved the republic.

But Léon Blum, Prime Minister of France, was prevailed upon by the British Government to announce a non-intervention policy on behalf of France and England, provided Germany and Italy would likewise pledge themselves to refrain from aiding their side. The British Government had taken the view expressed by Anthony Eden that Spanish nationalism would resent any foreign interference in the internal affairs of Spain and that the country which did intervene on either side would in the end be hated by all.

Even Winston Churchill, inveterate opponent of appeasement, expressed the opinion to a French audience, in the Théatre des Ambassadeurs in Paris, that the Spanish Government had committed a grave error in retaining the responsibility when it no longer had the power. He meant by this that the government should have abdicated when it threw open the arsenals and invited the people to arm themselves in defense against Franco. Applied to the European governments in exile, this principle would mean that they should resign because, owing to German aggression, they no longer exercise any power at home.

On the other hand, if the Spanish Government—rendered impotent by the defection of the army officers—had resigned, the people of Spain would have gone on fighting anyway. There would then have been no hope at all of receiving any aid from the democracies. The Spanish people might have done better that way, for all one can tell.

At any rate it was open to the British and the French navies to declare that they would guard the coasts of Spain against any foreign intervention and against the importation of Moroccan troops into Spain. In that case, the Franco uprising would have collapsed for want of mercenaries. But Germany had provided against this contingency by warning France that there would be war if France intervened in Spain, and Léon Blum did not feel free to plunge France into war without the aid of Britain and for the sake of a country toward which France had no treaty obligations. Three weeks later Blum admitted that he had erred. Undoubtedly he had hoped that the Spanish people would win without any outside aid. An uprising such as Franco had organized generally succeeds in the first twenty-four hours, or it fails for good. In Spain the first round had gone to the people. Then it no longer looked hopeful for the continuation of democracy in Spain, without French aid, and yet it was too late.

By that time France was pledged with England, Italy, and Germany not to intervene. While this pledge of course did nothing to stop the Axis from sending supplies and troops to Spain, it blocked all effective action for the democracies. Having secured their friend Franco against French and English aid to the government of Spain, German-Italian intervention became brazen and shameless. They sent whole tank corps and combat wings to Spain to aid Franco and denied that they were doing anything of the sort, while the British, French, and Russians—the last equally interventionist—at the "non-intervention" committee meetings gravely registered the official denials. With few noteworthy exceptions, the conservative press, for want of an excuse, invented the tale of a Communist uprising in Spain. The Spanish people were labeled Reds. It was enough to justify every cowardly retreat before Hitler and Mussolini on the part of the democracies. Yet the Spanish Government claimed no more for itself than England and France were going to ask of the American Government later on: the right to buy ammunition with which to resist the Fascist onslaught. Nor is it conceivable that the French, British and American rightist press was ignorant of the fact that there was no Communist movement in Spain and never had been, in spite of the eagerness with which the Communist press accepted responsibility for the unflinching courage of the Spaniards.

In Madrid and in some of the northern provinces of Spain there was a strong Social Democratic Party supported by Socialist trade unions, while in the rest of Spain—particularly in Barcelona and Saragossa—the working classes and the peasantry were loosely organized in Anarcho-Syndicalist trade unions, whose political ideals came from the anti-Marxist leader in the First International, Michael Bakunin, and the later exponent of Anarchism, Prince Peter Kropotkin. A moderate version of Anarchist philosophy, proposing the organization of Spain on a federative basis with a high degree of local self-government was supported by the liberal bourgeoisie, by the intellectual world of Spain in the Universities, and by most liberal writers.

Perhaps those who resisted aid to the Spanish Republic felt that a success of the Spanish Revolutionists would constitute as great a danger to the security of centralized democratic government and capitalism as the establishment of a Communist dictatorship, but by failing to aid the liberal republic they forced the government of Spain to turn for aid to Russia, the only country which was willing to assist them, even for a price.

Owing to this failure, the Spanish revolutionary movement could be compelled by the Russian Government to make a large and disproportioned place in its ranks and in the government of the republic for such individual Communists as could be found in Spain. Thus the plain fight of the Spanish people against oppression was allowed to degenerate into a conflict between Communism and Fascism to see which side would be able to seize the power at the expense of the people. A British Labor member of Parliament arose to ask the government whether it would not be wise to evacuate the people of Spain so that the Russians and the Germans might fight it out between themselves without bleeding the Spanish people to death.

By that time Italian submarines in the Mediterranean were sinking British merchant ships which were supplying food to the Loyalists, but the British and the French press spoke politely of unknown submarines. The very café tables in Paris shook with laughter. The suggestion was advanced to rename the Boulevard des Italiens the Boulevard des Inconnus (the boulevard of the unknown). Labor members in the British Parliament demanded convoys for British merchant ships, and Mr. Chamberlain arose to explain with unconscious humor that he would not allow selfish business men to plunge the Empire into war for the sake of profits. To the Socialists he sounded like the devil quoting scriptures.

Public opinion at last compelled the French Government to break its pledge. It tacitly permitted the Loyalists to smuggle a few planes and guns into Spain. At the start that might have been enough to save Spain, but now it was too late. Thus the long and dismal series of too little and too late was inaugurated in Spain. At the same time, Pierre Cot, Minister of Aviation in the Blum cabinet, was under attack in Parliament. The rightists had unearthed proof that he was selling planes to the Loyalists, and they trumpeted the charge to the world. The leftist press cried treason, and the conservative *Le Temps*, the only readable newspaper in Paris, mocked them in measured terms. How could it be treason to tell the truth in a free country?

Finally even the Catholic and Royalist paper, the *Action Française*, was appalled at the ferocity of the Spanish reaction. Bernanos published a report in that paper of his visit to Franco Spain. On the island of Majorca, he had witnessed the execution of eighteen republicans, humble fishermen and mechanics. They were placed against a wall and sprinkled with holy water, confessed and executed. No crime was charged against them save the heinous one of belonging to the republican party.

Although the democratic Catholics of the Basque country sided with the liberal government of Spain, most American Catholics saw in the Spanish opposition to Franco an anti-

Catholic movement and used their influence to stop any American aid to the Loyalists. Thus, abandoned by all the world, the people of Spain fought for two and a half years against overwhelming odds. In the end the country was exhausted to the point where the Fascist victory was hollow. Franco has been unable to repay to this day the services which Mussolini and Hitler rendered his cause. Even so, four French divisions guarded the Pyrenees when the German Army broke through at the Meuse, whereas no troops would have been needed to guard that frontier if a stitch had been taken in time.

The Dress Rehearsal

Spain proved an excellent opportunity for the Nazis to test their weapons, their military theory, and their strategy. In the war they waged on the Spanish people with the aid of Moroccan troops, they learned the weakness of their tanks and the weakness of the Allied anti-tank guns. France and England were surprised three years later to find that their anti-tank guns were useless against the armor of the German tanks, and a desperate attempt was made to bring out the old 75 to stop the Juggernaut. In Spain, too, Germany tested the effectiveness of her bombing planes when she wiped out Guernica as a dress rehearsal for the attack on Coventry and the Baedeker bombings of England. The Italian defeat at Guadalajara taught the Nazis the danger of piling up tank columns for lack of efficient traffic regulation, thus exposing them to wholesale destruction by the primitive home-made bombs of the inventive Spaniards. All German weapons were as yet in a tentative state of development. It was in Spain that they perfected them.

At the same time the people of Spain were kept in suspense by the democracies. Throughout the civil war, the hope of eventual aid was kept alive by the agitation in their favor in France, England, and the United States. This hope moved the government of Spain to abandon guerrilla war, the only method of warfare which might have brought success, and which was in harmony with the traditions of Spain and the temper of her people. The word itself is Spanish.

The ingenuity displayed by the Spanish people in fighting tanks and in the organization of anti-aircraft protection later served as a lesson to England when a few Englishmen who had fought on the side of the Loyalists brought home the knowledge they acquired in Spain. For many months, volunteer groups exercised in Hyde Park to learn the method of stopping an armored attack, by using crude anti-tank gasoline bottles, land-mines, and gasoline-soaked mattresses. When the Nazi armies invaded Holland and Belgium, the British Government had to follow the example of the Spanish, urging the formation of voluntary home guards on the model of the Spanish, an event which alarmed at least one English lord, who cried revolution.

The present highly trained commandos of the British Army are using many of the methods developed by the Spanish Anarchists. The Russian aviators and tank-drivers profited well by the lessons they learned in Spain, both for their mechanized armies, which stopped the Germans before Moscow, and for the guerrilla fighters in the rear of the German armies.

But the expectation of real and effective aid misled the government of Spain in the attempt to train an infantry army on the model of the French Army. Hundreds of thousands of guerrilla fighters were withdrawn from the front lines to be given intensive training in obsolete military methods which were growing daily more obsolete as the Germans were learning to apply the tactics of the Blitz. The Spanish Government wasted two years in training an army in the use of hoped-for material which never arrived, while the French Army learned nothing, though the greatest numbers of volunteer fighters for Spain had come from France. Only these had no standing in the French Army. They were not generals, nor did they belong to the aristocracy.

Austria and Czechoslovakia

Even before the Spanish civil war ended in a victory for Fascism over a devastated Spain, Czechoslovakia was abandoned to the same fate. At the outbreak of the civil war in Spain, France and England could have secured with very little effort a military base in Spain against Germany and a moral victory into the bargain. Two years later it was too late to save Czechoslovakia—the only genuine democracy born of the Versailles Treaty.

In conformity with the principles of German geopolitics, Hitler's diplomacy—after the political and military isolation of France had been achieved—shifted southward, to exploit the advantages of the alliance with Mussolini. In the spring of 1938 Germany marched into Austria, and Czechoslovakia was isolated. The Czech fortification lines were built on the model of the Maginot Line, but as they were designed later, the Czechs were able to improve considerably on the French system.

However, in the south, on the border of Austria, there were no fortifications. Using Austria as a base, the Nazis could have conquered Czechoslovakia with ease. But they did not care for war. The tactics of the Blitz had to be kept secret in their application as long as was humanly possible, so that when the time came it might be used to full effect on Great Britain. In *Mein Kampf*, Hitler wrote that the British fight to the last, even if their armaments consist of rifles dating back to the deluge. By the same token he expected that the continental nations would submit without a fight.

The investigation of crime is facilitated by a trait said to be common to all criminals. The burglar and the mass murderer develop a technic personal to themselves, and which never varies. The investigator can consequently tell at a glance the perpetrator of the crime even though he may not know the criminal.

By the time he was ready to absorb Austria, the pattern of Hitler's technic was already well established, but it was as yet imperfectly understood. Though he had used the method inside Germany before he came into power, and outside— when he left the League of Nations, reëstablished conscription, built an air force, concluded a naval pact with Britain, and remilitarized the Rhineland—every one of his moves came as a surprise to the western world. The method used by the Nazis may be described as demanding an apple from a tree in a neighbor's garden, obtaining the apple by tearing up the apple tree by its roots, taking possession of the garden and organizing it as a base from which to demand an apple from the next garden. The modest demand for an apple is made with a clamor as if the lives of seventy million famished people depended upon it. The entire machinery of the totalitarian state, the propaganda barrage of orchestrated lies, written by the Fuehrer and conducted by Goebbels, is coordinated into an ear-splitting din of convulsive howling, rising to a crescendo while two million disciplined Dervishes assembled at Nuremberg shout Heil and Victory, Heil. Heine described it a century ago in the essay already quoted, on religion and philosophy in Germany:

You will hear a roar such as has never before been heard in the history of the world. At this racket the eagles will drop dead out of the air and the lions in the furthest deserts of Africa will slink away to their royal caves with their tails between their legs.

A performance will be staged in Germany by the side of which the French Revolution will look like a harmless idyl. It is true at present it still seems to be fairly quiet. Here and there a few are somewhat lively, but do not suppose that these are destined to be the real actors. They are only the little dogs which are running around in the empty arena barking at each other and backbiting before the hour comes when the hosts of gladiators will appear who are to fight in a life and death struggle. And the hour will come. The Nations will group themselves around Germany as if they occupied the steps of an Amphitheater to watch the tournament. I advise you Frenchmen, beware, do not applaud. . . .

What did they want of Austria? What was all this noise for? Practically nothing. Freedom of speech for Austrian Nazis, granted; a Nazi minister in the cabinet, granted; a plebiscite, granted—but it must be a plebiscite conducted by the Nazis, so Schuschnigg resigned to avoid bloodshed. Austria fell without a shot, because Austrians must not shed a brother's blood in vain. But no such obligation is acknowledged by the aggressor for himself. Abel must put up no defense while Cain strikes him down.

And Czechoslovakia—Germany wants nothing of the Czechs. She is too proud to admit members of an inferior race into her new order. All Germany wants—and that at the price of world war—is what the Sudetens, her "blood brothers" are enjoying already: equal political rights with all other nationalities in Czechoslovakia. It is a demand which the Czechs can not grant, since the Sudetens have it already. Therefore, let them give to the Sudetens autonomy, self-government, self-determination: did not Wilson promise that in his fourteen points? . . . Have Jews got self-determination in Germany? Such a suggestion can not be made. It would outrage the feelings of the Nazis. How can the world apply equal standards to a master race? Perhaps Germany would like to have the Sudeten population handed over to her, so that they may live under the blessings of Nazi rule. By no means! She must have not only the apple but also the tree on which it hangs. That tree is the fortifications, the Maginot Line of Czechoslovakia, constructed inside the territory inhabited by the Sudetens.

In all Europe there was no one but England left to act. Russia and France were following the advice of Heine. They kept very quiet.

Russia had a mutual aid pact with Czechoslovakia, but it was an annex to the French-Czech alliance. Russia consequently maintained that she was not expected to act unless France went to war in defense of her ally. But France was isolated, cut off from all possibility of waging a frontal war on Germany, and between Russia and Germany there were the Baltic countries and Poland, whose government was eager

for a piece of Czechoslovakia. This too must be noted as one
more characteristic method of Nazi criminality in international
affairs: always associate a lesser criminal in the perpetration
of the crime; subsequently he can be robbed of his share in
the booty.

My German ex-school friend to whom I talked in Kaunas
had learned his geopolitical lesson well: England was not going to fight. When I met him I was on my way to Abbo, Finland, to visit Professor Edwin Westermarck, who had been
my teacher in sociology at the London University. The head-
lines caught me in Stockholm: *Chamberlain flikt ken Berchtesgaden.* I phoned my wife, Erma Rockhill, to ascertain her state
of mind and to ask after Michèle, our little daughter. Our
French friends had cried: "Treason! Chamberlain is going to
sell Czechoslovakia." The American consul privately thought
that it would be wise to return to the United States. Would I
come home?

Careless as usual about police regulations, I had neglected
to apply for a reëntry visa to France before I left Paris, and my
two-year visa had run out. As I had my permanent residence
in France I had no doubt that I would be able to persuade
the French consul to give me a visa without going to the
trouble of communicating with the Paris Prefecture. But in
Stockholm I came across a young French consul who had all
the makings of a Prussian bureaucrat. Why had I failed to
apply for a visa? I pointed to my French Carte d'Identité
good for three years of permanent residence. He was sorry.
He would have to write to the Préfet de Police. How long
would it take? About a fortnight. I pointed to my passport
giving me three days' stay in Stockholm on my way to Finland. While waiting for my French visa, I might get into
trouble with the Swedish police. There the bureaucrat had
me: Aha, you do not mind breaking French regulations, but
you respect the Swedes. He was going to show me. Did I not
realize that in Germany I would be arrested for such an offense as I had committed against France? I wanted to know
how he could think of comparing Germany with a civilized

country. We parted company hurling mutual defiance at each other. I was going to see the French Ambassador, who was a friend of my friends in Paris. He would see. For his part he did not care; after this threat he would not even write to the Prefecture. I could go hang myself.

I left to gather my bags and to take a plane to Paris. Arriving at Le Bourget airdrome I explained to the French passport controller that I had neglected to get a visa. He advised me paternally to be more careful in the future, and that was that.

While living in France we spent many summer vacations in Châtel-Guyon, a spa near Vichy. Both resorts are in the high central plateau of France which is inhabited by the Auvergnacs, said to be the shrewdest tradesmen in France. It is also the birthplace of Laval. We had discovered a gay little hotel at Châtel-Guyon which beyond dispute had the finest cuisine in France combined with a price low enough to permit the badly paid French Army officers to stay there with their families.

There were, however, a few non-military as well, who came there regularly every year for the "cure." The military rarely talked shop, preferring the company of the outsiders with whom they could discuss other things than the life of the garrison. The outstanding guests among the outsiders were Emanuel and Luce Passemard, both distinguished pre-historians who had fascinating stories to tell about pre-historic man and the magnificent paintings which he left behind in the caves of France. There were two French girl explorers, Odette du Pigaudeau and Marion Senon who were the only women to have traversed the French African colony, La Mauritanie on camel's back, living the life of the native Berbers, a white race of Mohammedan faith. Odette's book on their exploration entitled, *Barefoot Through Mauritania* is a classic in that field of literature. There was the deputy Scapini, who lost his eyesight in the last war and now represents Vichy at the armistice commission at Wiesbaden. There was M. Mangin, a manufacturer of corsets, a very wealthy man, a Protestant Frenchman and a pacifist. He and Colonel Huillet, mem-

ber of the French war council, had long debates on the merits
of pacifism. The gist of Mangin's argument was that if France
did not have any army at all she would be better off. Civilian
defense would be sufficient to resist a German invasion.
"What," he demanded to know, "would the Germans do if
they did succeed in occupying France. A country like France
could not be held by an invader any longer than the out-
stretched arm can hold a heavy weight." To which argument
Colonel Huillet replied that without her army France would
be lost; "there simply would be no France."

Most of the friends we made at Châtel-Guyon lived in Paris
and we saw them often. Before the Munich agreement the
Passemards urged Erma and Michèle to stay with them on
their estate near Nîmes in Provençe, for the duration; Odette
du Pigaudeau offered her little ancestral home in the Bretagne
—a much safer place from bombing, she assured us, than the
city of Nîmes. She also held that I had no business to fight
for France and I was included in the invitation. The owner
of the hotel in Châtel wrote to urge us to come to Châtel for
the duration. Being a watering place, there was no war industry or airdrome anywhere in the immediate vicinity.

Fernand Hommelynck suggested his country place in Belgium. He was certain that Belgium would be overrun in no
time and not suffer too much actual fighting. Stephan and
Nannette Simon had a villa in the south of France near St.
Tropez. Nannette and four children would go there while he
would drive a tank at the front. France short of man power
had to call even the fathers of large families. He begged Erma
and Michèle to stay with his wife. Michèle's nurse, Bertha
Stoker could have gone to her native Switzerland but was
determined to stay with us. None of our friends, though they
all feared massed German air-raids, had any idea that France
might be invaded. Listening, at the house of the Simons, to a
speech by Hitler before Chamberlain's second flight to Germany, everybody asked everybody else's opinion as to what
it meant—would it be war? When Simon asked Erma what
she thought of the speech, she explained that she had stopped

listening after the first three minutes: "I have been looking at you, fascinated at the idea of what a beautiful corpse you are going to be." They all laughed, realizing how well that described the atmosphere created by the voice of the boche.

Said Simon: "It is like a mystery story, with the crime hidden, the criminal ready to pounce upon the reader, and no saving detective in sight. It would be a pity if Hitler were assassinated. We would never know the end of the story."

Erma asked whether it would not be better to have him assassinated, and then see how History develops after that.

The Passemards were working in the Museum at St. Germain. A newspaper with a particularly incredible head-line, made Luce exclaim: "I am insane, I alone am insane. All is well in the best of all possible worlds. It can't be that what our statesmen are doing is insanity. It can't be that everybody is insane, and I am sane. That is an idea entertained by the inmates of insane asylums; I will not succumb to megalomania. It would be intolerable; life would not be worth the living if they should be wrong and I right. Oh, ye saints, what is to become of the state of France!"

Our friends besieged Erma with questions about the United States. What would President Roosevelt do? He had made a well remembered speech about quarantining the aggressor. Could England and France count upon the United States? What was the state of mind of people in America?

Erma had been back home to visit her mother in the far west. She had returned an admirer of President Roosevelt, though belonging to a family who had voted the straight Republican ticket since Abraham Lincoln, a record broken but once, when her mother voted for Eugene Debs as a protest against his imprisonment.

Erma explained that under the impact of the personality of President Roosevelt, American liberalism had at last reëmerged. It was now the most liberal and progressive country in the world emanating a warmth of heart and humanity which had been lacking during the period of perpetual prosperity. Then her countrymen had walked about with a frozen expression of self-satisfaction in their countenances. They had not only won the last war but they had also solved all economic problems. The business cycle had been licked: no more depressions and no more poverty and want; two cars in every garage. The United States had then been blind to events in the rest of the world, a snug little universe all by itself. Now, however, after the frightful ordeal of the depression, the common man was coming into his own. Puzzled and perturbed, people in America were asking searching questions about their economic and social order, which up to then they had taken for granted. As yet however the mind of America was turned inward. Erma believed President Roosevelt to be farsighted enough to know what was coming, but the people of America were inveterate isolationists. There was therefore little comfort that the rebirth of the liberal spirit in the United States could offer to our anxious friends. The burden would have to be born by Europe alone.

In the reduction of Czechoslovakia, the pattern of Nazi criminality emerged in all its purity. The fabric of European civilization was rent asunder. The human solidarity of its free people seemed to have been destroyed forever. In the history of Europe it was the bleakest hour, for the hour foreboding the doom of a civilization is more terrifying than the night which follows. The little republic could not be saved, because Austria had not been saved, and Austria had not been saved because no aid had been given to the revolution in Spain, and Spain was abandoned to its hangman because Ethiopia had been given to the enemy. The cumulative effect of past mistakes had gained a momentum which only Germany could halt, by a countermovement of her own—the cumulative horrors of which are the exact measure of what it took to set the world back on a road toward human and universal solidarity. Though the failure of the peaceful nations appeared at its height in the capitulation of Munich, it also set the stage for a different play which henceforth would be played by forces no longer under the control of the great dictator.

10

The Augean Stables of the Nazis

THE realization that Germany was once again on the war-path did not come until the rape of Austria. The demoralizing effect of that realization opened a wedge to Nazi propaganda abroad. Up to that moment, Hitler was using up the unreserved credit granted to the Weimar Republic by the western world. After the rape of Austria he began to move on his own steam and to sustain himself by his propaganda.

Invariably, propaganda, to be successful, must fall upon willing ears. The public must respond with the instant reaction of one who hears made articulate what he has hoped or feared all along. What the Nazis had to tell Germany in the years of their march to power and afterwards was eagerly accepted by the German people because they wanted to believe precisely what the Nazis conveyed to them. Most of those Germans who remained skeptical merely did not believe that the Nazis were the right people to realize their dreams. Abroad, however, Nazi propaganda had to work upon the fears of intended victims, since few outside the Reich could look forward to seeing the Nazis establish themselves as a superior race over the rest of Europe. But in the early days of their rule, no one feared them, and few believed in them. The very creation of a ministry of propaganda was rightly adjudged to be an open admission that they were going to spread nothing but lies.

Outside Germany no one believed that the Germans were in fact a superior race; neither was there any disposition to credit the Nazi tale that Germany had lost the last war owing to the collapse of the home front. Even if people believed it,

180

their comment could only be, "So what of it?" A small minority of twisted minds welcomed the Nazi campaign against Jews. Many more believed that Germany would prove a bulwark against Bolshevism. The vast majority of people, however, saw in them and their leaders a gang of cutthroats and vain boasters who would achieve the ultimate ruin of a Germany already ravaged by the severity of the economic crisis and the vast army of unemployed. The persecution of Jews, pacifists, leftist writers and politicians, university professors and scientists, the burning of all German literature of value, the worship of Wotan, the interference with the teaching of Christianity by the churches, the suppression of the trade unions and the confiscation of their funds, and the institution of concentration camps were little calculated to gain for Germany the admiration and the love of the world. Whatever excuse was advanced for the Nazis was in reality due to the much more subtle propaganda of the Weimar Republic which had preceded them.

People who had learned to see the origin of all evil in the Treaty of Versailles believed that they were vindicated. The war had been fought to make the world safe for democracy, and to hang the Kaiser. Now, behold, there was a man worse than the Kaiser. Those who had worked for an abrogation of the Treaty of Versailles thought themselves no less vindicated. The treaty had not been abrogated quickly enough to suit the hurt pride of the German people. The dislocation of industry and trade throughout the world was attributed by many not to the defects inherent in the economic system, not to the war itself and the subsequent war waged by Germany against the reconstruction of her own country and Europe, but exclusively to the conditions created by the Treaty of Versailles. Jean de Bloc's prediction of the consequences of a world-wide war were largely fulfilled, but the economist John Maynard Keynes entitled his book: *The Economic Consequences of the Peace*.

If Nazi propaganda had been designed to convert the world to Nazism and Fascism, it is no exaggeration to say that they could have gone on preaching their gospel forever without converting any more of the people of the world to their way of thinking than the comintern or the Italian fascists. Whatever unquestioned success they did have was due to the fact that no one believes a liar even when he tells the truth. They said that they wanted to conquer the world, that they intended to exterminate whole nations so that they could gain *Lebensraum* for themselves. They demonstrated daily at home what barbarism they were capable of committing. They boasted of immense armament plans. Nevertheless, the world remained convinced that they were lying. Even their best advertised victims, the German Jews, scrutinizing the first discriminatory measures taken against them, concluded that the Nazis were not nearly as bad as had been feared, and quite a few who had fled abroad returned home.

In France and England the character of Hitler was received exactly as Charles Chaplin depicted him, years later, in an untimely film, "The Great Dictator." He was a comic figure. His deeds and speeches aroused more derision than indignation. What indignation there was was expressed in the churches of France, where devout Catholics prayed for the persecuted Jews of Germany. For the first time in the history of the British Parliament the leaders of the three parties, Conservative, Liberal and Labor, rose in turn to condemn the action of a country with which Britain was at peace. Strong presentation by the British foreign office induced the Nazis to call off "the Night of the Long Knife," which was to be a Bartholomew's night. It became a mere boycott of all Jewish shops for one day.

People sighed with relief. The Nazis were amenable to reason after all. Representatives, religious and secular, of the German Jewish communities appealed to the world not to provoke the Nazis to further outrages by instituting a boycott against German goods. They begged that the protest in the press and from the pulpit be toned down. In this they followed the example of the political parties in Germany, who had likewise pleaded with their followers not to provoke the Nazis, though they, at least, had the excuse of being utterly helpless.

However, the attraction of Nazi successes, like slow poison, began to be felt abroad, at first only by those who were themselves consumed with desire for unrestricted power. The students in the Latin Quarter of Paris have the merit of having discovered the first product of this later era of Nazi propaganda abroad—one Ferdinand Lope, a man dressed in a redingote and wearing the rosette of the Legion of Honor. How he gained this distinction is a mystery except it be explained by the age old French quip: "Don't you know? He asked for it."

Ferdinand Lope dreamed that he would be the savior of France, though why France needed a dictator was not clear. One more personage on the payroll of the republic overburdened with civil servants could hardly help to balance the budget. That at any rate was the objection of my concierge to dictatorship. When the students discovered the ambitions of Lope, they were delighted. Two parties were formed, the Pro-Lopes and the Antilopes. They organized mammoth meetings, demonstrations and counterdemonstrations for and against the Fuehrer, up and down the Boul' Mich'. Those who played the rôle of hecklers at his meetings had a hard time, for they were bodily evicted as was customary in all movements of this type. Lope was an educated man and not without political acumen. Asked what he would do about the unbalanced budget he shot his reply with vigor and without hesitation: "I am going to balance it!" "What will you do about unemployment?" someone would shout, and his answer would be as prompt: "I am going to abolish it!" After every such incisive reply his followers would yell encouragement and break into wild applause. In short, Lope had everything it takes to become a dictator except a public which would believe in him, or a disastrous defeat of his country at the hands of the enemy.

A friend and I once sat next to a dignified gentleman who engaged my companion in conversation. In the informal atmosphere of the cafés of Paris this was not an uncommon occurrence. He talked politics with apparent good sense, but as the conversation progressed, it became obvious that he was arguing in favor of dictatorship, counting up all the short-comings of democracy. I begged to be informed who would be his choice as dictator of France: Jacques Doriot, Colonel de la Roque or . . . He dismissed them all with a large gesture. Something in the tone with which I asked the question had antagonized him. He would not tell me, but for my companion, a sympathetic and charming American girl, he graciously consented to write down his prognostication in her address book: "Ferdinand Lope." I said: "But the man is an idiot." Whereupon the stranger rose to his full height and, choking with indignation, repudiated my judgment: "Ferdinand Lope, an idiot! I will have you know, my dear sir, I am Ferdinand Lope!"

In Great Britain early Nazi propaganda was celebrated in the army at the officers' mess tables. After-dinner speeches furnished an opportunity to the least articulate to give a tirade à la Hitler, thus again anticipating Charles Chaplin's version of a thousand speeches, while everyone stood up with out-stretched arm and shouted Heil. In the refugee press in Paris, Walter Mehring, a German poet, published a fusion of all Hitler's discourses—and it made sense, Hitler sense. It takes a great poet to write the slanguage of the Nazis. Mere knowl-edge of the terms which they have introduced into the Ger-man language is inadequate. There is a secret in sentence structure, a use of adjective and invective, giving to the lan-guage a rhythm foreign to standard German, which only a master can hope to reproduce. Hitherto the world has known that there is poetry beyond prose, but the Nazis have created something which is as far beneath the prose of everyday speech as poetry is above it.

The nonchalance with which the great democracies re-ceived the outpourings of Nazi propaganda was based in the main upon a comfortable military theory: the theory of the superiority of defense over offense. It was not only the mili-tary experts in the army academies of the democracies, and the writers such as Liddel Hart, who believed in this doc-trine, but the great masses throughout Europe. Everybody had been in the last war, and everybody had discussed mili-tary strategy as passionately then as people are doing to-day.

The older generations had acquired a doctrine of militarism which they bequeathed to the younger generation. But that younger generation was not interested. A young French writer described a scene which nearly every one can corroborate from his own experience. His uncle had been an officer in the last war and was anxious to instruct his nephew in the art of mili-tary strategy. He drew for him a map of a battle field, set up the divisions and regiments of the French and of the enemy, and then asked his nephew what he would do if the enemy made such and such a move. The nephew, bored to death, indicated a course of action, whereupon the old man threw up his arms in despair: "Why, you are a bigger fool than Foch!"

The Bluff School of Thought

The impact of German propaganda began to be felt only as the European governments retreated before the German menace. As the German military might grew, so too grew Ger-man influence. This was all the more true since few people were able to fathom the mystery of their diplomatic success.

Outside Germany, before the Munich agreement, the pub-lic took no interest in military matters. In the fifteen years which I spent in England, the United States, and France I can recall only one solitary private conversation on the sub-ject of militarism. To-day everybody is a military strategist, but during those years a retired army general or colonel who would bring the matter up at a dinner party was looked upon as an unconscionable bore, and most of the time he was.

Except in Germany and Russia, there was almost no military education in the schools. In France, for example, the entire teachers' federation was pacifist and taught pacifism to young France. Schoolboys in Germany, on the other hand, before, during, and after the last war were given intensive instruction in the history of military strategy. On the whole it was very accurate history, at least up to the German defeats by Napoleon's armies. Napoleon's success at Jena and Auerstadt was attributed partly to the decline of military leadership in Prussia after the days of Frederick the Great and partly to Napoleon's miraculous luck. Also during the First World War, military theory in Germany as taught in the schools fell to the level of numerology and astrology as a passing phase. Students were told, for instance, that this was the third war of the German Reich. The first had been against Austria in 1866, the second against France in 1871, and as *"aller guten Dinge sind drei"*—three was a lucky number—Germany was bound to win again.

Cursed with a photographic memory, I drew my teacher's attention to the fact that the World War was either the first or the fourth war in the history of modern Germany. If he counted the Austrian war, he also ought to count the war against Denmark which Bismarck waged two years before the Austrian war. If on the other hand he had in mind the wars fought by Germany since the unification of the Reich, the Franco-Prussian War of 1870–71 could not be counted at all, since the German Kaiserreich was constituted after the victory over France. This show-off of unasked-for knowledge brought the wrath of the gods down on my childish head. There was the fact that I was after all an enemy alien only tolerated at school: the least I could have done in return for such kindness was to refrain from throwing cold arithmetic on the patriotic ardor of my history teachers. My father, persona grata with the German industrialists, had a lot of explaining to do.

Outside of school, numerology and other manifestations of wishful thinking were rampant. Some one had added up all the words in the Bible, divided them by the number of verses, multiplied the result by the number of chapters, taken the square root, and subtracted the New Testament from the Old. The result he got was the second year of the World War, which was taken as proof that Germany would win in 1916.

After the Battle of the Marne the predictions of the German General Staff were not much better than the predictions of the numerologists.

Very early in that war the idea of a peace offensive had dawned on German diplomacy. The theory was that they would make peace in the west and concentrate all their forces on Russia. As soon as Russia was knocked out they could deal with France and England at ease. But they could never bring themselves to make the peace offensive without attaching strings. At first they wanted only indemnities, but the more hopeless the situation grew the wilder were the conditions they laid down for any peace, however temporary. Every military offensive, spring and autumn, was presented as the last, the knock-out blow to the enemy. The unrestricted submarine warfare was to force England to her knee in two months. The United States was bluffing—she had no army. When she declared war, Germany was told that America could not send any troops to the continent. The German submarines would see to that. When troops began to arrive, we were assured that Americans would not know how to fight; they were bumpkins without military skill or tradition; France and England would be knocked out before America could make her industrial weight felt. When the submarines failed to starve Britain out, the Zeppelins were going to do the job of bombing Britain unconscious. When the treaty of Brest-Litovsk was imposed upon Russia there had been bread riots in Germany, but there was no cause for worry: the Ukraine was going to supply all that was needed. But the Russian peasant is a stubborn fellow; he refused to plant, and what he had in store was hidden. The food situation did not improve.

In the postwar world, however, Germany quickly returned to "reality." As early as 1921 I heard from my teachers the first tentative geopolitics, while from then on all the wishful thinking was done in the democracies.

Though military problems and the strategy of war were hardly ever debated in democratic countries, people had deep-rooted convictions on the subject—convictions born of the last war and the democratic victory. Wars, so it was thought, were won by three things: money, money, and money. In natural resources the democratic nations allied during the last war by far surpassed the total resources of Germany. Britain and her empire alone, possessed of the finest navy, could block- ade Germany until she begged for mercy. In addition there was the French Navy and her Army, the finest in the world, manning the impassable Maginot Line. Back of them stood the United States, with unlimited resources. Though she had a neutrality law, it was not likely that she would refuse to sell her goods to any one who could pay cash and carry the goods away. By the nature of world geography only England and France could trade with the United States during the war, whereas Germany would be isolated. In point of morale, the democracies might be divided in peacetime, but in time of war they had greater staying power than monarchical or to- talitarian countries. This was only natural, since free men are better fighters than slaves. Moreover, since the democracies would not be the aggressors, they would also have a just cause to defend, an imponderable which it would be difficult to overestimate.

Based upon this military theory, a school of thought devel- oped, after the remilitarization of the Rhineland, which at- tributed all Hitler's diplomatic successes to bluff. It was argued that the governments of the democracies needed only to call his bluff and he would back down. That school of thought was bolstered by many apparent successes. Barthou's objec- tion to German rearmament in 1934 had induced Hitler to postpone by months the reëstablishment of a conscript army. Mussolini's massing of troops on the Brenner Pass after the assassination of Dollfuss compelled Hitler to postpone the An- schluss by nearly four years. Again, in the case of Czecho- slovakia, two months after the absorption of Austria, in May, 1938, Hitler mobilized his armies on the border of Czecho- slovakia. The Czechs mobilized in turn and Hitler backed down.

He then proclaimed with self-righteous indignation that the

German army had been engaged in maneuvers only. The Bluff school of thought drew attention to this caution of Hitler. It also pointed out that the German Army generals had opposed all his moves as by far too risky. Hitler might be reckless, but the very caution of which he had given proof argued that he weighed the chances of war or peace, and that he knew well enough that he could not afford to go to war.

Even before war broke out, Germany's economy was in a sorry state. The *News Chronicle* in London illustrated the autarchic principle in force in Germany by drawing two identical factories side by side with a single chain of carts serving both factories, carrying butter to the coal factory and coal to the butter factory—a sort of vicious circle of economic incest. While children lacked nourishing food industrial products were being made of milk. The standard joke in Berlin described a noise in the overcoat: it was the knocking of a woodworm feeding in the wood fiber. The artificial production of gasoline and rubber absorbed an immense quantity of raw wood and steel which had to be imported. Private housing was severely restricted. The railroads vital in the conduct of war were being shockingly neglected for the sake of road-building. Transport by truck, however, would demand such an astronomical quantity of gasoline that Germany could not last six months through any war. Lacking iron ore, Germany was developing the low grade mines which demanded a greater outlay in capital and raw material than the mines could yield by all economic standards. If Russia fought on the side of the democracies, Germany's outside supply of iron ore from Sweden and Norway would be cut. Otherwise the Allies would buy the entire output of the Norwegian mines, the total harvest of the Balkan countries, and so on.

Nor was the human element neglected in the list of German weaknesses. There was well-nigh universal agreement on the fundamental decencies of the German people. Every indication of German opposition was being carefully collected and given wide publicity. There were instances where German manufacturers had expressed to foreign salesmen their contempt for the Nazis because of their cowardly maltreatment of the Jews. Jewish salesmen still allowed to ply their trade in the early years of Nazism were asked into the private office. The doors were carefully closed, and the individual German merchant alone with his conscience unburdened his heart and his mind to his Jewish colleague, feeling better afterward. A great virtue was made of the fact that few individual outrages were reported against Jews. Every act of vandalism and barbarism had been carefully organized by the government. The shop windows were marked, the concentration camps enlarged and new ones built, and when all was in readiness, the storm troopers were brought to designated street corners, and tally-ho, the chase would begin.

Wide publicity was given abroad to real or imagined disagreements between the German high command and Hitler. From time to time the rumors were confirmed by a mild purge, such as the dismissal of Generals von Fritsch and von Blomberg before the invasion of Austria.

There were rumors of strikes by German working-men, of an underground Communist movement, using ingenious devices to reach the German people. Much reliance was placed upon a possible revolution at the very outbreak of war. The people would then be armed and could pay the Nazis back.

The worst source of information about the state of mind of a people is invariably supplied by emigrés. German newspapers published by refugees from Nazi land were staffed for the most part by people who had their bags packed in readiness for the journey back to a purified fatherland. For wishful thinking is never so intense as among those who have been driven from the land of their birth. It would seem that the dust of the worst fatherland remains attached to the soles of those most cruelly used, even when they are driven out barefoot. The state of mind of those who had been forced to flee, of people who had been offered a new home in France, England, and the United States was such that they could not refrain from telling their friends: *"Bei uns in Deutschland,"* everything was so much better. Happy were those who were allowed to stay in Germany, could take their whipping at home and remain faithful to the Fatherland. Germans in exile were quite capable of repeating the whole unsavory mess of Nazi propaganda: the decadence of the democratic peoples, the rarity of private baths in cheap French hotels, etc. However, it would be wrong to assume that refugee optimism did more than confirm a view, well nigh universal, about the "fundamental" decencies of the German people.

When Emil Ludwig, for example, made the matter of fact statement, "Hitler is Germany," the New York *Times* saw fit to scold him. Six months after the German declaration of war on the United States, the *Times* just missed calling Ludwig a traitor to his country by reminding him that he was German, when he had shown a fine loyalty so rare among his countrymen.

These wishful thoughts about German economy and morale, in addition to pacifism, account for the complacency with which the people in England and France watched the growing might of the German armies. German armament might be as gigantic as the Germans claimed, but the giant had feet of clay. When Charles Lindbergh spoke of German aviation, he spoiled his case by letting his sympathy for the Nazis shine through, but sincere enemies of Fascism were just as suspect of having fallen victim to Nazi propaganda when they pointed out that all the restrictions of consumer goods in Germany added fuel to the war machine and made it, next to the Russian, the most formidable in the world.

Before the Japanese attack on Pearl Harbor much the same theory was rampant in the United States. The Japanese had none of the advantages which favored German propaganda. They could not whine about an unjust treaty ever imposed upon them, since they had never lost a major war, nor could they count on racial sympathies. Even the most rabid American isolationist had little love for Japan. Japan could not claim that in her war on China she was preserving herself or the world from the menace of bolshevism. There was not even the faintest suspicion that the United States Government or

American industrialists favored her because they feared Communism more. Japan waged war on China under the slogan of "Asia for the Asiatics," offering the establishment of a co-prosperity sphere. She complained about her "lack of access to raw material," but she nevertheless insisted on being invincible. Thus it was not Japan who spread the legend of her vulnerability in the United States. Yet most people in America were being assured that Japan had bled herself white in China and that she could be blown right out of the water. Military experts and radio commentators, free from any suspicion of being fifth columnists, assured the American public that Japan could be finished off "any Wednesday afternoon; just give the word."

Thus in the United States as in Europe overconfidence was due to the chain of subconscious and conscious military reasoning born of the last war, and above all to a total misapprehension as to the nature of the totalitarian state.

The bluff school of thought failed to see that the totalitarian states were bound to retain the initiative in any contest with the democracies as long as these followed a short of war policy. As long as Hitler refrained from any direct attack upon any of his immediate neighbors, the democracies could not act or maneuver. With every retreat he prepared an advance, while the solid support he enjoyed inside Germany protected him from losing face with his followers. With every break of a treaty came his assurance that this was positively his last demand upon the world. His very apparent readiness to back down contributed to the feeling that he was not wholly unreasonable. While he announced that he had given the order to remilitarize the Rhineland, for instance, he also asserted that he was willing to return to the League of Nations and participate in a general scheme of disarmament. People who listened to his speech in France congratulated each other: "It's all right. He says he wants to come back to the League of Nations."

Since most people belonged to the bluff school of thought, the retreat by the democratic governments seemed to be utterly incomprehensible. The *New Yorker* magazine, for instance, suggested in its column, "Of all Things," that Europe might try to say "boo" to Hitler and see what happens. It is not very difficult to guess what would have happened. He would have retreated if his army was not ready, but if it was ready Europe would have been at war.

Throughout the protracted negotiations regarding the Sudeten, while the world hung between war and peace, people would ask themselves what Daladier, Chamberlain, and their general staffs were talking about whenever they met in London or Paris: they were, after all, strong enough to force Hitler to retreat. There was only one among our French friends who thought he had the answer. The democracies were, according to him, in no position to wage war and their military and political leaders might therefore spare themselves the trouble of all this journeying backward and forward, were it not that people in trouble hate to be alone. He wagered that they just sat together and sighed. This was not quite as funny as it might sound. To understand why the obvious lies of the Nazis began to take root at the time of Munich one must recall the atmosphere created by the imminence of war.

During the days preceding the Munich agreement the lights of Paris were dimmed out. By all odds it was more macabre than a full blackout. The partial blackout was produced by a black cloth hood hung over all the street lamps, letting a cone of light shine through to the pavement. The town glowed ghastly, as if a dress rehearsal was being staged for the funeral of the city of light. The atmosphere of doom and evil foreboding was heightened by men digging trenches in the Jardin de Luxembourg where our nurse was promenading the baby. She stopped to ask one of the workmen what they were doing, and he replied philosophically, "Digging graves, Madame, for you, Madame." To complete the picture, the sirens of Paris howled disconsolately once a week.

Six months after Pearl Harbor, the efficient Mayor of the city of New York had not yet discovered a siren which could be heard. When the sirens of Paris were first tried some time in 1935, they were not good enough to awaken all sleepers. I would have slept through the first Paris trial warning, if Erma had not awakened me. Overhead there was the drone of what sounded like an armada of planes. We had not read the papers and for a moment we thought it was the real thing. I asked Erma why she was putting her shoes on, where she thought she was going, and she explained that out west men die with their boots on!

But by 1938 the sirens of Paris howled loud enough to wake the dead. They were tested every Thursday at noon. When her mother tried to tell our little girl that there was nothing to be afraid of, it was just music, Michèle at the age of two had the answer: "If this is music, music is wicked." Even after many months in the United States, the passing of a police car or an ambulance with its sirens going full blast would make us sit up with nerves on edge. The seeds of Nazi propaganda could sprout only in such an atmosphere—the atmosphere of imminent war and capitulation.

It was then that the ultra-reactionary elements in every nation looked upon Hitler as an ally in their own struggle for power, while they looked upon Hitler's enemies as their own enemies. Hitler cried that the Jews and the Bolshevists were in alliance against him, and all ultra-reactionaries stood ready to rush to his aid as their champion against the common enemies.

Anti-Semitism and Tolerance

France had been a home and a vacation to the rational, the kind of heart, the tolerant, and the gay, to all who had sympathies for the arts and the art of living, who loved good food and wine and the easy companionship of the people of France. But that was not the whole secret of her glory. People of means could enjoy this good living anywhere in the world for a price. However, those who knew France and loved her people best were not among the rich in purse or the mighty of this world who could stay in her luxury hotels, eat in expensive restaurants, and drink at the Ritz bar. Only men without fame or fortune could taste to the full the civilization of France, since only in France was the individual the center of the universe. Other nations had the equality of men on the statute books, but it remained an ideal as yet unattained. In France, it was a living reality. The finest human ideal men can hope to attain, the very ingredient which gives meaning to the word civilization is this—that men learn to evaluate men by their character and by their character alone. In France people did this quite naturally and unreservedly. They made one feel that one was of value merely by belonging to the human race. To Frenchmen this was so much a part of themselves that few of them have thought to dwell upon or to extol it. Foreigners were more likely to notice it. To the obscure sojourner in France this finest virtue of her people proved a source of happiness compared with which the pursuit of fame or fortune in his own country seemed an idle and dreary way of spending his life. In possession of this highest good, the bread and salt of French hospitality, the expatriated could taste the joy of life on a café crème, and cheap food washed down with *vin ordinaire.*

An American couple we knew in Paris moved to London. There, after having lived in Paris for years, they were struck by the fact that some of their English friends, without meaning to be unkind, were capable of speaking to them as follows: "You Americans . . ."

They resented this form of address. To be sure, they were Americans, but what was more important, they were Amos Stote and Dorothy Stote. This was the significant fact. It distinguished them for good or evil from 130,000,000 other good Americans, all citizens of a great country like themselves, with whom they had a republic and a glorious history in common. But every man's life is his own, and every individual has his qualities and his faults, and in that he is unique. As such he has the right to demand that he be appreciated or condemned as the case may be for what is his own and his own alone. No one in France had the occasion to make such demands, for every one was accorded this courtesy as a matter of course.

During the Munich epoch, however, the pest long contained in Germany threatened to poison the atmosphere of France. A young French medical student told us that his life was being made miserable at home, where his parents railed night and day against the Jews, without any provocation. At a dinner party I was informed by a handsome young woman who sat next to me that Pope Pius XI was a Jew and that his name was really Lehman. To be sure, in the words of a classic writer, God had created her with such precipitancy that he omitted putting the brain in.

But there were more serious evidences of the effect of Nazi propaganda. A plea for tolerance went out, from certain quarters. We ought to try to understand. Not all the Nazis had done should be roundly condemned. Perhaps the atrocity tales should be taken with a grain of salt. Particularly, French Jews were under suspicion, their opinions untrustworthy. They were decried as intolerant, blind to the merits of National Socialism. Thus the quality of mercy was strained to the point where tolerance was demanded for the intolerant.

Our host at one dinner party belonged to this school of tolerance. He expressed the opinion, with reference to the Sudeten, that since Hitler wanted it that way there was no help for it, and we would have to resign ourselves. One of his guests, a war hero of the First World War, disputed this defeatism with vigor, until the host asked him with much genuine kindness whether he was not prejudiced against Germany because of the persecution of the Jews. His Jewish guest was astounded. If his memory served him right the Jews were neither the first nor the greatest victims of Germany: it started with two German invasions of France and some four million French casualties in the last war, of which he was one, as his father before him had been in 1871. Had his host forgotten France, or was he deriving some unavowed satisfaction from the thought that the first casulties of the new war which was shaping up were Jews? By all appearances the coming war promised to be no war at all, but a universal pogrom against human liberty.

A few weeks after the capitulation of Munich, Horace Van Offel, a Belgian writer of tales for children, returned from a lecture tour through Germany. He came to the Café des Deux Magots to talk to his compatriot Peter Flammand, whose Flemish poems have the quality of Chaucer and Villon rolled into one.

We ordered a pernod for Van Offel, while I, unendowed by nature with any taste for alcohol, was having a mournful grapejuice.

Flammand looked at Van Offel expectantly: "What did you find, in Germany?"

"*Eh bien*," said Van Offel, "Hitler is doing constructive work, yes, that's it, constructive. . . ."

"Constructive? Constructive of armaments, no doubt, and soon that will prove very destructive of Belgium, eh?"

"Oh, no," says Van Offel. "They have assured me that Nazism is not an article for export. They have no wish to let their enemies benefit by what has proved to be such a blessing to Germany."

"Not an export article? Then why in the name of all the saints do they spend billions of marks on foreign propaganda?"

Van Offel (*indignant*): "They never gave me any money."

"Oh didn't they? Well, why on earth didn't you ask them? Ask and you shall be given. Were you tongue-tied? What ailed you? Were you not yourself? They are rich and powerful, gathering to their table the scum of the earth, yet you hesitated. Didn't you stop to think that no one would know? Besides, what if it were known: no one could accuse you of dishonesty, since you are speaking your own mind. This is most alarming. If virtue is to be its own reward what would become of the writing profession? You are a disgrace to your calling, a menace to my trade. How am I to live when you go and offer your services for nothing!"

Van Offel, ruffled, counter-attacked: "It is all the fault of the Jews. They monopolize the publishing business. You can't get anything printed nowadays without their having a share in the rewards of your labor."

"What! Don't you get your royalties?"

"On the contrary, they are too free with their money. Jews have no regard for it. Mind you, my best friends are Jews. Whenever I've been in trouble, they have never failed me. But what is one to do? I have done the best I can for them. Believe me, Peter, I have warned them not to support the Socialists, the scourge of Belgium. But they won't listen to me. How can one hope to save them, when they are all Socialists digging their own graves?"

"Are all Socialists Jews? That is the question."

"No, but they are misled by Jews."

"Vandervelde, Huysmans . . . ?"

"They are Jews!"

Flammand flared up: "What! Are all honest Belgians Jews?"

By this time delegates had arrived from all the tables in the café, each contributing to the argument in support of Flammand, a veritable Dreyfus Case in a coffee-pot.

Flammand calmed down: "Well, perhaps he is right: who can tell? Perhaps my publisher is a Jew, too, though he goes to Mass as regularly as I take a drink. Who but the vulgar can tell a Jew from a Gentile? I tell you there are no Jews in all the world, yet Van Offel knows personally fifteen million Jews, each blocking his road. A figment of his imagination. But his best friends are Jews! How is that, do they support rogues as well? Are they all things to all men or only to those who are less than men? Are they all of them rich enough to waste money, or are they poor and miserly, intelligent and decent, stupid and orthodox, well-groomed or dirty, the salt of the earth or the seed of corruption, the last to be resolute or abject slaves? Don't let it bother you, my friend and compatriot. Go start a publishing company of your own. Fifteen million Jews won't stop you, or by heaven, I shall take your part and join the Nazis myself."

Flammand fell in the Battle of France, while the Nazis made

Van Offel publisher of *Le Soir*, the largest daily in Belgium. However, after a few months of his services, he was fired. It would seem that the reward of the traitor can never exceed thirty pieces of silver.

Though I am telling the story of Nazi propaganda in France, because we lived there at the time, it was much the same in all other democratic countries, a variation on the theme as determined by local conditions.

Under the blood-curdling sirens, which seemed to amplify the howling of the disciplined Nazi Dervishes, it was by no means easy to escape Flammand's charge of vulgarity. That quality which, defying definition, distinguishes French Jews from other Frenchmen as it distinguishes English Jews from Englishmen and American Jews from Americans, began to preoccupy people who had never given it a second thought. Jew and Gentile alike started making mental notes, classifying their friends as Jews and non-Jews, while scrutinizing the doubtful or mixed cases.

But although the pigeonholes of the mind were filled with information and generalizations, it was utterly useless for the purpose of evaluating individual character, like the information contained in that other pest which, between the wars, made the life of travelers miserable with useless passports and visas adorned with hideous photographs. When and where were you born (and if so, why?); any distinguishing marks; color of your hair, eyes, and skin; what justifies your presence in our fair land; are you inflicted with a loathesome and contagious disease; do you intend to overthrow by force or violence the established order. (You and who else?) While spies, saboteurs, fifth columnists, and agitators traveled with diplomatic or bona fide passports, enjoying the privilege of extraterritorial rights, or the hospitality accorded to tourists in possession of permanent visas to all the corners of the globe, honest men were robbed of time, money, and sleep to nurture the overgrown weeds of bureaucracy. The innumerable governments of Europe had sown the seeds of authoritarianism in every capital and large-size city of the world, and these had sprouted into Embassies, Delegations and Consulates. No one could travel anywhere in Europe for more than twelve hours without being confronted with a wealth of foul-mouthed officials, bent upon discovering things that were none of their business, and inflicting the humiliation of physical and mental invasion on the person.

Just so the vulgar and profane constituted themselves amateur officials, staring at their neighbors with the intensity of the village gossip and the contumely of office. But this variation of anti-Semitism remains relatively harmless. Though it is an infernal nuisance, it belongs to the category of prejudices which affect all, Jew and Gentile, alike. It is the kind of prejudice which flourishes everywhere in the world—in the suburbs and on Main Street. Those who evaluate the worth of their fellow-men by the color of their skin or eyes also used to hate the fellow who goes abroad without a hat or wears a petunia in his lapel.

We are living at present in a suburb of New York. Recently a local music teacher offered to give lessons to our little girl. One of our neighbors advised strongly against entrusting our child to "that woman." The woman teacher being white Protestant, nothing was said against her religion or her race or indeed against her qualification as a teacher, but—"Do you know, although she is married, she uses her own name. She is often seen working in her garden clad in a dressing-gown, and is reputed to have once lived in Greenwich Village."

Even at the time of Munich, Nazi propaganda succeeded only in intensifying the existing popular prejudices. Without the support of the sword there is no future in propaganda. As long as the abuse of political power is prevented by safeguards of individual rights, anti-Semitism remains a parlor game of those who suffer from lack of self-respect and consequently try to derive some merit from the fact that they belong to that vast exclusiveness of 99 per cent of the inhabitants of this earth who are not Jewish. Verily an inflated aristocracy.

Protests against this vulgarity were not lacking, nor were

they confined to the intellectual world. Paris at times was
flooded with newspapers financed by the German consulate
and distributed outside the regular channels. They all died an
anemic death for want of buyers, but they were also invariably resurrected under different names and different direction. The German propaganda machine was carrying on a
game of trial and error to find out which line would take hold,
but only the native-grown anti-Semitism of the *Action Française* seemed to have any vitality. Their clerical anti-Semitism
was born of the grudge they held against the people of France
for the defeat inflicted upon them in the Dreyfus Case.

From the vantage point of the wide terrace of an elegant
café on the Champs-Élysées, we watched the auxiliary news-
vendors crying out their papers, replicas of Coughlin's *Social
Justice*. At a table near-by a woman, evidently a member of
the wealthy bourgeoisie, stood up and spoke her mind
calmly, but loud enough to be heard: "I am only a woman,"
said she, "but if I were a man, I should know what to do. Is
there no manhood left in France? Are you going to sit here
and listen to this voice which speaks French but is the voice
of the boche?"

She must have given expression to what was felt by many,
for she had no sooner said her say when little was left of the
papers except torn remnants, while the vendors were streak-
ing down the avenue in wild flight to escape a beating.

The protest as well as the attack upon the Jews outside of
Germany remained Platonic. No country except the traditionally anti-Semitic Poland introduced any discriminatory laws
against the Jews. Even Italy succumbed to it only after Mussolini had ceased to be master of his own brand of Fascism
and started taking orders from Hitler (March, 1939). But also
no nation thought seriously of interfering in the internal affairs of Germany to stop the persecution because intervention
would have been looked upon as the greater crime.

It was not realized that German anti-Semitism was an ingredient of the fifth column, different in kind from the exclusive spirit of restricted neighborhoods, and a direct menace

202 SHORTAGE OF VICTORY

to the freedom of the world. The Weimar Republic had succeeded in establishing firmly the principle that the victim and
not the criminal is guilty. France and not Germany was responsible for the war of 1914 and the post-war crisis. The
Nazis tried to accomplish a similar feat. Not they but their
victims were guilty. "Europe"—so spoke the great dictator—
"will not know peace until the Jewish problem is settled."
Such perversion of the truth of which imperfect man is capable
feeds on itself until it is all-embracing. It must expand, and
propaganda is the ferment which sustains the lie and makes
for growth. The denunciation of the Jews became a denunciation of the Jewish spirit and flowered into a denunciation of
the human spirit as such, the Nazi version of Emmanuel
Kant's, *Das Ding an sich* (the essence of things). The destruction of human liberty which Nazism meant to accomplish was
symbolized early in 1933 by the burning of the books, while
all decent men and women in the world whom the Nazis
could not yet reach were denounced as warmongers, bolshevists, and Jews.

My pretty dinner partner could well believe that Pope Pius
XI was a Jew, for he accepted the Nazi challenge: "Spiritually
we are all Semites." In Germany itself, Cardinal Faulhaber
and Pastor Niemoeller echoed these words. The Protestant
churches of Germany were filled to overflowing with ardent
Christians who sang the battle hymns of the early Protestants
in defiance of the Nazis: *Eine feste Burg ist unser Gott.* . . .
(A mighty fortress is our God). The Catholic Church of Germany protested against the compulsion of the state which violated daily the concordat which Rome had concluded with
Hitler.

But this courage of organized religion did not expand. The
leaders of the Catholic and Protestant churches in Germany
insisted that they were not concerned with politics, confining
their protest to religious matters. It is difficult to explain this
limitation which the churches in Germany set themselves except on the supposition that their members had no objection
to the political expansion of Germany. At any rate, religion,

exactly like the social and secular ideals, failed to inspire the people of Germany with the courage for civil disobedience.

When anti-Semitism becomes a weapon used by the government against the liberty of the people and of the individual, it never stops at the Jew. Its action and its thought have to expand, until it overflows the political frontiers of the state by means of the sword: in the end the Jews never lack company.

The expulsion of the Jews from Spain in medieval times took place simultaneously with the expulsion of the Moors and the flowering of the Inquisition, which burned heretics at the stake regardless of race, creed, or color. How well this connection was understood by the emancipated in those days may be deduced from Cervantes' protest in his *Don Quixote*. Though he disguised his indignation to escape the Inquisition, he left no doubt as to where he stood. He makes a Moor praise the wisdom of the measures taken by the Inquisition against his people, but he also shows this Moor to have been a good neighbor, beloved by all. Sancho Panza in his wisdom is too cautious to aid the Moor in the recovery of his fortune. Only Don Quixote, being mad, can defy the Inquisition, without getting Cervantes into trouble.

The early crusaders quite logically concluded that it would be folly to go all the way to Palestine to kill infidels when there were the Jews close at hand, and so they massacred them by the thousands, but at the same time just as many sorcerers and witches were burned, together with such heretical books as those by Erasmus, Descartes, and Spinoza. But for a near miracle the world may never have known the paintings of El Greco and will most certainly never know how many priceless masterpieces of art and literature did not see the light of day because the mind which bore them was burned at the stake. As long as the Netherlands were under Spanish rule as many Netherlanders as Spaniards fell victim to the Inquisition.

In one respect the medieval Jews were more fortunate than their fellow-Christians. The state refused to grant to the

Synagogue the aid of the secular arm, for lack of which the orthodox Jews have never been able to burn their own heretics at the stake. In the absence of any political power, the Synagogue had to remain nearest to the teaching of Christ. It could expel the philosopher Spinoza and denounce him to all Jews and to the world as an atheist, but it could not deprive him of his life or even of the bread which he earned by grinding lenses. Since the dispersal of the Jews, the Synagogue has lacked the power which it had in the days of Pilate. No power based upon force has ruled over its members, and no hierarchy has connected the separate synagogues of the world. In the history of medieval civilization it was a unique democratic institution. The rabbis enjoyed only the prestige they were able to command by the wisdom of their leadership. At no time were they powerful enough to enforce their rules at the point of the sword. If the Jews as a religious community have survived to this day, they owe it to the internal liberty of their communities, which the temporal tyrannies of Church and State have been unable to destroy.

To-day as in the Middle Ages the Jews have the company they will never lack as long as force, intolerance, injustice, and exploitation rule the world. The trickle of Jewish refugees from Germany finally grew into a torrent of uprooted humanity, from Spain, Austria, Czechoslovakia, Poland, Denmark, and Norway. In Holland, Belgium, and France, refugees choked the roads, impeding the movements of their defenders as a drowning man in terror chokes his savior. The splendid security in isolation was gone from the brows of anxious mothers in England who took their children to street corners and parted there from them, without knowing when they would sail or what boat would take them to the provisional safety of the western hemisphere. They remained behind in agony at the thought that they might have sent their children to death by Nazi submarines. They had not deserved such a fate: only a year earlier England and France had generously received all the children the German Jews were allowed to send abroad. In Germany, likewise, mothers were not allowed to accompany their children to the train. They, too, for a very different reason, had to part with them on some designated street corner, and wonder whether the Nazis would keep the pact or keep the children as hostages.

At the same time, in the Far East, the worthy replica of the German state, Japan, had set in motion the same process of evolution. Millions of Chinese were driven like chaff before the hurricane of unchained totalitarian fury. As in the west so in the east the aid given to the persecuted stopped short of war, while business as usual provided aid and comfort to the enemy until the fire of destruction jumped five thousand miles of ocean and scorched the fringes of the western hemisphere. Germany and Japan have proved Kipling a poor prophet: the twain *have* met. East or west, white or yellow, tolerant toward all religions as Japan has been to a greater extent than any other nation, or intolerant toward them all, like Germany, the totalitarian state remains essentially the same.

Adding insult to injury, the Nazi loud-speaker daily mocked the democracies for their failure to come to the aid of Manchuria, the Jews, Ethiopia, Spain, Austria, Czechoslovakia, Poland, etc. Thus the criminal put on a fool's costume, pronounced judgment, and executed the sentence upon the victims of his crime. The mills of the gods grind slowly. . . . To-day German refugees from R.A.F. raids travel the same roads once taken by their victims to Paris, Warsaw, Prague, and Vienna.

The Russian Revolution

THE historian owes gratitude to the Japanese. By their action they have supplied the acid test of the laboratory demonstrating that the enemy is the totalitarian state, and that religious or racial hostilities are only an indispensable ingredient of the brew. Where there are no Jews, the white race, the Chinese, or the Koreans fill the void. In the last analysis, anti-Semitism was a relatively unimportant horse in the Augean stables of the apocalypse. Had there been no Jews, the Nazis would have manufactured another scapegoat or ridden some other horse. In any case, strict adherence to the principle of non-intervention in the "internal affairs" of other countries would have robbed the democracies of the Herculean strength to clean the stables.

Anti-Bolshevism was a horse of a different color. It deserves a thorough analysis, since it has considerable bearing upon the present conflict and promises to remain a grave problem for the future.

In their endless string of abuses dignified by the word propaganda the Nazis throughout registered success only in so far as they were able to utilize existing prejudices and hostilities. At the time of the Munich agreement, Russia was isolated geographically, politically, and ideologically. This result had been achieved for Nazi Germany partly by Nazi and Communist propaganda. But in the main the isolation of Russia was due to the internal divisions of the democracies themselves.

The isolation of Russia began during the last war at about the same time as the appeasement policy toward Germany, and like the appeasement policy it originated in the democracies. Though the democracies were fighting in the west for the preservation of the principle of self-determination for all nations, and to make the world safe for democracy, their governments departed from the principle of non-intervention when the Second Russian Revolution broke out in October, 1917. For by that time, having largely suppressed all freedom of speech and press, they were no longer democracies but semi-totalitarian. The war had necessitated the creation of a united command and the establishment of government control over production and distribution. The allied governments consequently felt free to use a surplus in man power, and above all in ammunition, to intervene in Russia. The decision to stop the revolution was made on executive order without submitting the policy to Parliament or Congress and without regard for public opinion.

During the present war, made wiser by experience, England and the United States have adopted totalitarian measures in war production with the consent of the governed and without war hysteria. Abuse of governmental power to the point of oppression has thus been avoided. Press and speech are still free. But, in the last war, the Pacifists and Radicals were right in their criticism when they claimed that the democracies were fighting Prussianism abroad while at home they were rapidly falling victim to the same evil spirit.

The Allies had hailed the advent of a democratic government in Russia in February, 1917, because the provisional government created after the abdication of the Czar promised to keep Russia in the war, and because the February revolution did not appear to threaten the capitalistic system. But the Russian people had had enough of war. In the words of Lenin, they answered the question of war and peace with their feet; they walked home. Nor was it astonishing that they should have given up the struggle. For three years they had fought with inadequate weapons, against the powerful German Army, for the most corrupt régime in the world. At times the Russian soldiers had gone into battle exposed to the efficient machine-guns of the Germans without being able to shoot back. To defend themselves they were forced to wait until a comrade possessing a rifle fell. There was not sufficient ammunition or shoes or uniforms on hand, those that were on hand did not reach the soldiers, since the ordnance of the Czar was carrying on a lively trade in army goods and food supplies on the black market among the civilian population.

In spite of the squalor, poverty, and degradation in which the peasantry of Russia was forced to live—or perhaps because of it—it required nearly a century of agitation—from the uprising of the Decembrists in 1825 to 1905—for the peasantry to be ready for revolt. Supported by the bourgeoisie and the working class, all equally oppressed under the autocratic rule of the Czar, the Revolution of 1905 elected a democratic and leftist parliament. Had the Czarist régime possessed the wisdom to bow to the will of the people and been content with constitutional powers, Russia might have taken the road of the western democracies. But absolutist rulers, like the dictators of to-day, can not resign themselves to a curtailment of their power. The revolutionary impulse had no sooner spent itself than the court of St. Petersburg recovered from its fright and sent the Duma (Parliament) packing.

The Russo-Japanese War, which ended in defeat for Russia, had not been popular and was the immediate cause of the 1905 revolution. But the war of 1914 was popular. Even many of the extreme revolutionists supported it. France was under attack, and to revolutionary Russia, France was the France of the Great French Revolution, the original source of the revolutionary movement in Russia, and it was under attack from German absolutism, not as bad as Czarist rule but withal German and therefore hateful, if for no other reason than because Germany was in no small part responsible for the maintenance of absolutism in Russia. Undoubtedly the Slavs' antipathy for the Teuton played a part even in the mind of revolutionaries emancipated from racial prejudices. All revolutionary Russia hoped that the war would finally end in revolution, as the unpopular Russo-Japanese War had ended.

On the other hand, the Bolshevik Party, insignificant in size in spite of its name (majority party), under the leadership of Lenin, uncompromisingly opposed the war as an imperialistic enterprise of no concern to the proletariat.

Lenin proved of unusual foresight and political acumen. He expected that Russia would lose the war and that the lost war would produce a revolution not only in Russia but in Germany as well. At the same time he anticipated that his proclaimed opposition to war would catapult him into power as soon as the people turned against the régime which had led them to defeat.

The Economics of Revolution in Spain and Russia

In February, 1917, the revolution broke out, and from then on to the Ocober Revolution, the peasant-soldiers left the front to return home and to possess themselves of the land, while the workingmen took over the factories. It was then that the slogan was born which Lenin took up, proclaiming it as his own, though it was diametrically opposed to his program of centralization: The land to the peasants, the factories to the workers, all powers to the Soviets.

In the history of revolutions the six months of the Russian Revolution from February to October 1919 ranks unique for its thoroughness. There may never be anything to compare with it in the western world, not, at any rate, until the people in the industrialized western countries learn to manage the factories as well as the individual peasant knows how to plant potatoes and wheat, and how to raise livestock.

It is no accident that the Russian Revolution, like the French and the American revolutions a century and a quarter earlier and the Spanish revolutionary resistance to the Franco putsch in 1936, took place in an agricultural country. Only a peasantry and at that a comparatively primitive peasantry can destroy the entire economic, social, and political organization of the country and live. In a highly industrialized country the destruction of all communication and all means of transport would not only paralyze the economy temporarily but would lead to famine and pestilence and might wipe out the entire population. In England, dependent upon foreign food supply, such a revolution would find the country with no more than a few weeks' or months' supplies of food on hand, and unless the outside world came to the rescue the people of England would starve.

In the United States the dislocation of railways and road transport, the stoppage of all industry, would depopulate the great cities which would suddenly discover that they are nothing but stone deserts, dependent for their food upon the rest of the country. The industrialized and specialized agriculture of the United States would fare little better. Men do not live by bread alone, neither can they live on wheat alone or poultry, oranges and apples, or eggs and milk alone. Specialized farms of this type require a wealth of outside supplies, specialized fodder, e. g., which they do not grow themselves.

Although the Russian Revolution came from within, it was as devastating as a Blitzkrieg waged upon the nerve centers of an industrialized country. If Russia survived she owes it to the peasantry which took possession of the land, organized itself spontaneously in soviets or local councils and started tilling and planting the soil. In the making of this revolution which made tabule rasa of the past, the psychology of the individual peasant played the most important rôle, a rôle studiously ignored by the Marxists biased in favor of "Proletarian" revolutions.

The Russian peasant, like his French and American forebears, faced no financial or technical problems of high complexity. He knew quite well that he could get along without the landlord, his manager, and outside supplies. The landlords had demonstrated this for centuries by staying away most of the time from the estates. Some of the land belonged to the peasants as common land and this they cultivated without any aid from the bailiffs, and they knew also that more land would provide all their simple needs. Gogol tells in his novel *Dead Souls* of a landlord who asked his serfs how it was that their own wheat stood manhigh in the common fields, while the wheat on his ground hardly wanted to grow at all. His sly serfs had the answer: It is the climate, my lord. Obviously they took better care of their own than of that which was not their own.

In highly industrialized countries the division of labor has advanced to the point where skilled workers are specialized in one trade, and where most of them know only a subdivision of that trade. The industrial manager alone can see the work of the factory as a whole, but each factory in turn is dependent upon the supply of raw materials and semifinished goods from every quarter of the globe. If the working class took over the factories unprepared, they would not in the absence of managerial support know what to do with them.

And for this reason the industrial workers are not as a rule anxious to take over the management of the factories, but content themselves with demanding full employment, higher wages and shorter hours. Thus none of the driving force which makes the individual peasant of Europe long to own the soil he tills is present in the industrial working classes. When workmen took over the factories in Italy after the last war they were unable to organize production efficiently, with the result that they were quickly disillusioned and failed to put up any effective resistance against the reaction triumphant.

Factory Soviets in Russia during the process of their formation from February to October, 1917, enjoyed the coöperation of the old management and of the engineering staff. For a near century the revolutionary movement was led by the sons and daughters of the Russian bourgeoisie, and the class as a whole welcomed unreservedly the overthrow of absolutism. It is only after October that the bourgeoisie were antagonized by the arbitrary methods of Lenin and his party, the new rulers being unwilling to share a particle of their power with either labor or management.

Eighteen years later the example of the Communist Party dictatorship, the suppression of all economic liberty in Rus-

sia had a profound influence on the Spanish Revolution. The
revolutionary workers of Spain likewise gained the support of
experts and engineers when they seized the factories in 1936
and some liberals, skilled in management, also stayed on to
help defeat the Fascists. The Spanish Syndicalists were much
farther advanced in technical knowledge than their Russian
colleagues. In the organization of their trade unions they had
profited to some extent by the lesson of the Russian Revolution.

Better trained in industrial self-government, they were
able to keep the factories running. The entire textile industry
of Barcelona for instance, second in importance only to the
textile industry of Manchester, continued to produce almost
to full capacity. Workingmen organizations supplied the electricity for the towns, operated the railroads, the subway and
the tram-cars. They reorganized the Hispano-Suiza motor-car
factory and many others for the production of ammunition
and even succeeded in producing a few planes.

Nevertheless, the attempt to create self-governing democratic industrial organizations presented problems of greater
complexity than the Anarcho-Syndicalist organizations had anticipated. When the stocks of raw material, lying on the factory
grounds at the time the unions took over management, were
used up, and when the cash assets in the banks of the companies were exhausted questions of credit, finance, and foreign
trade arose with which the unions were not prepared to cope.

Control of the banking system had been centralized by the
government so that the unions had to appeal to the government for assistance. The Spanish Government maintained that
the war against Franco could only be fought by totalitarian
methods and summoned the unions to relinquish control of
the factories to the government. When the unions refused because they were opposed in principle to nationalization and
dictatorship, the government in turn refused them credit and
war orders. Instead of employing the productive capacity of
the Spanish textile mills, the Spanish Government, since the
unions would not yield, placed its orders for khaki clothes and

ready-made uniforms in Poland, where it paid twice the market price for these goods. Thus Republican Spain, fighting for its life against Franco, also carried on a second conflict between the working class and government.

The peasantry of Spain, on the other hand, did very much better than the workingmen in the towns. Independent of government control, money, foreign exchange, and so on, they organized communal farming on an unprecedented scale. In the province of Aragon, for instance, they succeeded in improving the productivity of the land to the point where they were able to supply Barcelona with food, whereas previously the province hardly had enough to supply its own needs.

But exchange between town and country on a basis of barter is infinitely clumsy and the peasants, though they had enough food, had to do without the products of the city. Part of the reason for the loss of the war must be ascribed to this internal conflict between a government dependent upon Russian aid and consequently subject to Communist principles and the revolutionary masses who wanted no centralization of power into the hands of the state. The Spanish Government discouraged guerrilla warfare against the invaders, but failed to produce a unified command and a disciplined army for want of equipment, nor did it succeed in establishing total control over industry. As neither side yielded, Republican Spain fighting the Fascist was neither totalitarian in organization nor wholly decentralized. Consequently the military conduct of the war could neither produce a unified command, nor an all-out guerrilla war waged spontaneously by the people themselves.

Foreign Intervention and Russian Reaction

Precisely the same fatal three-cornered battle between the government, the people and foreign intervention doomed the Russian Revolution. Insistence upon the continuation of the war against Germany brought about the downfall of the Socialist government of Kerenski in October 1918. Lenin and his party, but yesterday decried as spies sent by the Germans to undermine the war effort of democratic Russia, gained the confidence of the people because of their peace-at-any-price policy and also because the Kerenski régime had tried to keep the front intact by introducing capital punishment for desertion. The folly of Kerenski was all the greater since the law could not be enforced with the entire army deserting.

As soon as Lenin and Trotski had taken over the reins of government they started peace negotiations with Germany. The price the Germans demanded was the highest which had ever been exacted from a defeated power. Even so, the German rulers regretted the necessity of having to be content with so little owing to the exigencies of the western front, and no sooner was the treaty signed than the Germans violated it. Lenin on the other hand believed—as it turned out, rightly— that the exorbitant demands of the Germans could be accepted with little risk by one who had no intention of adhering to the terms of the treaty. The opportunity which would make a unilateral abrogation of the treaty possible was bound to come sooner or later.

At the same time reactionary Russia, up to then quiescent, began a counter-revolution and gained the support of the western democracies. Future historians may well agree that this intervention of the democracies in the Russian Revolution rather than the Treaty of Versailles was the supreme tragedy of the twentieth century.

The allies of Russia would have done better to support the Russian Revolution, even from the point of view of keeping Russia in the war. The people of Russia needed a breathing space, permitting them to reorganize their economy on the basis of the Soviet institutions which they had themselves created in answer to the need of the hour long before the Bolshevists seized power. At the same time, peace or no peace, they were fighting Germany, if no longer on a continuous front then by guerrilla warfare, to prevent the Germans from carting away their seed and their livestock. They compelled Germany to keep some fifty thousand troops in the Ukraine, troops which might have turned the tide on the western front.

But the Allies decided to keep Russia in the war by waging war on the revolution. They acted like the absolutist powers at the time of the French Revolution. On the pretext of trying to reëstablish the legitimate government of Russia with which they were allied, forgetting their own revolutionary origin, they chose to ignore the biblical warning to the children of Israel: "Remember that you too were once slaves in Egypt."

The Allies achieved their aim, but not as intended. Russia went to war again, but in defense of the revolution against the intervention. At the same time the democracies contributed mightily to the blackout of liberty in Russia which followed the revolution.

It has since been claimed by some Russian historians and corroborated by foreign eyewitnesses of the revolution, that the intervention was defeated in the main by guerrilla warfare and that the Red Army hastily organized by the Bolshevik Party acted only as an auxiliary to the guerrillas. That was unquestionably true in the Ukraine where the so-called povstantsi, peasant partisans, defeated the German efforts to set up a puppet régime (a device later perfected by Hitler in all conquered countries). The partisans crushed the armies of the Whites one by one under the leadership of Makhno, a warrior of the type made familiar to American movie audiences by the superb film *Viva Villa*. At one time Makhno was allied with the Bolshevik Government in Moscow, and he was then hailed as "the Napoleon of the Revolution." Later, he fell foul of Lenin and Trotski because he objected to the suppression of all individual liberty in Russia, and Moscow denounced him as a counter-revolutionary.

It is an open question whether or not the guerrillas might have defeated the intervention everywhere single-handed. The Bolshevist Party, at any rate, insisted upon the necessity of a unified command and a military dictatorship as the only way to victory over the counter-revolution. They pointed to the support which the capitalistic countries were giving to the Whites, proving that the Allies were secretly in league with capitalistic Germany to suppress the Russian Revolution. The necessity for a military dictatorship to defeat the intervention, feigned or real, gave them the opportunity to do away with all the freedoms established by the revolution. They abolished for the duration not only freedom of speech and press, but free elections in the Soviets as well. These spontaneously created organizations were thus deprived of their economic function.

In many ways the original Soviets resembled the early town meetings of New England, though their main function was economic rather than political. With the advent of the Bolshevist dictatorship, however, they were reduced to executive organs of the central government, with the state appointing its functionaries instead of the people electing their local leaders. The total decentralization of powers brought about by the revolution was thus forced to give way to a total centralization of power into the hands of the state, and the Russian totalitarian state, the first of its kind, was born.

By the time the intervention was defeated (1921), it was too late to revive the practices of the revolution. The peasant-soldiers returning from the front found that the revolution had failed. The Bolshevik Party was firmly established in power and had changed its name to Communist Party. The change between the days of revolution and the Russia which Lenin had created was so glaring that the illiterate peasantry which knew little of the change in name but saw the effect was in the habit of explaining that the Bolsheviks were splendid fellows, but that the Communists were no good.

Russia was disillusioned and exhausted after six years of war in which she had suffered even more than France, and the Communist Party made it quite clear that it had no intention of yielding one particle of the power it had acquired during the wars against the intervention.

Nevertheless, enough revolutionary fervor was left among the sailors of Cronstadt, who had been the first to rebel against the tyranny of the Czar in 1917.

After the defeat of the intervention they passed resolutions reminding Lenin of his promise to reëstablish freedom of speech and press, free elections in the Soviets, and to liberate all political prisoners. These same sailors had rescued both Lenin and Trotski when they were in hiding from the hands of the Kerenski police which meant to bring against them the unjust charge that they were spies on behalf of Germany. But the oppressed of yesterday had become the oppressors of to-day. Leon Trotski sent a telegram to the sailors of Cronstadt ordering them to withdraw the resolutions or he would have them shot like pheasants. They refused and the threat was made good. Troops not yet demobilized were brought up from the front. They were told that Cronstadt had to be reduced because the Whites had taken charge of Cronstadt and the revolution was in danger.

Cronstadt fell, though the sailors resisted to the death. Since that episode, resistance to the régime of the Communist Party rarely flared into open rebellion but continued underground, ever-present, insidious, sapping every purpose and proclaimed aim of the government. The Communist Party hit back. Throughout the five-year plans, the government press continued to charge Russian labor with drunkenness, sabotage, inefficiency, and non-coöperation.

Peace between Russia and the West

Although after the defeat of the Allied intervention in Russia the uneasy hostility between Russia and the western powers continued, there was no further danger of war between Russia and the democracies of the western world. After 1918, the democratic nations regained the liberties they had lost during the war. In 1920 a council of action formed by the British Trade Unions organized a strike of the dock-workers, who refused to load munitions which were destined for the interventionist armies in Russia. Lloyd George was thus compelled to withdraw from the war. Poland, with the aid of the French

General Maxime Weygand, was able to roll back the Russian counter-invasion which had brought the Red Army to the gates of Warsaw. Thereupon peace was concluded.

Any further intervention in Russia would have been effectively stopped by a general strike in the European countries.

In the United States a few boys and a girl were condemned to twenty and fifteen years imprisonment respectively for having printed and distributed leaflets threatening a general strike if shipments of munitions to White Russia were not stopped, and also for having called President Wilson all sorts of picturesque names.

The incredible conviction was upheld by the Supreme Court, Justices Holmes and Brandeis dissenting on the ground that the defendants had only exercised their right to free speech. The hearing before the Supreme Court gave council for the defense Harry Weinberger the opportunity to define the difference between abuse of the President and criticism. Said he: "When you criticize me, that is criticism, when I criticize you, that is abuse." Subsequently President Wilson commuted the sentence.

It is true that the hostility to the Communists remained intense in the United States, in all classes of American society. But this hostility could never again degenerate into war with Russia, because the working classes and large segments of the bourgeoisie, though hostile to Marxism and dictatorship, were uncompromisingly opposed to war in general and to war on Russia in particular. The controversy which raged between leftists and rightists with regard to the true nature of the Communist dictatorship precluded any united action against Russia, however much certain die-hards throughout the western world might have wished to see the Communists wiped off the face of the earth by war. An attack by Russia on the western world was equally beyond the realm of the possible. Russia would have been faced by a united front from Poland to Spain.

Nationalism remained strong enough in every country to transcend any sympathies for the "Great Experiment," par-

ticularly as these sympathies were due for the most part to
the proclaimed peaceful intentions and opposition to war of
the Russian Government. Inside Russia, even the total command over all channels of opinion could not serve the Russian Government to kindle any enthusiasm in the heart of the
people for a war of aggression. Russians are not Germans.
For centuries, Russian abhorrence of war had found expression in the songs of her people and the revolution had wrought
no change. The Russian agreement with Nazi Germany of
August, 1939, and the attack upon Finland and the Balkan
countries lost to the Communists not only whatever sympathy
and prestige the Russian Government still enjoyed in the western world, but the resistance of the Russian people to a program of aggression very nearly lost Russia a war waged on
such a diminutive opponent as Finland.

Fascism versus Communism in the West

Nevertheless, the short of war hostility between Communist
Russia and the western democracies projected into the sphere
of international politics the ideological element which had
been of little importance in 1914. Sight was lost of the fact that
military alliances and mutual love between allied governments
need not necessarily coincide. Beneath the mistrust for each
other, of governments based upon different ideologies, there
may yet be a justified mutual trust between allied peoples.

The deceptive retention of the framework of capitalist management by Fascist countries blinded the capitalistic and conservative world to the evolutionary process in the Fascist state
which gradually but inevitably deprived capital of all power
in favor of the military dictatorship. The conservative world
saw the Communist menace to its liberties clearly, because it
was naked, but it failed to see the far greater menace of
Fascism. At the same time the liberal and pacifist world—
misled by the phraseology of the Russian Revolution which
the Communist government retained, as the medieval church
retained the teaching of Christ—was willing to close its eyes

to the obvious tyranny of Russian totalitarianism. It is only
since the German invasion of Russia and the magnificent defense put up by the people and the armies of Russia, that the
controversy between two types of visitors to the Russian state
has been dissolved. Those who defended the régime as a work-
ingman's government, and those who attacked it as a dictatorship established over the proletariat, can now agree upon its
vital—its one—salient characteristic. It was, and has remained
essentially the same to this date, a military dictatorship which
was born of the war of intervention. Like all totalitarian states,
it sacrificed all but a minimum of the economic needs of the
people to the military needs of the state.

During the nineteenth century the state was deprived of
nearly all power to intervene directly in the process of production and distribution. Its function was largely confined to
police duty, that is to say, to the maintenance of the property
laws such as they had evolved since the American and the
French Revolution. Unable to intervene in the economic organization, the state could do no harm and the Socialist school
of thought consequently arrived at the easy conclusion that
governmental regulation of the process of production and distribution would be more efficient and equitable than that provided by private ownership and corporate management. The
theory carried the proviso that the machinery of government
must be in the hands of those who preached Socialism and
who were therefore presumably beyond suspicion of seeking
personal gain or satisfaction from the exercise of power for
the sake of power. Just give me the power, says the Socialist
politician, and I shall do the rest. The theory of Socialism both
in its democratic as well as in its dictatorial and subversive
version was thus ideally designed to foster passivity and apathy
among the masses.

In all of the traditionally democratic countries the vast
majority of laboring men remained faithful to the basic principles of democracy. But in all large-scale democracies the inventive capacity of the revolutionary epoch which created the
democratic systems had dried up. At the same time the dy-

namic force of the Communist dictatorship in Russia and the Fascist and Nazi dictatorship in Italy and Germany focused all theoretical speculation upon these two alternatives: Fascism versus Communism. Those who opposed Bolshevism and Fascism with equal determination only urged the preservation of that relative liberty which western civilization had achieved. They pointed to the incontrovertible fact that even in an economic crisis of unprecedented severity, the unemployed of the capitalistic system were still better off than the employed slave labor of the dictatorships.

But the satisfaction which could be drawn from such a comparison by those who suffered under the poverty amidst plenty of the capitalistic world was slight. Life, moreover, abhors stagnation. Where there is no progress there is invariable decline. Under the influence of Socialist doctrines, both of the democratic and the dictatorial variety, the world between the wars was blind to any road which might have led to a more generous conception of liberty than the freedom preached by the laissez-faire school of nineteenth century economics. That freedom was limited to those who owned or controlled the means of production, or possessed that peculiar mixture of business acumen and organizing talent which makes for success in capitalist economy.

Throughout the world the economic crisis had shaken the faith of the captains of industry in their ability to manage the national economy but, whereas in Germany capitalism capitulated completely to the state, in the United States and in England a compromise was worked out which helped to tide the two countries over the worst effects of the depression.

In America the severity of the crisis at the time the New Deal took over had paralyzed the economic mechanism of the country as if a revolution had taken place. A situation which, according to Marxian theory, must automatically be followed by a seizure of power for the proletariat. But "scientific" Marxism is a poor prophet. Like the Dow Jones theory of stock-market fluctuations it is right only in retrospect. Its predictions for the future never come off, and like chart readers of the stock exchange, the explanations Marxists offer for their lack of foresight reveal that they, too, are incapable of reducing life to a fool-proof formula. Instead of the dictatorship of the proletariat the new deal brought a burst of new freedom to the United States. In social thought it stimulated search for a solution without the compulsion of the police state. In the economic field it curtailed the power of management to do as it pleased with what was considered unreservedly its own in the past, and thereby increased the sphere of liberty for workingmen, dependent upon management for their livelihood.

But in the United States, as in England and in France, the expansion of liberty did not go far enough. The state as reformer mitigated the evil of a scarcity economy but it did not solve it. In the smaller European democracies in Denmark, Norway, Sweden, Holland and so on, a further advance was made in the struggle for freedom from want, by the organization of coöperative farming and marketing, financed by coöperative credit institutions.

No sooner had the captains of industry recovered from the fear which led to their temporary abdication, when the organized opposition to the New Deal began. Capital had not suffered from any curtailment of profits. On the contrary, a marked recovery took place everywhere, but management resented the curtailment of its unbridled power over the means of production which it had misused during the seven fat years. Labor on the other hand had not gained free access to the means of production and full employment. Idle factories still faced idle men. Thus both labor and capital were left on their hunger as it were.

The capitalist world of France might have been reconciled to socialist reforms if these had been sponsored, as in England, by some rightist party. French capital was antagonized by the stereotyped phraseology of the Socialist Party—nearly identical with the Communist verbiage—and since the crisis in France was less severe than in England and in the United States, French capital capitulated temporarily only because of the threat of revolution. Since they were never as badly frightened as their American colleagues they had never been moved to introduce the reforms themselves through their political representatives in Parliament.

The ideological controversy between leftists and rightists reached its greatest intensity at the time of Munich, brought to a head by the economic crisis and by the action, the propaganda, and the counterpropaganda of both Russia and Germany. The Liberal and Social Democratic press at times was closed to any objective criticism of Russian action. It feared that the internal evils of the Russian régime, if brought to light, would only add weight to conservative sympathies for the Nazis' and the Fascists. It minimized the revelations of the Russian trials, pinning its faith into some future development of democracy in Russia. The conservative world on the other hand developed in its midst a nucleus of influential and powerful people who constituted what became known as the Cliveden set.

These die-hards were assured by their German friends, the leading industrialists of Germany, that the Nazis were arming for an attack on Russia. The German industrialists thus acted as lead sheep to the slaughter and enslavement of their western colleagues. The members of the Cliveden set in every country in the world desired a Russo-German war so intensely that the wish to see it consummated became father to the thought. Since they never exercised sufficient power anywhere to plunge their own countries into war against Russia they prepared to sit back and applaud while Germany would do the job for them.

Meanwhile they did their best to obstruct any measure short of war, however ineffective, which might have been taken against the growing might of Germany. It was sincerely expected that the defeat of Soviet Russia would stop the agitation of labor for higher wages and shorter hours, and the right to bargain collectively; it being assumed that all these demands of labor were inspired by Moscow, as if there never had been any revolutionary movement or any fight for the emancipation of labor and for the curtailment of the power of industrial lords, monopolies, national and international cartels before the Russian Revolution. As it turned out the evil wish was not father but cuckold to the thought. Hitler played his own game against the German industrialists while he was making his bid for power in Germany and he likewise played his own game against the foreign "plutocracies" in the field of international politics. Those who had seen his game never doubted that he would attack in the west in order to destroy democracy and capitalism first, well knowing that the enemy he had to fear most was the liberty of the western world.

Though the Cliveden sets in France and England grew powerful enough to block any effective interference with Nazi propaganda and diplomacy their strength in the last analysis was based upon the unconditional opposition to war of all peaceful people. Democratic majorities everywhere were influential enough to stop any aggressive action by their own governments, but they were not powerful enough to move their governments to intervene against Japan when she attacked China, against Italy when she attacked Ethiopia, against Germany when Austria was overrun. They could not supply arms to Spain and they were helpless as their governments were helpless for want of arms when Czechoslovakia was dismembered.

When Chamberlain and Daladier arrived at Munich by plane to consummate the capitulation of democratic to fascist politics, the German people received them with sympathetic enthusiasm. The great diplomats and statesmen of the western world arrived to associate themselves in the crime against Czechoslovakia. Germany applauded the harbingers of the Pax Germanica. The breakers of solemn treaties were no longer only German, the democracies, too, had found an "elegant" way out. Thus Chamberlain and Daladier enjoyed a brief hour of popularity in the land of treachery. The prisoners used to their prisons magnanimously received the new men. The adored jailer this time had not only brought in helpless individuals, but he had proved that even the members

of the upper classes in society are no better than they should
be; for this all Germany was grateful.

The Fifth Column

After the Munich agreement Germany's hegemony over Europe was unchallenged. Hitler held the European states and
their governments in the palm of his hand. A protest from
him was sufficient to subject the British press to censorship,
a feat which no government on the continent had ever before
performed. The diplomacy of the unarmed can not prevail
against the mighty. It seemed as if he could go on reducing
every country in Europe to his domination as he had reduced
Austria and Czechoslovakia. He needed only to refrain from
such action as would re-unite a divided world. His game was
clear. No war! War carries risks even when undertaken under
circumstances most auspicious and most favorable to the aggressor. Some one might get shot while engaged in peacefully
invading a neighbor's garden. Therefore submission must be
obtained without war; it is demanded by virtue of the pacifism
of the chosen victim, and of the world. A peaceful world was
put upon its mettle to maintain the peace, so that the barbarian could reduce his victims one by one to slavery, or exterminate them at will.

Hitler had reached the highwater mark of his power. The
universal abhorrence of war had delivered to him, without a
fight, two nations. Not since the days of Jericho had such
fortifications crumpled before the noise of the trumpet-call of
propaganda backed by a show of arms. Strict adherence to
commercial principles, appropriate in a better world, delivered to Germany the gold stock of Austria which served as a
guarantee for the Austrian debt. It was deposited in the Bank
of England by the International Bank of Basel of which Germany was a member. The British Government justified its
failure to intervene at the bank by the technicality which
gave it no authority to freeze the Austrian funds, since Austria had not defaulted, and there was no reason to assume

that she would. The burglar who had cracked the safe and found nothing in it was thus handed over the bank account of the man he had imprisoned. Upon receipt of this money Hitler promptly defaulted on the Austrian debt.

The Czechs, rendered utterly defenseless by the loss of their fortifications, had also become economically vulnerable. They therefore asked Britain for a loan of thirty million pounds sterling. Mr. Chamberlain announced in Parliament that he would support this request. Some one shouted: "Blood money." Mr. Chamberlain went on to say that he had authorized the Bank of England to transfer ten million pounds to Czechoslovakia at once, on the principle that he who gives quickly gives twice. Thereupon he was corrected; a member cried: "Takes twice," and Mr. Chamberlain grew annoyed. "This house," said he, "can not hear the weighty matters which I have to lay before it, when the Prime-minister is continuously interrupted."

Acting on the assumption that Hitler was pursuing economic ends, the British Government offered him an immense loan which would enable him, now that he had had his last wish fulfilled, to readjust his internal economy for peace production. He did not deign to answer. The disintegration of Europe seemed complete. Poland had "profited" by the dismemberment of Czechoslovakia and secured for herself a piece of that unhappy country, and Paris promptly predicted a fourth division of Poland between Germany and Russia. By the action of her government, Poland had severed the bonds of sympathy which linked her to the western world in spite of her corrupt and ruthless government in the hands of army colonels. Slovakia, under the leadership of her Quisling, Monseigneur Tissot, was breaking away from the Czechs. The countries of the little Entente allied with France—Romania and Yugoslavia —could no longer resist after the keystone of their defense, Czechoslovakia—and her fortifications—were lost. Henceforth they were wholly dependent politically and economically upon Germany. Russia had apparently been eliminated from the concert of European powers. France was isolated, Spain and

Italy belonged to the axis dominated by Germany; Japan was about to join.

The men and personalities of Europe who saw clearly were pushed into the background. Churchill occupied the back benches in Parliament. In France, Henri de Kerelis and Emile Buré were voices crying in the wilderness. De Gaulle was unknown, an obscure officer in the French Army. The prestige of all democratic statesmen was gone, and their integrity was in grave doubt. The personality of President Roosevelt retained universal popularity, but the United States was far away and had given herself a neutrality law which removed all but her moral influence in Europe. The victory of 1918 was lost, and Great Britain was at the lowest point of her prestige. These were days in which England tried the soul of those who knew her history and who clung to the belief, in spite of all evidence to the contrary, that in the end she would fight and fight magnificently.

In every country in Europe midget Hitlers had sprung up, nurtured by a Nazi promise of power. Mosley had organized the black shirts in England on the model of Mussolini's Fascists but was now ready to swing into the Nazi camp. There was a Quisling in Norway, a Mussert in Holland, a Degrell in Belgium, the cagoulards, Doriot, Déat, Colonel de la Rocque, etc., in France.

In the small Baltic countries and in the Balkans, which had been democratic at their creation since they owed their existence, for the most part, to the victory of the democracies in the last war, the fifth column fascist and semi-fascist governments were already in power. The original parliaments were dissolved and the rights of national minorities suppressed.

While the growth of Nazi and the decline of British prestige abroad divided the countries of Europe within and without, it served to consolidate all the "anti" elements in each nation. The antiDemocrats, the antiSocialists, the antiCommunists, the anticapitalists, the antifreemasons, the antiJews, anticatholics and antiprotestants in every country in the world, though they had nothing in common were welded into a homogeneous anti-social bloc bent on destroying, in common action, the free-dom of their fellowmen—a freedom which cramped them, re-stricted their violence, and withheld from them the power which they thought their just due. It is of these that the fifth column in every country was composed. In this one respect Nazi propaganda contained an element of originality, although Imperial Germany had furnished a precedent in the Ukraine in 1918 and the Japanese in China had aped the example. The Nazis, judging others by themselves, discovered that a prom-ise of power is of greater attraction to the potential traitor than the traditional thirty pieces of silver. These are soon spent, but power is of greater non-economic satisfaction and the beauty of it is that it remains self-generating of cash as well.

In possession of power the puppet ruler can, as the col-loquial phrase has it, write his own ticket or print his own money. This promise of power which they made to all poten-tial traitors is the only promise the Nazis have been tempted to keep but could not for lack of even that honor prevalent among thieves. Their servant in the Sudeten, Henlein, has never been heard of again though his services among certain well-meaning people in England were inestimable. Mussert of Holland seems to have vanished as well, nor is there any news of Tissot, the priest of Slovakia, and Degrell of Belgium. If they are not dead or in disgrace, the power they exercise seems to merit no publicity.

Of all the deadly vices and seven sins of men, the desire for power is the most virulent disease. By the side of it the miser's hoarding of money is a quaint trait in an otherwise lovable soul. The Nazis needed to keep faith only with a Seyss-Inquhart of Austria to inflame the hopes of an army of rats in every country in the world. Of this army only one could hope to serve the Fuehrer in the capacity of valet-in-chief. The chances of success were, therefore, as remote as the win-ning of a lottery ticket, and that at the risk of life. But the greed for power is of such intensity that it banishes from the hearts of cowards all fear of the firing squad or the assassin's bullet.

Nevertheless, like Nazi propaganda, the effectiveness of the fifth column remained dependent upon the might of the Nazi armies and the weakness of the enemy. As the armies of the aggressor grow so grows the fifth column. The full fruit of potential treason can be gathered only by an invader overwhelmingly powerful on the battle-field. In England and Russia the method of undermining the country's government from within failed because the invasion of England failed, and because in the Russian case the Nazis were confronted with an army powerful enough in men and equipment to hold their own before the onslaught of the Blitz. What is even more remarkable, the Nazis failed in Sweden and Switzerland, as well as in England and Russia. Neither of these islands of civilization in the totalitarian sea, though utterly defenseless, has tried to win the enemy's favor by aping his régime.

Because of the shock produced by the military successes of the Nazis, people jumped to the conclusion that all countries which had fallen had succumbed to the fifth column. Nazi propaganda did its best to support this notion. When people begin to suspect that every neighbor is a member of the fifth column and that the government itself is honeycombed with them, the result may be as disastrous as if it were true. After the fall of Norway, and the sensational "revelations" of the press about Quisling and his works, the French Government herded refugees, sworn enemies of the Nazis, indiscriminately into concentration camps. The Vichy Government handed these twice-imprisoned and twice-betrayed back to the Nazis. The French people, on the other hand, showed better sense. In innumerable cases they helped refugees to escape as they gave sanctuary at the risk of their lives to English soldiers hiding from the Gestapo and the German military.

In the conquered countries the establishment of a puppet government is child's play. There are no more than a dozen, or thereabouts, specimens needed to make up a government. These can be picked up in any saloon. Swing the doors open and you will find them in line. The disadvantage is that they have to be maintained by the bayonet. In Poland, for instance, such a government would require the protection of too many guns, urgently needed on the Russian battle-front.

The former American Ambassador to Russia, Mr. Davies, has made the discovery that the trials of the old Bolshevik guard eliminated a fifth column. This is rather a startling bit of hindsight. There are no puppet régimes in the conquered regions of Russia and Poland because the Germans regard these territories as their very own and are proceeding methodically to make them into graveyards for the native population. In the western countries under their rule, on the other hand, there are industrial plants which for the time being are needed to supply the German war machine, hence the pretense of collaboration. Should Germany win the war the extermination methods used in Poland and Russia will inevitably be extended to the west.

As to the Russian trials, they were inspired by essentially the same considerations which led to the blood-bath in Germany in June, 1934. The totalitarian state thrives on purges. The old Bolshevik guard would have done well, in 1921, when they slaughtered the Cronstadt sailors, to remember the matter-of-fact statement of Kropotkin: "Those who advocate dictatorship do not in general perceive that in sustaining this prejudice they merely prepare the ground for those who will later cut their throats."

In Yugoslavia, China and elsewhere the fifth-column weapon has been turned against the invader. Guerrilla fighters join the fifth column, are supplied with guns and ammunition and with them vanish to rejoin their comrades. The corruption of the Japanese officers permits the Chinese to carry on a lively barter in goods vital for their armaments in exchange for such surpluses as they can spare. The same development is reported from Nazi-occupied countries where the demoralization of Nazi losses on the Russian front makes itself felt. Hitherto the Nazis were able to combat it. Far from trying to suppress graft and corruption, which would have been a hopeless task from the start, they established regular tariffs for each irregularity—such as the supplying of false passports to Poles, marking them down as non-Aryan so that they may obtain permission to leave the country, and so on. Now, however, this safety-valve is effective no longer, and regular German army supplies have disappeared to help arm the guerrillas, and feed the people in the conquered countries who can still afford to pay exorbitant prices.

While the promise of a share in the Nazi usurpation of power bred traitors and consolidated the antisocial elements in every nation immediately before the war, the Nazi armies of occupation have now reversed the process. Everywhere they now face a homogeneous population welded together by common suffering and ready to rise against the invader at the first opportunity, as the population of St. Nazaire rose to take part in the raid of the British commandos. In every country under Nazi rule a new spirit of human solidarity is born. The ideals of liberty and equality and justice for all, proclaimed a century and a half ago by the revolutions in America and France, have come to life again. When the conquered, but not subjugated, peoples of Europe will be liberated the world will hear of peace aims born in these dark hours which, like the liberating revolutions of the past, may once again carry civilization forward.

Words that had lost their force during the retreat of liberty between the wars have acquired a new meaning to those who live under the yoke of the oppressor, as well as to those who are still free and are working for the liberation of the conquered.

The Ides of March, 1939

Such power as Hitler wielded on the continent of Europe after his victory at Munich was barren of any creative and sustaining force. It was based on the bayonet alone. The economy of Germany was being exhausted to maintain the monstrous and unproductive machine which the totalitarian state had called into being. Every six months the régime had to show a victory to justify the sacrifices which it demanded from the people. Devoid of an economic and self-rejuvenating basis, the Nazi régime could not secure and consolidate its political power in Europe. The goal it had set itself and for which it was spending the wealth of Germany was being attained. The tanks, planes, and guns were rolling off the assembly line in the quantities required to subjugate all of Europe in the estimation of the German High Command. But the force which had been set in motion could not be controlled. The sorcerer's apprentice had become slave to the broom.

The products of the war industry could not be used to produce consumers goods. They were all lined up in an economic Dead End, designed to generate war and destruction and to spread this commodity on the conveyer belts of Europe: the roads and highways which, in time of peace, serve to transport food and drink to nourish a peaceful world.

The early experimental engines of the Nazi war machine, produced before the Spanish adventure, were exported to the Balkan countries and Turkey to pay for German imports in food stuffs and raw material. The finished war machine, however, stood poised to burst the confines of the Reich encircled by virtually unarmed nations, but which were rich economic units destined to feed the monstrous German war machine with their wealth and their blood.

The sorcerer's apprentice had forgotten the formula used by the master to stop the broom. There was such a formula which could have stopped the finished products of German labor: a German revolution. Even in the totalitarian story the people are master. They can frustrate the designs of their rulers if they so wish. In Russia, for example, the Communist state had not succeeded in establishing its total ascendancy.

But in Germany, and Japan, the master conspired with the apprentice, permitting him to time the attack before the planes, tanks, and guns produced on the assembly line would grow obsolete. The Nazi state would not have labored in vain. There being nothing to stop it, the machine exercised its compulsion, and on the fifteenth of March, 1939, Germany invaded Bohemia and Moravia—remnants of Czechoslovakia saved at Munich by the surrender of democracy.

The spell was broken. Instantly the last illusion of peace with honor was dissolved.

Up to that moment the world had been convinced of the futility of war, now it had learned of the futility of peace. Hitler had overplayed his hand. Until he broke the treaty of Munich he was using up the margin of what mankind would support for fear of a new war, but on the fifteenth of March his cards were on the table. Only those struck with incurable blindness could still fail to see, and only deliberate traitors could still glory in his aims.

The last non-aggression treaty signed with Chamberlain at Munich and later at the Quai d'Orsay with France had become a shred of paper. No government could still try to keep the open secret of the German purpose from the consciousness of the people in France and England. When Hacha of Czechoslovakia was subjected to the third degree in the foreign office in Berlin and signed his nation away into slavery, he also doomed his tormentors. The ides of March was the turning point in the war which Germany had waged upon the world since 1933. The force of pacifism was spent, the trumpcard of peace lost to Germany and, for the west, the diplomatic game was ended. From that day the stage was set for the military decision.

But before the curtain could go up on the trial by fire, there was still some preliminary shifting of the scene. Desperately, Britain tried to save the balance of power she had lost by appeasement. A treaty of mutual aid was concluded with Poland and a mission sent to Russia. It was too late to save Poland and it was also too late to save the alliance with Russia for France. The rulers of Russia were now prepared to take up where England left off. Excluded from the settlement at Munich and spared humiliation, Russia was now going to try the game of the Cliveden set, and by appeasing Hitler secure his rear while he attacked the west. In Moscow they knew

that they would have to fight Germany in the end, but, like
the democracies, they were going to let the Germans shoot
first.

They overestimated the military might of France, thinking that they might sit back and watch Germany and the
democracies exhaust each other, as the reactionaries of the
democracies had hoped to see Germany at war with Russia
while they continued their business as usual. Yet Moscow must
have had its doubts. It is not excluded that the Russian Government might have made common cause with the west if
England and France had been prepared to grant them military bases in Lithuania, Latvia, Esthonia, Finland, and Poland.

Russia was not going to respect the neutrality of the
small countries which lined her coast, or of Poland, which
barred her route into Germany. She would not yield them as
bases for German aggression upon her. The British and the
French governments, on the other hand, could not, after the
disaster of Munich, afford another loss of prestige by giving
their consent to the violation of the principle of national sovereignty. They would have been discredited, not only in the
eyes of their own people, but in the western hemisphere as
well.

Though the strategic argument of Russia was sound, to
yield would have been a greater moral disaster than the surrender at Munich. At Munich, France and England had failed
to come to the aid of a friend. Pleading impotence, they had
tried desperately to save what could be saved, but the surrender of the Baltic states and Poland to Russia would have
lost them in the eyes of their own people and in the eyes of
the world, the last imponderable of moral support.

The outcome of this dilemma was the non-aggression pact
between Germany and Russia. What France and England
could not do Germany did cheerfully. She abandoned to Russia what was not her own, as she had given part of Czechoslovakia to Poland. Thus the stage was set, the final backdrop
in place, the final fake document drawn up and presented to

the British ambassador in Berlin several hours after the German commanders had opened their secret instructions and the German Panzer divisions had stumbled into Poland.

The "eternal friendship" pact between Germany and Russia coincided with a shift to nationalism and isolation in Russia. While the German totalitarian state reached full Socialistic development, Russian and German propaganda talks became indistinguishable. The Russian radio denounced the war of the democracies as plutocratic and imperialistic in the same terms as the Nazi radio. Communist spokesmen in France, England, and the United States ascended the Utopian mountain peaks to join Hitler and Goebbels. The propaganda chorus was synchronized. The factories of ready-to-speak phraseology fused when the two great houses had reached the same high standards in the production of words. The Nazi factory, made up of the uniform material of abuse and whole cloth for mass production, adapted itself to the requirements of eternal friendship by dropping the Bolshevist line from its string of abuses while the Communist propagandists proclaimed grandiloquently that Hitlerism could not be destroyed by force. Perish the thought of revolution.

The Russian-German accord caused profound consternation, though it did not come unexpectedly. The division of the world seemed consummated. Global war between the forces of tyranny and the forces of liberty appeared in outline as hopeless for the democracies. They were faced with the terrifying possibility of a German, Russian, Japanese, and Italian alliance, an alliance which seemed more probable than the intervention of the United States on the side of France and England. All the totalitarians were well prepared while the democracies were destined to suffer a long series of defeats for lack of arms.

Every little country in Europe and Asia was doomed to be crushed between the millstones of the larger powers. After March 15th, Germany annexed Memel and Italy took Albania, as a curtain raiser. Poland was lost before September 1, 1939. Even a fully armed England and France could not have saved her from partition among her two giant neighbors.

Yet England and France did not throw in the sponge. To be sure they remained on the defensive, hoping to delay as long as possible the test of arms, but the German-Russian accord merely served to drive home the fact that they were fighting for their lives.

On the ides of March Pacifism breathed its last and the combined effort of totalitarian propaganda had lost the force of conviction. A world dedicated to the proposition that war was hell had been converted to the view that peace with totalitarians was hell and war a deliverance.

Manchuria, Ethiopia, China, Austria, Czechoslovakia, Albania, each was a part of the pattern of aggression and each had reaped the fruits of sovereign isolation alone, and now Poland was fighting alone. She was isolated. Neither France nor England could give her any material aid. One year earlier her rulers had thought her safe, safe enough to participate in the crime against Czechoslovakia, while Germany furnished the first in what was going to be a long series of exhibits to prove that she was incapable of even that honor which Plato found must prevail among thieves if they wish to survive. Although Germany, on the ides of March, had broken the myth that any understanding with her was possible, the force which she had generated was bound to carry her from victory to victory of unprecedented sweep and power.

The strategic problem which the German war machine was intended to solve was set by British naval power. Four-fifths of the globe are covered by water. Theoretically there are innumerable bases at the disposal of naval power which can be utilized for refueling, overhauling its combat units, and reloading with ammunition. Its mobility gives it the advantage of the offense over the defense. Theoretically a land power at war with a naval power is compelled to thin out its defenses along the coast lines to prevent the sea power from landing an expeditionary force. To defend its coast lines the land-bound army is compelled to try to defend everywhere and thus risks being weak everywhere. To beat a naval power, a land army must consequently move with greater speed than the navy can move at sea. It must go on the offensive and seek to cut off the naval power from its bases without which a navy is as powerless as a gun without ammunition.

In his war on England, Napoleon had furnished precedent by a string of victories, and by his alliance with Russia. Britain was compelled to try to get a foothold on the continent. She invaded the European continent twenty-four times and was evicted as many times, until the guerrilla war of the Spaniards against Napoleon gave her a permanent base.

The German machine was built to cope with British naval power. The mechanized army moved on land with a speed rivaling the modern navy. It enjoyed independence from the nature of the terrain; land had become as navigable as water. The heavy, medium, and light tanks performed the same function as the battleship, cruiser, and destroyer, while they were all screened by an umbrella of air power and by reconnaissance units on fast motor-cycles far in advance of the main force. Its transport system by truck is to the modern mechanized army what the supply and transport ships are to the navy.

But, although the German Army could theoretically move along the entire coast line of Europe as fast as its slowest tank it was, like the navy, dependent upon bases, and after each conquest these had to be organized, consuming more time than the conquest itself. Poland was conquered in three weeks in spite of her army of one million and a half men. That army was organized on the French model and, though it fought with determination and ferocity, it was doomed before the fight started. But in spite of the quick conquest, the organization of the Polish territory for a later attack upon Russia and the preparation for the assault upon Denmark, Norway, and the western powers consumed some six months—months which were not fully utilized by the western powers, because the nature of the German war machine was, as yet, imperfectly understood. One demonstration of German prowess was not enough to shake the complacency and self-confidence of the western democracies, or even to awaken fully the small democratic powers to their danger.

These remained neutral. In England and France much emphasis was put upon the revelation of a German fifth column in Poland, the corruption of the Polish state, the absence of fortifications on the model of the Maginot Line, the intervention of Russia—all of which explained the final collapse of Poland. Every reason but the military reason was admitted.

Liddel Hart still advocated reliance upon defense. Daladier, disciple of Mahan, spoke of the superiority of naval power over land armies, and pointed out that Germany had not had the time to build up an efficient corps of petty officers, the backbone of the infantry, while England and France had them in abundance. Chamberlain illustrated in the newsreel by a large sweep of the arm, that the German merchant marine was swept off the seven seas. The phony war was on. It was utilized by Germany to rehearse the assault on Norway, and to prepare the documents proving that the United States had encouraged England and France to wage war on Germany as she had encouraged Poland to resist the fair German demands for Danzig and the Polish corridor. Thus farsighted Germany prepared the "moral" ground for war on the United States.

Peace Offensive

At the same time Hitler began the series of peace offensives. Germany's demand for the Polish corridor had been her very last demand, henceforth she was prepared to maintain the peace. It was not she who had declared war on Poland, but Poland had threatened her with invasion. Nor had she declared war on England and France. Winston Churchill was the guilty person. It was he who had maneuvered France into declaring war on Germany. As always, England was prepared to fight to the last French soldier. Germany, on the other hand, was reasonable. There was no sense in bombing Alsatian cities and have German cities bombed in return.

There were several reasons for the peace offensive after the fall of Poland, and again after the fall of France. The democracies had not yet realized the full might of German arms, but neither was Hitler quite certain of the weakness of the democracies. In fact the ease with which France was conquered was a surprise to the German High Command, though throughout they were quite confident of their superiority. Uncertain of their own overwhelming power they wished to make doubly sure, by the peace offensive, that nothing would interfere with their preparation for the next war offensive. Home morale was kept up by the talk of peace which in German eyes was sufficient proof that the Fuehrer meant peace and that the Allies "wanted war." The offensive, moreover, might help to lower morale in France and England and drive a wedge between the two allies.

But the principle reason for it was this: The whole scheme of world conquest, it was realized in Germany, would require a longer breathing spell than the six months needed for the preparation of the next local war offensive. The conquest of Europe plus the British Isles, might not yet assure the fall of the British Empire. Though deprived of a base on the European continent the British Navy would still rule the Far East with bases in India, Singapore, and Hong Kong. With the backing of the United States, the British dominions might hold together, and the productive capacity of America might permit the preparation of a counter offensive to meet which Germany would be in need of a very long pause to overhaul her war machine, put entirely new and advanced models of planes and tanks in production, and prepare an invasion of the western hemisphere by acquiring the stepping stones across the North Atlantic, Iceland, Greenland, and Canada while a southern line of approaches would be prepared across the Canary Islands, West Africa (Dakar), and the South American countries. To be sure, the attack upon Russia was to precede the attack on the United States as a means of winning the sympathy of American isolationists and perhaps the entire "plutocracy."

That all peace offensives failed was due to the ides of March and the violation of the Munich agreement. The non-aggression treaty with Russia, itself concluded only six months after the invasion of Bohemia and Moravia, was meant as a peace offensive, as conclusive proof that Poland could not be saved and that it was therefore futile to go to war against Germany for her sake. The easy diplomatic victories Hitler had won by the mere threat of war had convinced him that his early teachers in Vienna had been indubitably right, when they talked glibly around the beer tables, of the decadence of the democracies. He had fooled everybody to date, the method had worked and as the practised criminal does not change his method, neither could Hitler change the pattern of his diplomacy.

But after March 15th the magic formula of peace no longer worked. Had it succeeded the world would now belong to Germany. Such a peace inevitably would have been a total surrender. It would have robbed the conquered nations of all hope of deliverance, stamping out the last remaining faith in the integrity of Britain. If England had laid down her arms, even the French and the Polish people might have been ready for submission. The United States would have lacked the impetus to prepare her industries for war by aiding England. There would have been no lend lease and consequently no arsenal for democracy. The people of Britain who worked ten hours a day and more in a seven-day week to make up the losses of Dunkirk would have relaxed. The demoralization of the world would have been complete. But Hitler lost the Pax Germanica on the fifteenth of March, 1939. It was never to be regained.

12

The French Debacle

IT is a truism that no army is either good or bad except in relation to the army which it has to fight. Yet this truism received scant notice in pre-war days. The French Army was regarded as the best fighting machine on the European continent, a view which was based almost exclusively upon its intrinsic values. Such comparisons as were made between the French Army and the growing German forces were made on the assumption that no new revolutionary methods of warfare had been developed since the Armistice.

Yet the character of these revolutionary changes had already begun to form itself toward the close of the First World War. The story was told of a conversation which took place, before the entry of this country into the war, among the members of an Allied mission to the United States. The discussion reflected the deep gloom which the stalemate on the Western Front and the bloody and indecisive Battle of Verdun had spread among the Allies. Only Winston Churchill was undaunted. He confessed that he did not see how the Allies would win the war, but win they would.

What finally won the war were the superior industrial resources and man-power of the United States, England, and France, and the appearance of the tank and mass-produced airplanes which enabled the Allied armies to take the offensive and break through the German lines.

Furthermore, while victory appeared swift and sudden, a long period of evolution preceded the climax. When the United States entered the war she was totally unprepared. The first American Expeditionary Force had to be fitted out almost en-

241

tirely with such reserves as French and British industries had been able to accumulate. It took the United States more than a full year to switch over from peace production to war production, and this in spite of the fact that many American factories had been delivering ever-increasing quantities of munitions to the Allies. In the short period between 1914 and 1917, the year of America's entry into the war, the time needed to prepare a nation for war—even the almost static type of trench warfare of those days—had already lengthened from a few months to a year and more.

Long before the development of the conveyer belt, the adaptation of industrial production to increasing demands of the armies and the ever more complicated weapons of war necessitated the creation of a central coördinating agency in the United States. Previously, England had created a "Ministry of Munitions" to speed up war production, and Germany had anticipated both. France continued to rely primarily upon expanding large-scale war industries, privately owned, and upon the individual initiative of innumerable small workshops spread throughout the country, which had switched over to the production of munitions with no trouble at all in the weeks following the Battle of the Marne. The individual French craftsman, turning out munitions almost by hand, contributed in no small measure to the staying power of the French armies, permitting them to hold the fort of western civilization until Britain and the United States, with their combined resources, could come to the rescue and deliver the final blow in the autumn of 1918.

The United States had hardly begun to hit its stride when the still powerful German Army, fully realizing that the war was lost, begged for mercy. Erich Maria Remarque has since told the dramatic story of the consternation among German soldiers when, at home on leave, they realized that the civilian population had been kept in total ignorance of the overwhelming superiority in equipment and reserves which the Allies were bringing to the front, and against which the hungry

German Army was fighting with inferior and diminishing ma-
tériel.

The Armistice cut short the evolution of new methods in
the production of munitions and of the newly invented implements of war. While the victorious Allies did not intend to
disarm, that is what in fact they did. Their war industries re-
verted to the slow pace of pre-1914 armament production, and
all the converted peace industries returned to consumer goods
production. The net result, unforeseen, was a state of almost
complete disarmament of the victors, a disarmament no less
complete than that of Germany. This was so in spite of the
large war budgets maintained by all the powers. War budgets,
like armies, are large or small only in relation to the capacity of any given national economy and to the size of the war
budget of the potential enemy. Such war budgets, which were
maintained on an even keel, shrank constantly in relation to
the ever-growing production capacity of industry.

The evolution of new industrial methods of production,
which had taken place during the war, was continued in the
peace industries. The methods of production which had developed proved readily adaptable to the production of consumer goods. The rapid rise of the motor-car industries, the
chemical combines, the agricultural-machine and the home-
appliance factories, the large staple-foods factories and mills
—all the stupendous increase in productive capacity of the
nineteen-twenties and even during the crisis-ridden thirties,
was made possible by the application and development of
methods of production evolved during the war. The conveyer
belt in industry was the crowning achievement of this evolution.

France participated less in this development than either her
former allies, or the enemy. Reeling from more than four million deaths and casualties, with all of her most productive provinces devastated by the invasion, France took even longer than
the defeated enemy to return to normal. Never a highly industrialized country, French economy remained evenly bal-

anced between agriculture and industry. By the year 1933, when Hitler took power and Germany started rearming in earnest, France was as disarmed industrially as Germany had been in 1927, when the Allied Control Commission reported to Paris the completion of German disarmament. Moreover, with only half the population and industrial capacity of Germany, the war potential of France remained at half that of the defeated nation.

To offset this ratio, the Maginot Line was conceived in 1927 by Paul Painlevé, statesman and mathematician. It presented a very real advance over the primitive trenches of 1914–18 and would have proved a formidable barrier to any new German invasion if no revolutionary method of warfare had been discovered. A series of well anchored defenses, the Maginot Line did not lend itself readily, once it was built, to any revolutionary improvements. Little more than multiplying indefinitely the various forts and extending them ever farther back for depth could have been done to improve its effectiveness. It was not extended to the sea, because reliance was placed upon similar Dutch and Belgian defenses, which were thought to be adequate and because of Belgian sensibilities.

Industrial production, however, is not static, and the development of new methods in large-scale peace industries proved as adaptable to war production as the methods of the 1914–18 war industries had proved to the post-war peace industries. And just as, during the First World War, the time needed to translate a plan of production into implements of war had increased, so, in the years of peace, the time needed before, say, the first of a series of mass-produced motor-cars could roll off the assembly line, had grown constantly. When the Ford factories switched over from Model T to Model A, it took one of the most efficiently run factories in the United States, hence in the world, two and a half years to establish the new assembly line.

Because of the time required to gear national economy to full wartime production, *1936 was the very last date, the zero hour, for France to begin assembly-line production of war ma-*

terials. Even that year might have been too late for victory, but with her war potential fully developed she might once again have been able to hold out until the other democracies could come to her assistance.

For the totalitarian state, war begins years before the first battle is fought. It begins in the factories and in the revolutionary transformation of the national economy at home. When the armies take up battle position the decision has already been made and needs merely to be confirmed. For an understanding of the French debacle, the actual course of the six weeks of fighting which started with the German invasion of the Lowlands in May, 1940, can be no criterion whatsoever.

Because for the democracies war does not begin until it has been declared, a French national peace economy sent to the front an army equipped as for large-scale peacetime maneuvers. It was beaten before the first shot was fired. The story of the Battle of France as it has been told in the press and in a deluge of books, is the familiar story of all defeated armies in the long history of human warfare. As the army disintegrates, as commands are no longer given or executed, as positions are abandoned which could have been held and others held which should have been abandoned, as the general staff lose their heads and the ministries at home resign or are overthrown, each soldier ceases to be part of an integrated whole, and, realizing that the common cause is lost, begins to think of himself. Few men die for lost causes. Decent men take to flight, while cowards stay to receive the reward of the traitor.

The Battle of France has been badly told. That a defeated army is routed is not news, but that an army in dissolution, without hope of victory, could still have to its credit the action of the French rear-guard which fought on against overwhelming odds to permit the British to escape at Dunkirk—*that was news.*

The best equipment, such as it was, at the disposal of the Allied armies, went with the troops which marched into Belgium. General Gort has since told how inadequate that equipment was, yet with that in hand the French rear-guard reenacted the heroism of their fathers at Verdun. By this act, and at a tremendous cost in lives, this French rear-guard possibly saved Britain from immediate invasion and consequently brought the defeat of Germany within the realm of the probable. Their sacrifice was made so that Britain might continue to fight, and so that France might live, not without hope, while under the enemy's heel. It is to be regretted that this story is over-shadowed by the fall of France. If it could be rescued from obscurity much might be learned about the elusive ratio between equipment and morale.

Was France Betrayed?

According to Mark Twain, there is too much human nature in the best of us, and one of the most unhappy manifestations of this abundance is the temptation to damn the loser. Few who have dealt with the causes of the French debacle have been able to resist this temptation. Even a writer of the quality of Somerset Maugham, who had lived in France for twenty years, presumably because he liked living in that country better than in his native England, attributed her defeat to a breakdown in the morals of her people. He emphasized that he meant "moral" without the "e." In his opinion the simple decencies of everyday life, the habit of speaking the truth and dealing fairly with one's neighbor, had disappeared in France.

Westbrook Pegler in the New York *World-Telegram* described France as a single red-light district of decay and corruption living at the expense of unsuspecting tourists poor in arithmetic.

The danger of this cant lies in the implication that the victor must have possessed all the virtues so sadly wanting in the vanquished. The low morals of the loser argue for a very high standard of morality among the Nazis, a proposition which once stated reveals itself as an absurdity. But until it is so stated, the implication remains that success in warfare and moral worth are somehow inseparably intertwined. Many of the writers on the fall of France, both French and foreign, even those who do not despair for the future of that country, have yet to learn of Heine's dictum:

> But War and Justice have far different laws,
> And worthless deeds are often done right well.
> The rascal's shots were better than their cause. . . .

So far only a one-sided story has been told, since among the list of the causes of the French debacle the human qualities of the French are missing, the qualities which, in fact, contributed more to the disaster than the very real shortcomings of French democracy.

Among the causes usually listed is the civil strife which threatened to tear the state asunder. There was the failure of the ruling classes to realize that Nazism was a far greater danger to their security and their possessions than the Moscow-directed Communist Party at home, a lack of discernment which made them inclined to regard Nazi Germany as a bulwark of capitalism and Hitler as a possible savior willing to come to their aid, provided they could seize the power to open the gate. Political corruption, a venal press, an army commanded by monarchists and Fascist sympathizers, a working class unwilling to work more than forty hours in a five-day week—the week of two Sundays, as Paul Reynaud called it, a treacherous Communist Party taking its orders from abroad, prepared to vote for or against the war budget, call strikes in the war industries or call them off in accordance with the ever-changing will of Moscow: all these were in retrospect offered as the principal causes of the defeat. The fact that defeat was followed by the establishment of a Fascist régime in Vichy headed by some of the military and political leaders of the old régime tended to substantiate this interpretation. Accordingly, abroad as well as in France itself, the verdict was final: France had been sold out.

But this list of evils, if properly worded to fit local conditions, would apply to all countries and would not nearly begin to cover the evils rampant in the totalitarian states. If bad social and economic conditions, immorality and corruption, lawlessness and abuse of power were responsible for lost wars, France should have come through with flying colors in any war with Germany. In reading this list of French shortcomings one might be inclined to believe that France was in chaos instead of being the most pleasant of all European countries, as it was. The truth is that the shoulders of society are very broad and that French democracy could bear with ease in time of peace the political strife of which so much has been made in retrospect.

The evidence of French politicians now in exile is particularly untrustworthy. In a futile attempt to justify themselves, they are inclined to continue abroad the political debates which were interrupted by the German invasion. The story as told even by very able French writers in exile is not free from bias. Many Frenchmen are inclined to take the qualities of the people to which they belong for granted; while they are critical of their country, its people, and its institutions. The legend of French decadence, for instance, which was so trustingly repeated by the Germans before the Battle of the Marne, originated in France. Revolutionary and creative ideas are not born of complacency, and French thought was never complacent on the subject of social and economic conditions at home. The very dissatisfaction with these conditions was the ferment which made for growth. The merciless exposure of festering sores on the body politic acted like the surgeon's knife when applied by the rational French mind at home. But abroad the effect is likely to be different. The "it-can't-happen-here" complacency is apt to be reinforced when the reader fails to note that the same logic applied to his own country might reveal it to be in a worse state of decomposition than was the France of 1939.

The prototype of political corruption, Pierre Laval, has his counterpart everywhere in the world. Every financial and political scandal during the life of the Third Republic the other democracies could match with an equal number of their own. Such phenomena as Stavisky are not peculiar to

French governmental graft. The United States had its Tea Pot Dome, Great Britain the Hatry Trusts and Sweden her Ivan Kreuger whose Match Trust was financed in America.

The labor organizations of France, on the other hand, were free from the evils rampant in the American Federation of Labor and the C.I.O. No local union president in France ever contemplated browbeating the rank and file by a threat of violence. Labor leaders in France were not necessarily better men: they, too, indulged in compromises dictated by the desire to preserve their power and influence, to the detriment of the best interests of their unions. But none of them were gangsters or racketeers enriching themselves at the expense of labor and of capital with impartiality. They were more virtuous because an attempt to use force would in all probability have brought a speedy end to their careers, if not by the intervention of the police, then by the rank and file of French labor.

Substantially the same weaknesses as those supposed to have led to the fall of France were to be found in Great Britain. The incompetence of the Chamberlain cabinet would have been difficult to match anywhere. Britain's ruling class was as blind to the menace of Nazism as were the French capitalists. The British Labor Party supported collective security, demanded imperiously that Hitler be stopped, and at the same time opposed conscription and armament. Yet Great Britain survived, found unity and purpose, and is to-day dedicated to fighting for victory.

Again, the France of 1940 was not radically different from the France of 1914. In 1914, France also suffered from internal strife, with the powerful voice of the Socialist leader Jean Jaurès calling for peace at almost any price. There was even an influential Partie de Prusse, which, enamored of German "order and efficiency," held France in low esteem. French monarchists and reactionaries commanded the Republican armies fighting a monarchistic invader, and a liberal and radical populace was given an ally as detestable as the absolutist and pogrom ridden Czarist Russia. Yet in 1914 France fought a magnificent fight during four interminable years, while the France of 1940 went down in six weeks.

In one respect all France was united during the long Armistice from 1918 to the German attack on Czechoslovakia in 1938. A nation divided in many other ways, France was unanimously opposed to war. It is true that the motive which inspired this unity was not of the purest in all classes and among all individuals, but the net effect was the same. Even if all Frenchmen had been devoted disciples of Tolstoyan pacifism, France could not have met the invader of 1940 less well prepared.

Before Munich, French unity for peace had been subjected to an acid test by Nazi Germany. When Hitler remilitarized the Rhineland, he gave France every moral and treaty right to declare war upon Germany, and what is more, France then still had a chance of winning the war. No fifth column but a leftist government was in power, headed by Albert Sarraut. The Locarno Treaty, which Germany had signed freely, without the compulsion of Versailles, declared expressly that *the remilitarization of the Rhineland was to be regarded as a casus belli.* Had France declared war, Britain would have been forced to do likewise, however unwilling she showed herself to be. Nevertheless, in all the land of France there was no newspaper, no individual whose opinion held weight, either reactionary, conservative, or leftist, no party, no voice *to urge* a declaration of war upon the government.

That government, for once more far-sighted than the public, stood divided five to four against a declaration of war. Commander-in-Chief Maurice Gamelin, consulted by the cabinet on measures the army could take to meet the German challenge, requested an order to mobilize the armies. Asked how long it would take, his answer, "Three weeks," caused consternation. Moreover, he revealed the fact that the Maginot Line would have to be manned before the order of mobilization was given, because it was without its garrison and could have been overrun with ease by the advancing German Army.

When this news leaked out there was laughter in France at the incompetence of the general staff.

Subsequently, the story was told that the German officers carried sealed instructions from Adolf Hitler to retreat if the French Army should march. It is true that such a retreat would have given Hitler a chance, once again, to act the part of injured virtue, but an examination of the progress made by German war industries from 1933 to 1936 makes this story somewhat doubtful. However this may be, the French Government felt that in any case, lacking popular support, they could not order mobilization and avenge the affront three weeks after the psychological moment for action had passed. In the meantime, French correspondents in London cabled home: "England tells us to use strong language, but to negotiate."

Thus Germany, exploiting the French will-to-peace, celebrated a major political and strategic triumph, certain now that the France which failed to fight in her own behalf was not likely to go to war either for Austria or for any of her allies in southeastern Europe.

At this precise moment, while Germany was continuing her war preparations with renewed confidence and on a scale unequaled in history, the France which for a century and a half had been fighting with varied fortune for a better and more equitable life, the France of the great revolution, came to life again.

The Popular Front

The Popular Front, which was formed in 1934, was an agreement among the Radical Socialists (liberals), the Socialists, and the Communists to support each other in the coming regular elections of 1936. This union of the leftist parties which had fought each other as bitterly as the other political parties was provoked by the attempt made in 1934 by a coalition of reactionary forces to overthrow the liberal institutions of France. The pretext for this attempt was furnished by the

Stavisky scandal. Stavisky's large-scale thefts were greatly facilitated by the graft he paid out to high-ranking officials in the state, in Parliament, and among the judiciary. The reactionaries considered his crimes particularly heinous since he did not swindle any small investors or laboring men, but like a modern Robin Hood operated exclusively among the rich and powerful insurance companies. Only unlike Robin Hood he failed to distribute his gains among the poor. Although many reactionary and Royalist functionaries had benefited by his generosity, reactionary France sought to hold Parliament, the symbol of popular rights in the detested republic, responsible for the scandal.

Accordingly, on February 6, 1934, a supreme attempt was made to set up a royalist dictatorship. It was a pitiful performance. A rightist mob tried to storm across the bridge which leads from the Place de la Concorde to the Parliament. The Guard Mobile fired without warning, or so it was claimed, and several men were killed; the rest fled. In the meantime, the demonstrators had managed to burn a few harmless autobuses and to sack a few cafés, subsequently blaming these misdeeds (they were all honorable men) upon irresponsible Communist elements which, they claimed, had managed to enter their ranks unperceived.

Two years later this incident, in itself no more serious than a riot during a factory strike, brought the Popular Front into power. With Hitler Germany before their eyes, the great majority of the French people were determined to nip in the bud any effort of French imitators to establish a Fascist régime of their own. Not content with a political victory for the leftist parties, French labor took direct action. Shortly after the elections of 1936 and Hitler's remilitarization of the Rhineland, spontaneous sit-down strikes broke out in all French industries and commercial enterprises. By what amounted to a general strike, French labor won social reforms long overdue, reforms for which they would have had to wait indefinitely, even with a socialist government in power, had they failed to make clear by their action that they meant to have their way.

In many instances labor had not been content to strike only,
but had started to operate the factories on its own account.
The strikes threatened to develop into a full-fledged social
revolution, and industrial management was sufficiently impressed to accept without delay the compromise solutions offered by the Blum government. The government itself was
surprised by the revolutionary temper of French labor. There
is no room in either the Socialist or the Communist program
for direct and independent action by labor while either party
is in power. Léon Blum saw himself compelled to plead with
labor not to strike against his government and to trust to
parliamentary reforms. Maurice Thorez, leader of the Communist Party, thundered against "those irresponsible elements"
which did not know when to stop striking.

All political parties urged moderation, pointing to the enemy
at the gates who was making feverish preparations for war
while France chose to set about the creation of a better and
a more equitable social order. But few knew that the zero
hour for the defense of France had arrived. At that precise
moment when French industries should have been working
day and night trying to make up for lost time against heavy
odds, French labor closed the heavy metallurgical industries
in August, 1936, and left on the first joyous paid vacation in
its history. They invaded the Riviera, hitherto the exclusive
vacation spot of the upper classes, much to the annoyance of
the latter. The victory over the enemy within was celebrated
in high spirits. No one who saw France in those days, kindly,
humorous, and full of high hopes, could have failed to join
in the spirit of general good-will and fellowship which permeated the nation.

This is not to imply that the outcome of the Battle of France
would have been different if labor had stuck to the job. In
the absence of a comprehensive program calling for the production of at least twenty thousand tanks and an equal number of combat planes, it was quite immaterial whether labor
worked eight hours a day in a five-day week, or sixteen hours
a day in a seven-day week at the production of consumer

goods. Moreover, the sit-down strikes of labor were answered presently by a sit-down strike of capital. Capital had consented speedily to the Blum reforms as long as labor threatened revolution, but as soon as the danger was passed industrial management began to sulk. Industrial operations were deliberately reduced to a minimum, and gold was hoarded or exchanged for foreign currency—an action which drained the gold stock of the Banque de France and led directly to the periodic devaluations of the franc.

The democratic régime has no machinery at its disposal to compel private capital to work, any more than it can impose long hours of labor against the determined opposition of the working class. But here again, even if Léon Blum had adopted the methods of totalitarianism and instituted government control over all imports and exports of money, as he confessed he was tempted to do, such action would not have altered by one iota the fate of the French armies in the Battle of France. Government control over foreign currency might have kept the value of the franc stable, it would most certainly have stopped the outflow of gold, but it would have done nothing to convert that gold into ammunition, tanks, and planes.

Consequently, it was just as well that labor took its vacation and worked only eight hours a day in a five-day week. It was just as well that office-workers bought family bicycles and spent long week-ends in the country with their sweethearts or their families. Perhaps these moments of leisure brought about an improvement in their physical well-being, a respite from toil, which is now helping them to bear the ordeal of Nazi occupation.

In any case, reactionary France had been administered a sound drubbing. Once again, as in the Dreyfus Case at the turn of the century and in the movement of General Boulanger after the lost war of 1871, the people of France had demonstrated their undying opposition to tyranny. Small wonder Royalists and dyed-in-the-wool reactionaries found cause for despair. Realizing that they could not hope to establish a

royal dictatorship as long as the people remained free to react, they began to look for help from abroad.

Socrates and Poison

At first, Mussolini looked like the most promising candi-
date. He was a dictator under a king, and the Latin sister nation therefore appeared to be blessed with that happiest of
all syntheses in government—a king for royal splendor and
a dictator to keep the unruly populace in order. In the early
days of his reign, Hitler looked less promising. He was vulgar
and ruled a barbarian country, the traditional enemy of
France. Moreover, he seemed to be but a small imitator of his
master, Mussolini. The French public, however, manifested
early a finer sense of perception. Whenever Mussolini appeared in the newsreels, the audience laughed with unrestrained gaiety. Hitler, when he appeared on the screen, was
regarded in grim silence.

Gradually even the Royalists perceived that Mussolini was
but a sawdust Cæsar, and under the provocation of the popular front reforms, some French reactionaries began wishing
aloud that Hitler might come in and restore order. But talking treason is not yet committing it, particularly in France,
where the love for conversation often leads to worse excesses
than the habit of the apéritif, usually taken in moderation.
Nor must it be assumed that all Royalists were Fascists or
sympathizers of the Nazi régime. Most of them sincerely loved
their country and opposed the action of the working class and
the Blum régime not only because their pockets were menaced
but also because they saw the danger to France from without
more clearly than the people who never doubted that they
could beat the Germans as their fathers had beaten them before.

One of the Royalist leaders, Charles Maurras, now a Vichy
man, argued in his daily paper *L'Action Française* against this
kind of loose talk which would prefer a Hitler to a Léon Blum.

He reproduced the text of the treaty which Germany imposed upon Romania in 1918 and which reduced the entire male population of the country between the ages of sixteen and sixty to abject slaves. Maurras reminded his readers that when the Romanian delegate broke into tears on having to sign the death warrant of his nation, the German commander drew his attention to the fact that the Romanian treaty might be regarded as a pact of friendship in comparison to the one Germany was going to impose upon France, England and the United States.

Charles Maurras was no exception. Only a very small minority among the reactionaries of France, the so-called cagoulards, contemplated treason before the French armies were defeated, nor would they have had, in the absence of that defeat, any great opportunity to carry out their intentions. Quite a few Frenchmen were invited to join a Franco-German friendship society for "cultural exchanges." Jules Romains lectured in German Universities in an effort to make the French will to peace understandable to a Nazi audience—a truly futile undertaking. They understood only too well, hoping that pacifism might remain alive and vigorous in France, while Germany armed. But in the last analysis there was very little in all this foolishness that might be called treason in the narrow sense of the word. It is difficult to imagine that the number of Frenchmen in the pay of German military intelligence was noticeably greater in the Hitler area than what could cynically still be called normal.

For the rest, most of the men regarded as reactionaries in France might very well have passed as radicals in other countries. Though none of them would admit any good to have come from the great French Revolution, it was nevertheless obvious that they were all deeply affected by the spirit of that revolution. If they opposed the ideas of Voltaire, Rousseau, and Diderot, and extolled the virtues of the kings of France, they nevertheless attributed to the *ancien régime* such a spirit of liberalism that one could not help wondering why the revolution had taken place at all. To believe them, all the kings of France were just so many Voltaires, Rousseaus, and Diderots. But above all, the France of Louis XIV had been the greatest military power on the European continent, only to be surpassed briefly by the France of Napoleon I, whereas the France of the Third Republic was born of the defeat in 1871, and won the war of 1914–18 only with the aid of Great Britain, Russia, Italy, and the United States. A whole world had to come to her assistance, and no sooner was victory won than the leftist politicians managed to lose the peace.

A friend of this writer, Henri Davoust, a great lawyer, a fine poet, and an excellent cook, sympathized with the Royalists mainly because he believed that a republican government had dangerously weakened the military power of France. Davoust had passed the entire four years of the last war at the front as a high-ranking officer. He had also acted as lawyer for the defense in court-martials. One of the cases he tried involved three common soldiers who had stolen several barrels of wine from the cellar of an abandoned château and divided the loot among their comrades. The three soldiers, as it happened, belonged to different branches of the army. One was attached to the artillery, one to reconnaissance and one to the ordnance. Davoust pleaded not guilty. He claimed for his charges devotion beyond the call of duty. The reconaissance soldier had found the cellar, the supply man had handed up the barrels through the cellar window, while the artillery man had loaded them on the cart which they had brought along. The men were acquitted.

Several months before the remilitarization of the Rhineland by Germany, Davoust spoke of his fears for the future of France, deploring the irresponsibility of democratic government, of the party spirit in Parliament and the egoism of the bourgeoisie, which had cast France adrift without the guiding hand of a strong government. He suggested sardonically and perhaps prophetically that to save something of French civilization, the national library should be transported to the Rocky Mountains, where the books would be beyond the reach of the Nazis. As he unfolded a somber picture of

the state of decomposition in which he saw France, we were
being served luncheon in his vineyard in the south of France.
The table was spread in the garden under an olive tree. The
meal was prepared by the caretaker, a woman of the country,
and would have satisfied the most fastidious taste of any of
the kings whose passing my friend deplored. The servant was
as joyous as the meal and talked to both master and guests
with the friendly equalitarian spirit of the people of France.

Trying to dispel the deep gloom of my friend, I asked him
to look at the scene. Was not France a country organized for
peace and the joy of living to a degree reached by no other
civilization? Could he then wish for the order of Germany, so
well governed, so efficient in the business of war, so mur-
derous of liberty and, consequently, of life itself? Was not
France one happy land, a magnificent garden, still the greatest intellectual force, the Athens of the modern world, the
second fatherland to every man of good-will and the spiritual
home of all who fight against their bondage? "What is wrong
with France except her neighbor?"

"But we have these neighbors," he cried, "and yet Frenchmen are allowed to quarrel among themselves as if they were
at peace. As to being the Athens of the modern world—ah,
my friend, we lack but a Socrates. There is enough poison on
hand."

Citizen Tusque and Anti-Militarism

A cruder man than my friend, a retired army officer, would
not despair of seeing his own personal ideal realized. He did
not believe that Frenchmen were too individualistic to submit
to discipline. The Germans in the last war had taught Frenchmen how to behave. He recalled that after the return of the
French authorities, French peasants would tip their hats in
profound respect whenever they passed a French officer. Now
he blamed himself and his fellow-officers for their failure to
preserve this happy state of affairs. A well disciplined France
could take on the Germans any day. Cross-examination

brought out the fact that he had been stationed in Alsace after the Armistice.

It is clear that he was wrong. In fact, no threat from without, however great, could change the anti-militarist spirit of the people of France. The business of organizing the defense of the country had to be left for the most part to the defunct French aristocracy, as few commoners would seek, in time of peace, a career in the army rather than in a respected civilian occupation.

To give an example: The son of General Tusque wanted to study medicine, but his widowed mother could not afford to send him to the university on the meager pension accorded to the widows of French generals. He consequently entered the army medical school. During the roll call of the first day at school the students rose to give their names: Marquis so and so, viscount so and so, count so and so. When the turn of Tusque came, he was thoroughly annoyed at this inflation of titles, and gave his own: Citizen Tusque.

Whatever influence the small Royalist minority enjoyed in the state of France they owed to the anti-militarism of the "commoners." Because of Germany the French submitted to conscription in time of peace; they would go to war in defense of their country, but they never lost sight of the fact that militarism and war were afflictions without which mankind would be far better off.

For a full realization of the anti-militaristic spirit of France one must have listened to casual conversations on the subject among the civilian population. In the talk on café terraces and in village *bistros,* where no abstract theories of social and economic problems are expounded, the spirit of a people reveals itself without restraint. Taking their apéritifs, a few peasants and village craftsmen, the local teacher, the druggist, and a few loafers would talk over their wine of their experiences in the last war. One such scene among countless others stands out particularly in my memory of the post-war years in France.

We were seated around a table in front of a restaurant on the Île de Ré at the foot of the lighthouse. The owner of the restaurant and the guests had taken us into their company with the easy grace of village hospitality. The man seated next to me had participated in the Battle of Verdun, but he menioned that only in explanation of how he had happened to rise to the rank of corporal. The slaughter had been so terrific that for want of good men they had had to advance him. After that he proceeded to demonstrate how his neighbor, a common soldier, had to stand at attention before him. "Get up," he cried. "Show them the respect which was due to me as your superior." Amid general hilarity they then performed a comic pantomime of officer and underling. One of the audience, evidently an incorrigible skeptic, doubted the veracity of the story. Indignation took hold of the raconteur, and despatching a boy to his home, he had him fetch his officer's pants, to exhibit with mock pride the stripes covering the seam.

Not all opposition expressed itself in laughter at the tomfoolery of military discipline. Frenchmen had an explanation for the mystery attached to the high proportion of active officers killed in the opening months of the war of 1914–18. They were allegedly shot by their own men whenever they abused their powers. Whether this grim tale has any basis in fact or not, it is revealing enough that it was widely believed to be true. The Gauls are soldiers, not militarists, was the universal boast. Trust them to fight the enemy with all the resources of their individual intelligence and you will not be disappointed. But humble submission to foul-mouthed officers whose powers have gone to their heads—leave that to the Prussians along with their goose-step, sauerkraut, and beer!

Frenchmen were not unaware of the growing menace of Nazi Germany, but from knowledge to action there is an abyss not easily bridged when such action goes against the grain of one's very nature. To meet the danger from without, France would have had to give up a way of life and a way of letting live which was dear to her people. Years before the outbreak of war they would have had to submit to a régime which, in form, if not in substance, would have been exactly like the totalitarian state. It was felt that if France adopted the economic and social structure of her enemy, she would thereby deprive herself of the moral right to fight for a way of life which her people had abandoned. The sit-down strikes of 1936 were in part inspired by the idea that only a France immeasurably better in her social order than the enemy had a right to ask her children to die in her defense. Neither corrupt politicians of the Laval type, nor the reactionary army command, nor an economic system based upon capitalistic exploitation, were thought worthy of the sacrifice.

Neither Parliament nor the public ever brought pressure upon the government to increase substantially the war budget. It was taken for granted that the army and navy asked more than was needed without urging.

Opposition to the Maginot Line

In justice to the French officer caste, it must be admitted that they failed in their duty because of this absence of popular support. A few of them, probably, were as abusive as the Prussian officers, but on the whole they were unlike any other army men in the world. Reactionary as the French thought them to be, they were nevertheless deeply imbued with the splendor of French civilization. They were well read, they patronized the arts, and above all they had that innate respect for the human personality, universal in France, which is the antipode of Nazism. But no institution in a democratic country can remain alive and vigorous when it lives in an atmosphere of hostility and indifference. It is then that deadly bureaucracy replaces action and a sea of paper masquerades as thought.

The desire for peace and security which permeated the nation determined military strategy in France. The vigorous school of thought to which Charles de Gaulle belonged opposed in vain the construction of the Maginot Line. That school maintained that the line would prove to be not only militarily useless against tanks and planes, but politically harmful. Its construction would proclaim to friend and foe alike that France would not fight an offensive war either in her own behalf or on behalf of her allies. Its psychological effect at home would be the creation of a false sense of security, which would prevent France from taking suitable action in time and hence permit the enemy to make all his preparations unperturbed. Furthermore, by its changeless character and its immobility, such a defensive fortification is an assurance to the enemy that he has nothing to fear from the element of the unknown, which ere this has brought to naught the best laid plans.

Against these considerations, which incidentally received very little publicity, there was the certainty that in any future war France would have to bear alone the full brunt of a German attack. This time no reliance could be placed upon Russia. Britain had no army, and the United States was, as a result of the last war, more isolationist than ever before. The French army command thought that France could not survive another loss of blood similar to the last one. Based upon the experience of the war of 1914–18, it was calculated that the enemy compelled to a strategy of offense would lose three times as many soldiers as defending France. As France had no intention of committing an act of aggression against her neighbors, there was no need for an expeditionary striking force of armored divisions such as was suggested by Charles de Gaulle. The importance of aviation was minimized. It was thought that bombing would cause great damage, but the plane could not hold any territory. Only the infantry could accomplish that and consequently was still the queen of battle.

Charles de Gaulle succeeded in convincing Paul Reynaud that the infantry had fallen from the position of queen to the humble place of the pawn on the military chess-board. As member of Parliament for Paris in 1934, Reynaud introduced a bill authorizing the government to create such an expeditionary force as that suggested by de Gaulle. Parliament voted against the bill not only because such an offensive force would be in contradiction to the non-aggressive foreign policy of France, but also because a professional army of 250,000 men would constitute a potential danger to democratic institutions at home. Universal conscription, regarded as undemocratic in England and the United States, was a very real safeguard of democracy in France. As long as every member of the nation served in the army, the rank and file of the army and the nation remained identical. No pronunciamento of a reactionary army command could give the order to march upon Parliament, or shoot at the mob, and expect that order to be carried out by the sons of the peasants, the workers, and the bourgeoisie. But an expeditionary force of the type suggested by de Gaulle might in a crisis have proved to be a subversive instrument in the hands of the enemies of the Third Republic.

Thus France, fearing the enemy within, was deprived of a weapon against the enemy without, a weapon which would have been instantly effective when Germany remilitarized the Rhineland and which in 1940 would most certainly have saved her from defeat.

In the days when the world went sentimental over the injustices of Versailles, France was accused of being a bad winner, unable to forget and forgive. Her enemies described her as a chauvinistic country anxious to establish a military hegemony over Europe. Had these accusations been justified, had France been a belligerent nation, none of the shortcomings of French democracy could, by themselves, have brought about her defeat. She would not have hidden behind fortifications. The same revolutionary spirit of France which found its expression in the struggle for a better economy in the sciences, in literature, in art, and in the fashion industries, would have supported revolutionary ideas in warfare and forced a change in the antiquated High Command.

As it was, Charles de Gaulle and his school found a ready public, as might have been expected, in Germany, but became known to France only in the last hour of her agony, when the enemy demonstrated to the people of France with unrestrained fury the military worth of revolutionary ideas in war.

Relief and Shame

France remained united in her determination to stay at peace until the Munich agreement. As the storm over Czechoslovakia began to gather, two valid but conflicting moral arguments divided the nation: the moral argument for peace, and the equally moral argument for keeping the promise of aid to Czechoslovakia, the friend and ally. This conflict divided the nation across all party lines. All political parties split into anti-Munich and pro-Munich groups. Even the Communist Party, officially adhering to the line laid down in Moscow, was divided in its rank and file, as was manifest after the Munich agreement. The circulation of the *Humanité*, the Communist newspaper, fell by 50 per cent. It had called for war. Pointing to the two years of heroic resistance of the Spanish people, as yet unbroken, and to the military might of Russia, it argued that it was not too late to stop Hitler. But when the boys came back from the front after the pre-Munich mobilization, they had had a most harrowing experience, sufficient to disillusion them in the military might of France.

During the dark days, when war or peace hung in the balance, when Chamberlain and Hitler seemed to have broken off all negotiations permanently, France had mobilized several classes and brought the Maginot Line fortress troops up to full wartime strength. The men who had fought in the last war had taken their sons to the Gare de l'Est, the station from which, only some twenty years earlier, they themselves had left for the front. Many, still fit for service, had gone with their sons. It was a mobilization totally unlike the older one. Instead of war fervor there was the grim determination to make "an end of it, once and for all," but the atmosphere was that of a vast funeral. The blood and tears of the old war, shed in vain, hung like a heavy cloud over that station of the east, the symbol of the seemingly immutable fate of France.

The muddle and inefficiency of that mobilization proved to be appalling. The general staff had tried to accomplish in a few days what normally needed several weeks. As a result of this haste, there were no blankets and no food. Some of the troops even lacked uniforms. But the disillusionment was greatest at the discovery by the men that they would not all be stationed in the safe underground fortifications of the Maginot Line, that the line itself had to be defended by troops stationed in front and out in the open. There they were cut off from communications with the rear. For days on end they had been without news and expected the guns to go off at any minute.

Those who knew of the state of unpreparedness of the French Army had argued strongly for peace at any price; actual experience had borne them out. We were told by a friend in the air ministry that France could not go to war, having no aviation whatsoever. He maintained that no more than 150 planes of all types could pass as front-line planes and that all aviation factories together were producing no more than one plane per day. It was difficult to believe him, and as he belonged to the Royalist faction, his opponents in the tense atmosphere of those days suspected him of giving out information which he should have kept to himself. At the same time, and irrationally, they tried to console themselves with the idea that after all he may not know everything, holding, as he did, but a small government position.

"And what about our army?" one would ask anxiously. "Will it be equal to the task?"

"Why, it is the finest in the world, the whole world judges it so. Besides, you can be sure that the Maginot Line is not only a defensive barrier, but has been designed to serve the offensive as well."

"Yes, but the British are not ready! Those fools, have we not told them what was coming? The stubborn, stolid Britishers; there is no way of figuring them out."

"Will France fight?"

"Do not worry; France has never broken her pledged word!"

When word came of the signing of the Munich agreement, Léon Blum expressed the feeling of the nation when he said that he had received the news with a mixture of relief and deep shame. The relief was manifest everywhere. In the countless little shops of Paris, relatives and friends of the soldiers soon to be returned to their families gathered to discuss the dramatic events leading up to the Munich agreement. Aware of the secondary rôle played by the French Prime Minister Daladier, the peaceful shopkeepers of Paris were lavish with praise for Chamberlain and his umbrella. What a man of courage to have flown into the lion's den at his age, and to have snatched their children from the hell of war in the nick of time.

On a more theoretical basis, among the experts in political science, wishful thinking ran high. Perhaps for the first time in the history of France, the idea of isolation began to strike roots. Czechoslovakia appeared suddenly in the light of a liability to France, an entangling alliance, if France were obliged to come to her assistance; whereas the alliance had been intended to secure the assistance of Czechoslovakia in case of an attack on France. The newspapers secured the opinion of a learned professor at the Sorbonne, who showed that there were quite a number of loopholes in the French treaty with Czechoslovakia, permitting France a way out.

The moral situation was made even more appalling by the intervention of that other ally of France, Poland, who joined Germany in the attack on Czechoslovakia and secured a share of the loot for herself. France had to swallow the humiliation of not being strong enough to stop the action of a government which had been dependent on France for its very existence. The tendency to blame the victim rather than the aggressor manifested itself when the charge was made that it was all the fault of Benes. He should have known better than to refuse his consent to a return of the Hapsburgs to the throne of Austria. The exclamation, "Rather Hitler than the Hapsburgs!" was attributed to him; therefore, his country got only what it deserved. The future policy of France was now perfectly clear, and perhaps it was all for the best.

France would abandon for good her unprofitable alliances

in southeastern Europe and in the east with Poland and Russia. She would henceforth concentrate on the development of her empire overseas. War in Europe had now become physically impossible. It was clear that the Germans could not break through the Maginot Line, while at the same time Germany could feel secure from any French aggression, now that she had in the West Wall a defensive barrier as powerful as the Maginot Line. Germany now had security, the lack of which had made her so belligerent. Economically, she could expand in southeastern Europe. France would not stand in her way. She could have the Balkan countries, which had been nothing but a liability to France. Up to now, France had lent immense sums of money to these countries to permit them to arm, loans which these countries never intended to repay.

These arguments sounded logical enough to people who were deeply ashamed. Many of the Frenchmen who tried to console themselves with this newly born ideal of isolation for France had been convinced that Hitler was bluffing. They had argued that it was only necessary for Great Britain and France to remain firm and unyielding, to call his bluff, and he would be forced to retreat. Instead, Czechoslovakia had been mercilessly abandoned to her fate. France had broken a solemn pledge for the first time in her history. It seemed unbelievable that she should have humiliated herself in vain. But only a few days after the Munich agreement it became apparent that Germany was not going to rest on her laurels. Hitler made a speech at Saarbruecken as violent and aggressive as ever. The possibility of a Russian-German alliance for the division of Poland began to loom large on the eastern horizon. In the British Parliament, Chamberlain called for greater efforts in British rearmament, and France began to look to her own defenses.

An abrogation of the advantages won by labor through the sit-down strikes of 1936 was answered by a call to a general strike, a protest strike of twenty-four hours, but the government under Daladier remained firm, and labor did not press its demands. On the other hand, no stupendous increase in armament production could have been realized in the short time still at the disposal of France. An inquiry abroad for more machine tools to permit a greater production of combat planes revealed that the Swiss tool-makers, the best in Europe, were working to full capacity on German contracts, with a five-year backlog of orders. Even if the French Government had placed orders for thousands, instead of only hundreds, of combat planes in the United States, the year 1938 was drawing to a close, and it would have been too late. The United States aircraft industries, with their negligible capacity, could not have delivered these planes in June, 1940, when Paul Reynaud made his pathetic appeal for clouds of American planes to save the armies of France.

The Image of France

As we have seen, when Germany broke the Munich agreement on March 15, 1939, by the complete occupation of what remained of Czechoslovakia, it was clear that time could no longer be gained by further concessions. A continuation of the appeasement policy would have demoralized the people of France and England completely. Time gained at the expense of morale would have been wasted by an internal decomposition of the state.

Hence Britain declared war when Poland was invaded. After several hours of hesitation France followed suit. During these hours, the Commander-in-Chief of the French armies, General Maurice Gustave Gamelin, was still worrying the government with his demand for three weeks to mobilize the armies of France to full wartime strength. But further delay had become impossible. There was nothing left but a prayer that the enemy would grant him the grace of this time. The enemy proved generous. France had nine months to prepare for the onslaught which was bound to come. The German general staff knew by experience that they risked nothing by waiting. No country, no complex organization such as that which a national economy represents to-day, can switch over in nine months from peace production to war. French war factories were scheduled to go into full wartime operation by 1941 and 1942. By that time hundreds of new factories were to be completed, turning out quantities of planes, tanks, and guns with which to start an offensive after the enemy had exhausted himself against the invincible defenses of the Maginot Line. At no time had there been any serious doubt that a united France would face the enemy. Always, it was argued, Frenchmen had forgotten their differences, however violent, when faced by a foreign foe. Paul Reynaud's classic phrase, "If to-day I were told that only a miracle can save France, I would believe in that miracle because I believe in France," assuredly would not have been spoken in vain had the Maginot Line proved to be as effective a barrier as the English Channel to the Nazi war machine.

France had a good plan, a logical plan of defense for a people determined to go to war only as a last resort, when all else failed. The plan went awry. A new element in warfare, the time element, sufficed to destroy the closely knit fabric of the plan.

In the post-mortem on the Battle of France undue emphasis has been placed, in the daily press, upon the evidence of treason and a fifth column in the French Army. It is understandable that the most judicious selection of the news as practised by the best newspapers should have failed to give the facts in their true perspective. But the historians who have followed suit should have known better than to confuse cause and effect.

The French Army was not defeated by treason and a fifth column. These phenomena made their appearance when the enemies within began to see defeat in battle as inevitable. Traitors are rarely courageous, and like the proverbial rats stay aboard as long as the ship is safely afloat. Laval could not have reëmerged from obscurity if the French lines had held. Pétain and Weygand, though they dreamed for a lifetime of the restoration of the France of Louis XIV in all its glory, would have continued to serve the despised republic as long as they saw a chance for victory. It was, after all, the same fatherland which they served in 1914–18, if not too well, yet well enough. Even the most unscrupulous of the French Fascists, Jacques Doriot, should be given the benefit of the doubt on the assumption that he would have much preferred, if this had been possible, to see his personal régime established in a France free from foreign domination. When Italy introduced anti-Semitic laws under German pressure, a French cartoonist gave the dog on the phonograph records of "his master's voice" the face of Mussolini. It is safe to assume that Benito would have been much happier in the rôle of Dictator to Hitler than he is in his present position as Statthalter for Italy. Pétain has hardly improved his personal position, now that he no longer commands the Republican armies under a Democratic government but has to take orders from the erstwhile enemy.

Once before, in the battles of 1914, a French High Command, discredited by the Dreyfus case, succeeded in restoring its prestige with the people of France, but in 1914 a Battle of the Marne could still take place; in 1940 the battle was lost with the first breach in the defenses of France.

During the long and unbroken retreat of the French armies in 1914 before the Battle of the Marne, the same deep suspicions as to the loyalty of the French army command were voiced. Had the Battle of the Marne been lost, failure would have confirmed these suspicions. The commanders of the French armies in 1940, in all probability, were neither better nor worse than their predecessors, but they lost a war for which they had not been prepared.

Much, too, has been made of the low morale of the troops, the rank and file of the army. But although it is true that the morale of an army may remain high in spite of inferior equipment, there is a minimum of effective weapons which an army must have and failing which no devotion, however great, no morale, however unflinching, can save it from its fate.

For the absence of that equipment, one must look backward to the years 1934 to 1936—years during which both Laval and

Léon Blum, the two opposite poles of French politics, were at the helm of the state; years in which the people of France thought of a preventive war as a crime too horrible to contemplate, in which they would have none of militarism and centralized government; years in which they would not admit that war with Germany was inevitable, and when it seemed incredible that even Nazis would unhesitatingly inflict a new blood-bath upon Germany and upon a world which still mourned the dead of the last war; years during which a proud people would not let a foreign foe impose upon them a way of life which in centuries of struggle against absolutism they had learned to abhor.

The story of the fall of France can be read in the drama of the ancient Greeks, where Fate, personified in the Furies, relentlessly pursues an innocent victim to his utter destruction. France fell because after victory was won she would not tighten the chin-strap of her helmet, because her people believed in the futility of war, a concept shared by the whole civilized world. So when, in the hour of her agony, she appealed to the United States not to let the motherland of human liberty die at the hand of barbarism, the New World was neither spiritually nor physically prepared to come to her aid.

When the armies of the Kaiser were defeated in 1918, the success of the democracies inspired a democratic revolution in Germany. But it was a revolution not without mental reservation. It was argued in Germany at the time that a democratic government, disavowing the Kaiser, would find favor in the eyes of the American President who had fought his war to make the world safe for democracy. This strategem succeeded in the end. In vain did Clemenceau warn France and the allies of France not to be deceived. To him Germany remained the eternal wolf, though momentarily dressed in sheep's clothing. While the victory of Germany over France in 1940 failed to inspire a popular uprising in favor of Fascism, it succeeded in depriving the people of France of all means of defense against the enemies of the French Revolution within. Hence Pétain and Laval were able to set up a régime in Vichy patterned on Fascism in emulation of the victor.

But if they hoped to soften the heart of Germany by the flattery of imitation they failed dismally. For once Germany has proved true to the letter if not to the spirit of her propaganda. She had informed the world that Nazism was no export article but was designed to serve Germany alone. The meaning of this claim has been made abundantly clear. It is impossible to placate Hitler by adopting his ideals. Nazi Germany has no ideology to offer the world for its salvation. It is out to establish domination, absolute domination, over all the nations of the world, and even a government which apes its methods of subjugation remains a thorn in its side as long as that government maintains a pretense of independence.

The German terms for France are therefore free from the spirit of compromise which in the long run nullified the Treaty of Versailles. Terms of absolute surrender tempered only by the German desire to gain mastery over the French fleet were imposed upon France. To tempt that fleet to surrender, a fictitious state of non-occupied France was created. Southern France was to be administered by Vichy, with a "free" Mediterranean coast as a bait with which to hook the fleet. But for the action of the British Navy at Oran and Alexandria, that fleet would have returned. The Vichy government, believing itself powerless against the enemy, wished to remember only the failures and crimes of its ally in the past. Trying to justify its abject surrender to the people of France, it sought to drag Britain with itself into the abyss of defeat.

But with continued British resistance, hope has returned to the people of France and with hope the courage to continue the war in the only way now left open. They have made it clear in innumerable ways that the Vichy government is a self-appointed one which lives only by the grace of the enemy. Were the Germans to be driven out, that government would not survive by one day the loss of German support. Paul Collette's attempt upon the lives of Laval and Déat bears witness to the irrepressible revolutionary temper of France. He made no attempt to escape. Calmly handing over his revolver, he stated his case and declared his willingness to bear the full consequences of his act. And such is the power of revolutionary tradition in France that his two victims, to save face, had to plead for the life of their assailant. Vichy pardoned him, but should he fall victim to the brutality of his jailers, a civilized world will be moved to regret the advance in modern science which has made more difficult the task of the would-be assassin.

The balance of the achievements of the Vichy régime is easily made up. The credit side is a total blank. Labor and capital are deprived by Fascist legislation of all independence. Germany still holds 1,400,000 French prisoners: only some 100,000 of the old and the sick have been released for Vichy to feed, as they are unfit to work for Germany. Collaboration, like peace, is a one-sided term in the German vocabulary. Germany holds all the territory of France which she occupied on the day of the Armistice. It is all she needs, as it contains the most important resources and industries of France. Paris, the administrative center of France which was promised to Pétain, has not been evacuated, but thousands of the inhabitants of Alsace and Lorraine have been dumped into Unoccupied France without ceremony. In tribute, France has already paid more to Germany than Germany was asked to pay as compensation for the devastated French provinces of the last war.

French commercial and industrial enterprises have become German property by sleight-of-hand of Nazi finance, and even those still in French hands are working to supply the Nazi war machine. The entire stock of French raw material and most of the treasure accumulated in centuries of civilization that was not nailed down has been carted away as German loot. Continuous tribute, apart from monetary payments, include shipments of 14,000 head of cattle per month; quantities of coal, wheat, butter, eggs, poultry, potatoes, and fruit go in a constant stream to stock the cellars and larders of the insatiable conqueror, while adults and children are cold and hungry in France. In their anxiety for quick victory the German armies kill without hesitation the goose which lays the golden egg. Thus, France is not left either machinery or seeds to renew her stock of food for further German milking, and the men needed for work on the land are kept in captivity.

All that Pétain and his followers have been able to realize of their dream of resurrecting the France of Louis XIV in all its splendor is the pitiful pronoun, "We." "We, Henri Philippe Pétain," is the manner in which this dull man introduces his decrees. His insistence upon a personal oath of fealty to him, Henry Philippe Pétain, brought bitter laughter to the Gallic soul of France. Frenchmen stopped each other in the streets and demanded an oath of fealty from their friends in imitation of the great example.

Inspired by De Gaulle, by British and Russian resistance, and by American preparations, the youth of France is escaping from the Vichy régime in ever increasing numbers.

Pétain could find no judges and no law-courts willing to sit in judgment over Daladier, Gamelin, and Blum for a crime committed by Germany. The charge that these men were guilty of the war had to be dropped, but the enemy insisted on a trial and he got it. The prisoners of Vichy were tried for their responsibility in the lack of French preparedness. It will remain to the eternal glory of France, that her courageous jurists and the accused turned this trial into a triumph of the human spirit, over naked force. The criminal at the bar became Germany and those who surrendered to her while her prisoners, even in defeat and at the mercy of the enemy, still wore the image of France.

13

Britain Fights

THE defeat of the French armies on the continent of Europe opened the gates of France to the enemy. Hannibal was inside the gates. Once the German Army had taken possession, it could temporarily paralyze the action of the French people and render defenseless the highly centralized French Empire, by destroying its nerve center: metropolitan France. Even without Vichy connivance, Indo-China was at the mercy of Japan and could have put up no better defense than Syria. Only after the enemy dispersed his forces inside France could the French people begin to organize resistance to his rule.

The defeat of a British Army on the European continent, however, is a different story. It need not be fatal. While France lost a war Britain only lost a major battle which brought the enemy to the gates of her Empire, but did not open the gates to him. *Hannibal portes est!* (Hannibal is at the gates) is a war cry stimulating to the utmost the will to resist.

Even if the British Isles had been conquered, the decentralized Empire would have been left intact. Each of the self-governing dominions: Canada, Australia, New Zealand, and South Africa could have continued the fight on their own and could have counted on the support of the United States. But instead of having to surrender the hub of the Empire, the people of Britain were given a task to do: Save the army at Dunkirk!

Though the signal was given by the naval command, the flotilla of motor-boats, sail-boats, row-boats, and coastal steam-

275

ers appeared like a spontaneous armada of salvation and performed a feat of heroism which a government can ask but can not command.

The defeated British Army derived as much glory from failure as the French in 1914 from their victory at the Marne. The British Tommies waited on the beaches, against which the German air force concentrated its fury, with the calm of the Londoner waiting for his bus on his way to work. No pushing and no crowding. Many of them stood in line for three days and nights waiting their turn; none lost their heads and few their sense of humor.

The stories which have been told of the legendary evacuation, whether invented or true, are a faithful portrait of the British spirit. There was the story of the soldier on the beach of Dunkirk who listened to a minute-by-minute account of the evacuation broadcast by the B.B.C. from London. He had to switch his radio off: He explained that it was too depressing.

Two cockneys conversing about their experience at Dunkirk: "Were you there on Wednesday?"

"Yes, wasn't it bloody awful? Rained all day long."

When France surrendered, world opinion gave Britain up as lost. In the words of Winston Churchill it was expected that she would have her neck wrung like a chicken. But like Winston Churchill himself she had quite a neck and after Dunkirk Britain showed the enemy a more formidable front than before.

A friend wrote me from London that he was not to be congratulated for his courage: "Courage is contagious. We all caught it from one another and from Winston Churchill." There was more to this modesty than the words conveyed. My friend is a London solicitor and, though a young man, he is sickly and looks it. A puny fellow with a yellowish skin drawn tightly over his face, he suggests anything but the hero except for a pair of dark eyes shining with kindly intelligence. He was always much worried about his health. Once, after a long rest in the country, he asked me hopefully how he looked. Devotion to the rules of common politeness tempered by years of friendship prompted me to tell him that he looked fit within the framework of the possible.

Like all our contemporaries he was a pacifist. But men can stand being pushed around "just so long." When a certain point is reached one fights, and, if the platitude about human nature always being the same has any meaning at all, it is not likely that this will ever change. Against the enemy of freedom within there is ultimately no defense except civil war or revolution. When the enemy comes from without the acceptance of the fight he offers is called war, but the phenomenon is essentially the same.

Winston Churchill's speeches to French audiences in France and to British audiences in England, had enjoyed wide publicity. Before this war he spoke the same words as in the days of Dunkirk, yet they acquired real meaning only when they were confirmed by the action of the enemy and the spirit of Britain. What the immortal lyric and music of the Marseillaise had been to France in the days of the French Revolution, Churchill's orations were to the people of England, rallying them to the defense of homes, hearths, and liberty. He resurrected words that had lost all meaning during the era of debunking between the wars. And, like the wars of the French Revolution, Britain's fight, waged alone and without "triumphant prize in store," deserves a different name; Winston Churchill addressing himself to the people of America compared the struggle to the civil war fought by Lincoln to preserve the Union.

The globe having become one and indivisible, liberty or slavery are one and indivisible. The stereotyped wars of the past between governments were different in kind from the present war. In the old-fashioned wars the people had no part, except as pawns, in the hands of their rulers. Every such war was followed by a treaty which contained the answers as to why the war was fought. The acknowledged loser yielded a bit of his realm plus the people in it and agreed to pay indemnities. The political treaty was followed by a commercial treaty and a slow recovery. The winners grew soft and the losers prepared for revenge. But for the hurt to national pride there was little loss to the people who changed hands from one sovereignty to another. Economically it was immaterial to the people of Alsace-Lorraine whether they were under German or French rule. Little was changed either way in the internal economic structure of the two provinces. But the kind of war which the totalitarian states have imposed is literally a war of life and death, for each and every one.

After Dunkirk it was expected that the Germans would make an immediate attempt at invading the British Isles. The moment seemed propitious. A great part of the British Army had been saved, but was without weapons. Such inadequate equipment as the British and French had at their disposal was lost in Flanders. Britain seemed defenseless. . . . But the successful evacuation itself was a victory. It proved that the British Navy was not yet scrap-iron. The R.A.F., though outnumbered 10 to 1, was a match for the massed German air force owing to the quality of its machines and the stamina of its pilots. Of little use in the distant Battle of France the British air force conceived for defense—gained command of the sky only over Dunkirk. Concentrated on the tight British Isles it was invincible; dispersed over the wider battlefield of France, far from its base, it would have been outmatched.

"History," said Oscar Wilde, "does not repeat itself, historians do." But Dunkirk, like the Battle of the Marne in September, 1914, was a turning point in the war. If the armies of France after the first Battle of the Marne had possessed sufficient ammunition they could have ended the war in 1914 by destroying the German Army. The British in 1940 held the Germans, but could not launch a counteroffensive of sufficient scope, for want of arms.

Hitler did not make a mistake in failing to take advantage of Britain's weakness, for an all-out attack after the fall of France. It was physically impossible for him to do so. A foolish version of his difficulties had it that the victory over France had taken him by surprise and found him unprepared for the invasion. If this version described his difficulties accurately it would be the first time in history that a victory came too soon.

The fact is that Hitler was licked by the same problem which thwarted previous would-be conquerors of the British Isles. The necessity of establishing bases for his army, air force, and navy on the opposite shores of the British Isles delayed his action too long. Before the fall of Holland, Belgium, and France he could not have made these indispensable preparations. Geography prevented it. After the fall of France the German Army accomplished the impossible in building the necessary airports, bringing up ammunition for its bombers and fighter planes, and laying in stores of gasoline all ready for the all-out attack in three short months. But it was too late. Military geography for twenty years had been uppermost in German plans of conquest, nevertheless it defeated the German armies within reach of their goal. Germany had not won a battle too soon but she had launched her war too soon. The long-range armada of bomber planes which could lay in ruins the centers of armament industry and communication were still in the blue-print stage. It took another two years before British and American industry had built such an air armada, and even then the armada was still far short of the goal set for it in Major de Seversky's book, *Victory Through Air Power*.

The three months of grace which the geographical position of the British Isles granted to the people of England would not have sufficed but for Britain's industrial preparations. Credit for the defensive victory won by England over the German air force must be evenly divided between the continental resistance to Hitler, British labor, and the R.A.F. From the Battle of France to the Battle of Britain and after, British labor stuck to the machines for seven days a week ten hours a day, while the civilian population remained calm under indiscriminate bombings. The unbelievable had happened. The civilian population was in the trenches, while the army was comparatively safe. The anticipation of ruthless bombings by the Germans had had a large share in the formulation of the peace at any price policy of Britain and France. Now, however, the reality proved to be less terrifying than the threat.

"In calamity England has the pulse of a cannon."

A crowd of spectators watched a London cockney furiously sweeping away the debris of his house. Looking up, he explained: " 'itler's blooming 'ousemaid, that's what I am."

Rebecca West has told the story of the bombing of London in its human implications. Miss West wrote of her conversations with the Janitor in her apartment house, while they passed long hours in the air-raid shelter. The Janitor was a veteran of the last war and recalled the days he had spent in the magnificent scenery of Yugoslavia's mountains as the most beautiful of his life. He spoke of the many landslides which occurred in Yugoslavia, some of which buried whole villages. A German cannonball had removed the top of one mound and revealed that it contained the skulls of men, women and children who had been buried there alive by a landslide. Miss West, knowing her history, asked for details, and was able to explain that these villagers had not been buried by any landslide. It was the work of the Turks in the last century. The Janitor disputed this. It was not possible in his opinion, since as he had already explained there were women and children among the dead. Miss West, certain of her ground, insisted: "That was the way they carried on war in those days." Finally convinced, the Janitor commented: "Well, who would have thought such a thing possible?"

The Janitor's inability to translate his experience into terms of reality is perhaps the ultimate reason for the six years which Germany had at her disposal to prepare for war.

The inconceivable becoming reality still remained inconceivable.

For a brief moment the German war machine surrounded the British Isles in a wide arc from Norway to the Pyrenees then, unable to advance, it flooded backwards through the Balkans, while the bombing of Britain went on throughout the winter to April, 1941. In September, 1940, Britain defeated

German daylight bombing. In April, 1941, night bombing began to be too expensive for the German air force.

Germany had lost not only the Battle of Britain but a propaganda campaign as well. She could have won victory only if the war had remained concentrated upon the British Isles. It was not to her interest for the time being to extend the war, if submission could be obtained without. German propaganda fired rapid broadsides against war. In seventy different languages Germany proclaimed that the criminal rulers of England and the United States were intent upon spreading the war. But since the German Army marched into Bohemia and Moravia, words no longer availed against the dechained forces let loose by the sorcerer's apprentice.

Even the friend and ally, "the eternal friend the best," Mussolini, no longer obeyed according to plan. As a neutral, he had been of inestimable value to Germany, pinning down part of the French Army on his frontiers, and part of the Allied Navy in the Mediterranean. The Allies had no alternative but to supply him with goods as long as there was still hope that the Maginot Line would keep Germany in check. Totalitarians are poor allies. When France fell the balance of power threatened to deliver Italy to Hitler without a fight. The fruits of victory would be Germany's alone and Mussolini knew what that would mean for him. Desperately trying to save himself from his friend, Mussolini could have chosen to side with Britain, but Britain was lost. It was wiser to put Germany in obligation to one's self. And Mussolini took the road traveled before him by the industrialists of Germany. "The hand that held the dagger struck it into the back of its neighbor," and got nothing in exchange. Rarely in the history of international relations has retribution been as swift and deadly. While Britain was fighting for her life she still had enough energy left to tear the Italian Empire to shreds. "The little one trotting by Hitler's side" had to fight even for a bone. Like a gambler throwing good money after bad Mussolini attacked Greece, and the Greeks—virtually unarmed, like the Spaniards four years earlier—forced the willing Italians to retreat. It was then that

Anthony Eden cracked a joke: "Never in the course of history have so many run away from so few."

The French had the satisfaction of seeing their *agresseurs latins* behave as they had expected them to behave. At the Paris World's Fair, in 1937, Italy was represented by a splendid pavilion. Its inauguration was celebrated by a banquet attended by French and Italian dignitaries and army men. One of the Fascist officers got thoroughly drunk and boastful. "Our Duce," said he, "ordered us to wipe out the Spanish reds, and no sooner was the order given than it was carried out. He commanded us to visit the wrath of God on the savage Ethiopian and behold it was done, if now he ordered us to march into France who could stop us?"

There was an embarrassed silence, until one of the Frenchmen supplied the answer: "Aren't you forgetting the customs-inspectors?"

At Mentone, on the Franco-Italian border, the French put up a warning sign to the Greeks who were pursuing the Italians: "Stop! This is France." The newsboys in Marseilles rushed into the restaurants with their papers, ambitiously crying out the news: "Macaroni well-cooked!"

The British began to regain prestige in France.

While the German air force continued to bombard Britain with lessening intensity the German Army prepared to secure its flanks for the attack on Russia and to take command of Italy into the bargain. Nazi diplomacy as usual proceeded to soften up the ground for the army. Hungary consented to let German troops pass through and enough of them stayed to take control of that country. Romania had received a guarantee from Britain, but, like Mussolini, her reactionaries—and in her case that meant all political and military leaders—judged Britain lost. Hitler took his personal revenge on King Carol for having accepted British guarantees and loans. Several native Fascist groups in Romania massacred Jews and fought for the privilege of exercising power on behalf of the Fuehrer while the German Army took over, and gave part of the country to Hungary. Hungary also being under their control, it did not matter either way. Bulgaria followed suit and all necessary bases for the attack on Yugoslavia and Greece were in German hands.

The Serbs revolted against the established government which had sold out to Germany. At the eleventh hour, surrounded on all sides by the same German war machine which had reduced France in three weeks, the Serbs, like the British after Dunkirk, decided to fight—against the heaviest odds.

But, like Holland and Belgium, Greece and Yugoslavia had waited too long. Once again, as in the Battle of Belgium moral considerations weighed more heavily for the democracies than military strategy. For Britain it would have been the better part of valor to continue the pursuit of the Italian armies and establish contact with General Weygand in French North Africa. Nevertheless it was decided to come to the assistance of Greece and Yugoslavia. Inadequate equipment, as in the Battle of France, doomed the enterprise and Britain suffered a second Dunkirk.

Germany followed through with an air-borne attack upon Crete which furnished the most heroic of all battles fought by the British to date. In distant Japan, the *Times Advertiser* described British heroism in terms which should have given pause to the military dictators of Japan.

The German reputation for invincibility seemed firmly established. In the United States the America First Committee through its spokesmen announced that Britain had lost the war.

Yet the victory at Crete had convinced the Germans that the invasion of the British Isles would be more dangerous than an attack upon Soviet Russia, while in the mountains of Serbia the Chetnicks, undaunted, elected a leader, General Mikhailovitch, and began the guerrilla war.

The Twenty-second of June, 1941

The totalitarian state is as sterile in conquest as it is in diplomacy. In 1938, after the fall of Czechoslovakia Hitler was diplomatic master of Europe, but could not maintain his mastery because it was based upon an unproductive military machine falling victim, with relative rapidity, to the tooth of time. In the spring of 1941 totalitarian Germany was military master of Europe and was still unable to maintain mastery. Every country she had conquered was coerced into feeding the machine of conquest with its life blood, while receiving no restorative life force in exchange. The machine absorbed all that the land and the factories could give. To be sure the accumulated wealth of centuries of labor would last several years, but after that there would be nothing. At the same time, robbery can not forever be justified by propaganda. The "spiritual" force, the will to power, which sustained the ascendancy of the Nazi machine in Germany meant nothing to the vast millions of Europe who had known liberty. While taking their bread the conqueror could not provide the conquered with any ideal.

Hitler Germany, therefore, had to fall back upon the old and tried method of the pre-Munich days which no longer worked. The conquered and the unconquered were to be tricked into a crusade against the "arch-enemy" Communist Russia.

And Rudolf Hess flew to Scotland.

He had been the only faithful dog of the master. But for that reason he had also been the least conspicuous and, therefore, the least esteemed among the powerful. All the honors and the glory went to those who pushed, while he had to be content with third place. In the totalitarian state, third place is as good as oblivion. After the Fuehrer's death there would be Goering and Goering would have plans of his own. There might even be a free for all in which such as Hess would be the first victim. A deputy Fuehrer who could not even make his own speeches would be without the ghost of a chance, a sheep among wolves. From 1923 to 1941 Hess bore his rôle without flinching. To him the Fuehrer had dictated the book, and to him he had confided all his plans, even the most secret, as lonely people are wont to do to their dogs. At last Hess thought that he had learned all the tricks his master could teach him, and ambition stirred in his dull soul. He was as good as anybody and he would dazzle the master with his brilliance. He came to Hitler with an idea: He, Hess, would fly to Scotland. He had it all planned out. He would go to see the Tory, the fool who had been his friend and with his aid he would either overthrow Churchill or swing him and the British cabinet into line for an attack on Russia.

But Hitler would have none of it. Hess was not to go and bungle the business. The British might give the story away to the Russians. There would be no surprise, hence no *Blitz*. It would be much safer to play the old game, the *fait accompli*. Attack first and then offer peace, or an alliance, to Britain; a common crusade against Bolshevism. Who would dare question Hitler's good faith once he had started war on Bolshevism, risking all on this trump card? If Britain then failed to fall into line Hitler would denounce her to the conquered peoples and to the United States as being in league with Bolshevism. It would be convincing, since the war effort was transforming England into a totalitarian state. There would always be sufficient fools in the world to believe Nazi propaganda, and the attack on Russia would make plausible all Goebbels had to say. To the statesmen of the western hemisphere, all "dwarfs" when compared with Hitler, he would be as convincing as to their stupid masses.

And so Hitler forbade Hess to fly a plane and Hess went away to brood over his master's motives. Could it be that Hitler himself was jealous of his brilliant pupil? Was the plan rejected only because he, Hess, had hit upon it before his master? When Hitler, eternally suspicious, had a watch set over him Hess was convinced he was being persecuted. The worm turned. He would show Hitler and all of them how wrong they had been in underestimating him. When the British treated Hess as a prisoner after he had announced, in true Nazi style, that he had come to save the world, he was indignant. Who did they think they were? How dare they treat thus a pure aryan and a Nazi?

In 1939, the British under Chamberlain and the Cliveden

set might have watched a German invasion of Russia through Poland with equanimity. Before Hitler broke the Munich pact by invading Bohemia and Moravia it is not excluded that if Germany had declared war on Russia, Poland might have been urged to permit passage to German troops against certain "guarantees." Now, however, it was too late for all Nazi diplomacy. After the Hess episode Russia knew that she was next on the list. Suspicious of Britain's honesty, Stalin still waited for a German attack, but took his precautions. Much to the indignation of the German High Command, as announced in the first days of the Russian campaign, the German Army found the Russian forces deployed for a counterattack. At first it looked as if the *Blitz* would work once again. The advance salients of the Russians were encircled and many Russian planes on the ground destroyed. But the Russians fought their way out, retreated in orderly fashion, leaving well-organized guerrillas behind and scorching the earth as they fell back.

Hitler's attack on Russia calls for a modification of the initial analysis we have made of his character. To be sure, he was no longer master of his own broom, but no other power had been given as much insight in Russian military preparedness as Germany. Newspapers are, after all, no adequate source of information. A little reading might have saved the Fuehrer from this colossal mistake. Had he read *War and Peace* by Tolstoy he would have learned that the Russians defend their soil—even if they can call little of it their own—to the death. Against Napoleon and again in the last war Russia fought stanchly before and after the revolution against foreign invasion and intervention. Though the peasants of Russia opposed collectivization of the land with a tenacity which caused a famine in 1932, of which some five million of their kind died; though the trials revealed a degree of passive resistance in the factories and on the collectivized farms unknown in the German and Japanese states, it stood to reason that so vast an Empire as Russia does not labor for fifteen years in vain. To be sure Russia is still dependent for aid upon the democracies, which did not start to arm in earnest and by total methods until after the fall of France, but, like the France of 1914, Russia has sufficient on hand to make Allied aid effective and to enable her to hold out until such time as Britain and the United States could open a second front on the continent.

The one pact which Hitler should have kept faithfully was his agreement with Russia concluded in August, 1939. There should be no dishonor among thieves, neither should there be war among totalitarians. By attacking Russia in the summer of 1941, Hitler finally justified the British faith in him, to wit, that if given rope enough he would get the noose around his neck.

In the afternoon of the twenty-second of June, 1941, Churchill moved to tighten the rope: "Any man or state which fights against Nazism will have our aid. . . . We shall bomb Germany by day as well as by night in ever-increasing measure, casting upon them month by month a heavier discharge of bombs, and making the German people taste and gulp each month a sharper dose of the miseries they have showered upon mankind. . . ."

When Hitler decided upon the Russian war there were still a few alternatives open to the German war machine. Should the German state survive an Allied victory, these alternatives will receive full attention in Germany and we might as well examine them beforehand.

After the conquest of the Balkan countries and Crete, the route to India via Turkey, Syria, Iran, Irak, the Suez Canal, and Egypt was open to the German armies in the east, while in the west Spain, Northwest Africa, the Cape Verde Islands and Dakar were equally accessible. Any of these routes could have been taken with fewer difficulties than the route to the Caucasian oil wells through the Ukraine if only the German High Command had known. The argument against taking the West African road was impressive. It would advertise German designs upon the United States before Germany was ready for her, while it would not paralyze the British Empire. Spain had no food, and Africa no oil. The Middle East was more promising.

The Turks might fight, but they would fight no better than the Serbs for lack of modern weapons. The British Army in the Middle East was not powerful enough to defend both flanks, Egypt and Turkey.

On the other hand, beyond the Middle East there was India and on the road to India, the German communication lines would be dangerously extended over thousands of miles of difficult roads and mountains. The Kaiser's régime had shown a great deal of military foresight in the projected Berlin-Baghdad railway line, but the line was still incomplete. The German armies on the road to India would have become vulnerable to the growing might of the Russian armies.

Meanwhile England and America were arming, and might catch up with the German war machine in spite of intensified submarine warfare. Britain was still master of her isles, ideal base for her navy and for the reconquest of the continent. Russia was supplying the German war machine with food and oil and by threats more might be squeezed out of her.

Past-master in treachery, Germany knew that Russia knew that sooner or later she would be attacked, although, taking a leaf out of British diplomacy, she was determined to wait and see. She was not going to shoot first and thus help to preserve the capitalistic democracies.

Thus the arguments for an attack on the Middle East or on Russia were fairly evenly balanced. Political considerations tipped the balance in favor of the attack on Russia.

Hitler could not resist the temptation of impersonating the crusader. But crusades are literally sacred. The profane who undertake them suffer the punishment of the blasphemer.

"It is true," says Hobhouse, "that devotion to a lost cause may waste much energy and wreck the life of the individual, but the spirit which sustains such devotion is the most vital force in the world, and it is better that it should go on acting unwisely than perish by not acting at all." So much for the rebellious elements who are in revolt against the injustice of men and the universe. The hypocrite, however, who sets out on a crusade and fails, perishes the fool and no poetry is written to his memory.

14

The Pathology of Peace
in the United States

A FEW weeks after Munich, France followed the example of Chamberlain and signed a non-aggression pact with Germany. Ribbentrop came to Paris for the ceremony. He was on his best behavior and made an excellent impression. A high dignitary of the Quai d'Orsay who had witnessed the signature of the solemn pact, told us that Ribbentrop was "a splendid fellow, yes, my friends, a splendid fellow."

On March 15, 1939, this dignitary gracefully ate his words. Erma and Michèle had left for the United States after the "victory" of Franco in Spain. We began to feel trapped. I was now being advised to join my little family by the man who had spoken so highly of Ribbentrop. "We can do without people who are not skilled in warfare. Do not imagine that this war is going to end before it has engulfed the world. We are at the mercy of German arms. France can not win this war. The only hope now must be that America will not wake up too late like ourselves. In any case there is no escape from war, death, and taxes. It will catch up with you. Remember," he added cheerfully, "American widows are paid better than the widows of those who die for France."

Michèle was born on the night the German armies marched into the Rhineland. Our second child John Peter was born in the United States on the day Paris fell. The war machine of the totalitarian state was indeed catching up with every one. All of the western hemisphere was experiencing, on a terrifying and sinister scale, the fate of the legendary American settler, who—isolationist without guile—alone at first, finally beheld the smokestack of another pioneer miles away. It was a signal to move farther west because it was getting crowded. The settler could move or stay as he pleased, there was nothing sinister about the new neighbor. But the United States could not move on. Isolationism in an interdependent world had become an illusion.

Perhaps it was the same American farmer who, in 1914, learning that war had broken out in Europe looked at the sky and drawled: "Well, they sure picked a fine day for it."

After Pearl Harbor, isolationism became taboo. It is being held responsible for crimes which are none of its making. It was shortsighted not to fortify Guam. Near disaster was avoided by one vote when the bill prolonging service in the army beyond one year was passed. But American isolationism was born of a genuine will to peace, and not of love for Hitler or the Japanese, or—in the days of the German-Russian pact —of love for Joseph Stalin.

Though the fifth columnists, Fascists, or Communists talked isolationism, they were not isolationists. On the contrary they were anxious for company from their likes abroad. There was an infinitesimally small but very angry variety which consciously or unconsciously was bitten by the same bug which destroyed the brain cells of Ferdinand Lope; the Huey Long variety, reinforced by a somewhat larger element of "the hate Britain worse than Germany" crowd, with several subdivisions of Communist coloring; "Churchill worse than Hitler" or more kindly "just as bad as Hitler" variety.

The term isolationism has been loosely applied to cover a multitude of motives. At the furthest extreme of the American pioneer who loved the solitude of the wide open spaces, there was the insufferable self-righteous chauvinist who thought that the geographical isolation of the United States was an expression of his own personal virtue. During the Czechoslovakian crisis an isolationist visitor to Paris, of this variety, pronounced sentence on Europe: "We can never straighten you out, you will always be at war." Emanuel Passemard offered him an exchange of neighbors: "Give us the Canadians in exchange for the Germans, we shall then sit back comfortably and watch the United States preserving peace in the western hemisphere. Every old lady in Europe will knit her socks and wonder vaguely about those belligerent Yankees who simply can not learn to hold the peace."

To-day isolationism has found a last refuge in the Argentine where it is being justified on the ground that Argentinians must retain sanity so that they may have a moderating influence on the peace. This pompous conceit was also to be found in the United States. Some isolationists were inclined to confound peace when there was no peace, with sanity; and aloofness from the fate of their fellowmen, with good sense.

If the isolationist viewpoint, that Americans should not meddle in affairs outside the western hemisphere, were an ideal susceptible of realization few could honestly quarrel with it. There is no resentment against the inhabitants of the planet Mars, if such there be, for not forming entangling alliances with nations on Earth. But the inhabitants of Mars, for the time being, are also safe from the conquerors of this Earth. None of the victims of totalitarianism would have hesitated to trade places with the lone American settler of the pioneering days. There is simply not enough room on the globe for all those who would be happy to leave the vicinity of the totalitarian states which are choking off the *Lebensraum* of freedom.

Without the totalitarians Europe would never be overcrowded. Though there were few wide-open prairies uncultivated and untilled—as in America—exercising an irresistible lure, one could be quite alone in the cities of Europe, more easily in fact than in the villages and in the country. But with the development of trade and communications in a shrinking world no city or production center is safe from long-range bombers operated by aggressors. The world has become too crowded for democracy and totalitarianism to live side by side. One of them must yield.

By 1917, the smokestacks of the aggressor became visible in the Americas in the shape of German submarine telescopes.

The United States then declared her solidarity with the victims of aggression, but after victory was won the smokestack disappeared from sight and mind.

The Era of Debunking

In no country had disillusionment after the last war struck such deep roots as in the United States. While the democracies of Europe were as pacifist as the United States, the era of debunking celebrated its greatest triumphs in America. In Europe the extreme materialistic interpretation of the last war was largely confined to the Socialists and the Communists; in the United States it was universal and enjoyed as much support among the conservative American Legion as among isolationists, liberal intellectuals, college youths, and radicals. This is all the more remarkable since the American Socialist and Communist parties combined were hardly ever bigger than could be contained by Union Square in New York. Such an insignificant minority can not be held responsible for so great a result.

In part the great expectations awakened by President Wilson's proclamation of a war to end war, and making the world safe for democracy, must account for the intensity of the American post-war reaction. The fabulous fortunes made by the war-industry and the subsequent economic crisis of 1922, the failure of the war to settle any problem except to banish the immediate danger of German world domination, the wrong interpretation of the character of the Weimar Republic and the French and English default on their American debt, all contributed their share to discredit the motives which had caused American participation in the European war.

On my first visit to the United States in 1929, I was surprised to hear from my brother-in-law, who had volunteered in the last war and had seen action in France, words that in Europe were spoken only by radicals and socialists. A practicing catholic and a member of the American Legion, he explained that he was resolved never to fight again unless all wealth as well as soldiers were conscripted in the next war. It was widely accepted as gospel truth that the house of Morgan, plus British propaganda, had tricked America into the war. As an employee at the Vanguard Press publishing company I edited a book by Hartley Grattan which purported to prove among other things that the *Lusitania* had carried ammunition.

Yet all these half-truths, plus those later unearthed by the Nye Committee, dealt with the effects of war and not with its causes.

At the outbreak of war in 1914 the world had no expectation that war would be profitable. A panic ensued on all the stock-exchanges of the world simultaneously with a run on the banks. The governments had to step in and close the exchanges and the banks to prevent investors and depositors, big and little, from throwing away their savings, and from ruining the national currency. This happened in spite of the fact that all belligerents expected the war to be over by Christmas with a victory for their side. It is only after immense war orders began to pour in that the capitalist world perceived the profitability of war.

In the course of the war the neutral countries carried on a lively trade with the belligerents. They bought French raw material and sold it to Germany and German raw material which they sold to France. After the war this trade was given exaggerated importance in leftist and pacifist literature. It was deduced that international capital had been in conspiracy against international labor. Evidence was presented that the Allies, or Germany, dependent upon the bias of the exponent could have won the war very much earlier, but that the capitalists did not wish it to end, because of the vast profits they were making. It was pointed out that the Krupp works and the Schneider-Creusot factories were never bombed during the war. French investors owned shares of the Krupp corporation and German investors had interests in Schneider-Creusot or vice versa. That clinched the argument. But the counter-arguments were at least as plausible. The war would

have continued to the end even if there had been no exchange
of goods of any kind through neutral countries, and no common ownerships of large scale industries.

In 1925, I saw a play in London entitled *The Old Adam*. It
showed the British Cabinet assembled to await the outbreak
of a new war. When the curtain went up an ultimatum of the
enemy had just been rejected. The ministers were nervous but
confident. Seated with them at the conference table was an
inventor. He had discovered a means of stopping the machinery of the enemy. Every motor, whether driven by electricity,
coal, gas, or oil would cease to function as soon as he pressed
a little button on the instrument-board of his machine.

The declaration of war came promptly as the clock struck
twelve. The inventor pressed his button. All lights went out,
and traffic stopped. Had he directed his rays against his own
country by mistake? By no means; the enemy had the same
invention and both countries were paralyzed. Both had refused
to yield because both had been confident of victory. It was
too late to start negotiations for peace. Instead the museums
were emptied of all primitive weapons, spears, bow and ar-
rows, which could be found. The British Navy was marooned
in the harbors, but there were plenty of yachts, sail and fish-
ing boats with which to carry the war to the enemy.

In the public imagination, between the wars the ammunition manufacturers emerged as the chief culprits. The prosaic
figure of Basil Zaharoff, large-scale traveling salesman of ammunition, spooked in the imagination of every dime-novel
reader and of all searchers of the news behind the news. It
was not perceived that wheat, for instance, was as important
an item in the conduct of war as ammunition. No one suspected the powerful farm bloc in the United States Congress
of having engineered the war for the sake of securing two
dollars a bushel for the farmers.

Preparation for, and conduct of, war are the business of
government. As the only agency which can declare and wage
war defensively or offensively the state alone must be held
responsible for its occurrence. In the structure of the state am-

munition manufacturers and wheat growers are only elements
of the whole. Basil Zaharoff owed his wealth and influence
to the generous commissions he received for supplying a governmental need. Without the opportunity furnished by the
military needs of the state the manufacturers of ammunition
would be anxious to produce sewing-machines and cash-
registers. The history of the International Business Machines
Corporation, and hundreds of other large-scale corporations
producing civilian goods should be conclusive evidence that
civilian production is at least as profitable.

The Failure of Neutrality

During the epoch of appeasement the same materialistic
dish which, when hot, had served to explain the origin of the
last war, was served up cold to explain capitalistic resistance
to war.

In 1935, when the American Neutrality Law was passed by
Congress, the effects of war were still mistaken for its causes.
The law consequently contained safeguards against the effects, but did not touch upon the causes of war. It provided
against American ships sailing into the war zone so that American lives and property could not be attacked by enemy submarines. It forbade the granting of credit to belligerents, so
that no capitalistic pressure could be exercised upon Congress
to declare war in order to save American investments. Even
travel on foreign ships in designated war zones was made a
penal offense for American citizens. Like the Maginot Line in
France the American Neutrality Law proclaimed to all the
world that the United States would not fight to safeguard her
interests until directly attacked. It was an assurance to all potential enemies that the United States would not interfere with
them while they made their preparations. It also held out as
bait to the potential aggressor the island bases in the Atlantic
and Pacific. Like the small countries of Europe these bases
were neutralized so that the enemy had reason to believe that
he would be free to take them at a time of his own choosing

and prepare them as advance bases for his attack on the western hemisphere.

But before he could take Guam, Wake, and so on, in the Pacific, and Iceland, Greenland, Dakar, and the Cape Verde Islands in the Atlantic he had to secure his flanks by conquering many nations on the continent of Asia and the continent of Europe. Japan was the first totalitarian power to take advantage of the assurance that she would meet with no United States opposition in violating the nine-power pact, which guaranteed peace to China and an open door to world trade. The desire to continue trade relations with the United States for the time being prompted Japan to avoid a formal declaration of war on China. Instead the war was coyly described as "the China incident." It might be noted in parenthesis that all totalitarian states have felt the need of creating a terminology and a phraseology of their own, as a final tribute to international morality.

The United States saw itself compelled to accept the Japanese terminology. The invocation of the Neutrality Law would have worked to the sole advantage of Japan. Thus, two years after its passage, the law had become inoperative. It had been conceived to stop the same sequence of events which presumably had led to American participation in the First World War. But even that kind of history did not repeat itself. The war began in the Far East and not in Europe.

The law proved inapplicable in Europe as well. Conceived to favor the two western democracies, without involving the United States, it worked to the sole advantage of Germany. While the democracies were still living on a basis of peace economy, totalitarian Germany was able to import all American raw materials she needed for war before the blockade was clamped down upon her. At any rate she imported enough to conquer the resources of Europe.

Moreover, the psychological cause of which the American Neutrality Law was the result imposed the burden of extra good behavior upon France and England. It is true that it was conceived in the same spirit which inspired European opposi-

tion to war. The niceties of democratic diplomacy in dealing
with Germany can therefore not be blamed wholly upon
American pacifism. But under the influence of native opposition to war plus the necessity of proving to the people of the
United States that neither France nor England could be
blamed for the war which was shaping up, the governments
of the democracies leaned over backwards in their concessions
to Germany and to the susceptibilities of the small democracies. It is not difficult to imagine the outcry against France
and England if they had disturbed the phony peace from
September, 1939 to May, 1940 by coming to the assistance
of Denmark, Norway, Belgium, and Holland without waiting
to be asked.

American isolationism is a variation on the theme of the
sovereign democratic state which can not go to war until directly attacked or threatened with attack.

The malice aforethought in the American version of Britain's
ideal of "splendid isolation" is less pronounced. The American
who wants to mind his own business does not lack the shrewd-
ness to perceive the advantages of a wait and see policy, once
the bus has been missed, but that foresight of which he is capable in his own affairs is diluted by the space which separates
his country from the centers of aggression. In Europe and Asia
the enemy is well camouflaged by the distance which separates
him from his last obstacle to world domination. To recognize
him at once consequently taxes to the full the famed shrewd-
ness of the Yankee.

Those who deny to themselves the advantages of designat-
ing the enemy and pronouncing him guilty of criminal intent
on circumstantial evidence, must wait and see. They have no
choice. And with or without premeditation the military advantages of isolationism are the same for the United States
as for Great Britain.

The March of War placed the United States last on its time-
table. Separated from the European continent by 3,000 miles
of ocean and from Asia by some 5,000 miles, Americans can

afford to wait and see for a longer period of time than the British.

A potential aggressor on the European or on the Asiatic continent has a long route to travel before he can get at the United States. In Europe and Asia he must first vanquish all nations barring his route to the sea or threatening his rear before he can organize the assault on the United States. In Europe as in Asia the last obstacle barring his way is the Empire, and sea power of Britain. The British Empire is either in possession or stands between the geographical bases needed by the aggressor of east and west as his last stopping place on his time-table before he can concentrate his forces against America.

What the defense of the continental nations by their land armies is to Great Britain, the defense of the British Empire is to the United States. When the Low Countries, France, and Norway were conquered, the enemy was at the gates of the British Isles; when China is encircled and Indo-China in the hands of Japan, the Asiatic enemy is at the gates of the British Empire. But not until Britain is vanquished in Europe and Asia, not until her navy is deprived of all its vital world bases can the enemy prepare to storm the gates of the United States. The United States being the last stop on the time-table of aggression in a global war enjoys at the start the full balance of power in time and space. As she waits for the threat to become clear and unmistakable that advantage is whittled away, but at the same time she can, like Great Britain and very much longer than Great Britain, study the nature of the beast, his methods and his aims, and prepare a vastly better military machine to thwart his purpose. Benefiting by the experience of friend and foe alike the United States can incorporate into her army, navy, and air force all the lessons taught by the course of the war as long as that war is confined to other continents.

The disadvantages of her position are equally clear. The bulk of American isolationists were as pacifist as the European democrats and even more intensely so. Like France Americans wanted none of war and like England, America had no peace-time conscripted army. The United States, like the European powers, was dedicated to the proposition that one must wait until the enemy is ready, and like the European democracies she was therefore doomed to miss the first bus; to lose the first battle, which otherwise might be the last, and a bloodless battle to boot. Bloodless because a war fought against the totalitarian state at its inception finds the people of that state reduced to slavery but not yet in possession of arms. On the other hand, so long as Britain, China, and Russia do not submit without a fight, the time to prepare is still at the disposal of the United States. Thus to date it has not only been a legend but a fact that the United States loses every battle except the last. In this sense the "interventionists" were perfectly right when they insisted that Britain was fighting the battle of the United States, exactly as Poland and France had been fighting the British battle, and as China was fighting for both the United States and Britain.

Since the success of the German armies focused attention upon Nazi geopolitics, several attempts have been made to work out a geopolitical theory for the democracies. Those bitten by the bug of geopolitics, as conceived by the Germans, have simply followed their example and done the job cold-bloodedly, thinking that this was "real politics." But such slavish imitations of Karl Haushofer are unreal in the full sense of the word, because the governments of the democracies are not free to shape a policy without a decent regard for the opinion of their people, and it is to be hoped that this will for ever remain beyond their power. If democracies could act upon German geopolitical principles without regard for moral content they would not be democracies but totalitarians, and in that case it would be idle to write on the subject. The ingenuity of those in power could be trusted to develop the most devilish schemes of their own without any aid from the armchair political theorist.

Even in the case of Germany, the cold-blooded geopolitician

has done his masters a disservice, by failing to oppose the attack upon Russia. If Germany loses the war, no historian of the future will be able to deny that the attack upon Russia spelled out her doom.

The necessity of adhering to international standards of ethics is pressing upon free men if they wish to survive. The most generous solution to international problems for each country and for each people of reasonable good faith in an imperfect world is still the best, as illustrated by the failure of the democracies to stand together. The shop-worn but only possible defense against an enemy who practises the equally shop-worn method of picking out his victims one by one, is still the only guarantee against hanging together. Though both methods are shop-worn, each generation seemingly must discover them anew.

Every new generation on earth is born with its head in the clouds and does not see the ground until it is cut from under its feet. The geographical position of Great Britain and the United States is a blessing only because of their next-door neighbors. Holland, Belgium, and France are Britain's geopolitical assets as Canada and Mexico are the most precious possessions of the United States. Yet both powers treat their neighbors to a dose of cold geopolitics. And the penalty of taking the virtue of one's neighbors for granted is invariably cruel.

Virtue can be its own reward only in the esteem of those who possess it. Those who benefit from the non-aggressive character of their neighbors should cherish them as the apple of their own eye, if they wish to survive. *Honor and aid thy neighbor who has no designs upon your liberty so that you may long live upon this earth* is a commandment upon which even an Clemenceau would not be tempted to exercise his wit.

There was prevalent in the days between the wars an insane version of Stephen Decatur's principle of allegiance to his country. "My country right or wrong," had become distasteful to the democratic peoples, but instead of adopting a more generous and universal principle in its place they acted on the principle that the enemy of yesterday must be right, and searched in their souls to find what it was that they did to wrong him. Nor was this the total measure of their insanity. Wrong as each one of them thought themselves to be, the peaceful neighbors by the side of whom they had fought the bloody battles of the First World War, were adjudged more grievously at fault.

There are still people in the United States and in Great Britain who would see a virtue in their own geographical position and a vice in the geographical position of the friend. Instead of concentrating their emotions upon the enemy who has done his best to merit destruction they prefer to remember the sins of omission committed by the ally in the past.

Fifty Thousand Planes

During the Battle of France wishful thinking still ran high in the United States. Military commentators reassured an anxious public that in all wars new offensive weapons were finally neutralized by the invention of new defensive methods. Of course, said the late Colonel Mason, France has not found these defensive weapons yet. . . . For France it was too late. When General de Gaulle arrived in England he stated that "Germany won with ten thousand tanks and twelve thousand planes; we can beat her with twenty thousand tanks and twenty-four thousand planes." It was as simple as all that, but the weapons had to be produced and only the United States could still produce them.

The fall of France brought home to many people that France had not only been a civilization but an empire as well. Indo-China, a virtually unknown geographical concept, swung into view. The three powers, France, England, and the United States, unperceived or unacknowledged by their people, had formed a structure of peace dependent for support upon each of the three pillars. The defeat and surrender of France left western and southern Europe at the mercy of Hitler's armies. England could now be subjected to mass air-raids and in the Far East a vital keystone of democratic defense was removed when Vichy surrendered Indo-China without a fight. If Vichy had instructed Indo-China to fight it could have put up no more than a token defense. The United States would not have come to the defense of Indo-China and since Britain was in no position to take on one more enemy, the colony was doomed to fall into Japanese hands. Establishment of Japanese bases in Indo-China presaged the fall of the Philippines, Malaya, Singapore, the Dutch East Indies and Burma, as well as the cutting off of China from supplies from the western powers.

After the break through at the Meuse, President Roosevelt, addressing Congress called for what appeared a fantastic number of war planes: Fifty thousand. The people who had most determinedly opposed rearmament now criticized the administration the loudest for neglecting the defense of the country.

But paradoxically it was just as well that America had no accumulation of weapons on hand. Had there been such they would have been obsolete or obsolescent, and therefore useless. If the United States had joined Britain and France at the outbreak of this war and sent an expeditionary force to France she, too, would have shared in the defeat since her arms and equipment would have been inadequate and her army would have been modeled on the French. The United States would have become even more vulnerable to Japanese attack. Both flanks of the western hemisphere could not be guarded by a one-ocean navy sufficient only as long as Britain guarded the Atlantic coast. Timing of production for war had thus become of the essence in the making of victory.

What March 15, 1939, had been to Europe, the fall of France was to the United States. To judge by the American press, Americans saw more clearly and earlier the meaning of Hitlerism than many Europeans. Perhaps this is not wholly explained by the excellence of American newspaper reporting. The danger of war at this distance could be regarded with less alarm than in Europe. Americans, not fearing imminent involvement, were consequently less inclined to wishful thinking on the subject of peace with Hitler.

At the time of Munich many American pacifists were disgusted with France and England for their cowardice, but in retrospect it is less difficult to understand the relief with which the public in France and England received Chamberlain's peace with honor. It is true that they did not know how defenseless they were, but disaster was feared and the respite was consequently received like manna from heaven. The day after Munich Madeleine Huillet, daughter of Colonel Huillet, telephoned to invite us to tea. Talking to me she asked: "And what do you think of Munich?" "I think," said I, "that you will now have to mobilize every six months." This opinion was passed on to her father, who asked her to tell me that I was an idiot, which she did.

The Mind and the Guts

Even after the fall of France there were still some American isolationists who believed that they were charitable in looking upon the interventionists as fools. Most isolationists, however, discovered that they had been isolationists only because they believed that France and England would stop Hitler without American aid. The author of the phrase: "America First," Mr. Jerome Frank, for instance, changed his mind on the day of the break through of the German Army at the Meuse.

The so-called interventionists had been in reality as isolationist as their opponents. They, too, had hoped that America might be spared the ordeal, but had thought that the lesser risk was all-out aid to the Allies. America had no war-mongers. Like France she had had no use for revolutionary thought in the art of warfare. William Mitchell suffered a worse fate than De Gaulle. De Gaulle was ignored but General Mitchell was court-martialed because he would not keep silent.

And exactly like France and England after the fifteenth of March, 1939, the United States rearmed at her leisure. There were to be cannons and butter, and business was to continue as usual at home, and with Japan. America worked at rearmament without an awakened instinct of self-preservation. The knowledge of the coming attack was of the mind rather than of the guts.

All had counted upon the Maginot Line as much as the French, all had relied upon the heroism of the French, upon French unity in the face of a foreign foe, upon French generalship, upon new millions of French casualties, dead and wounded. America's frontiers in Europe were on the Rhine but the defense was entrusted to the French alone, because in time and space it was first and foremost their business. When France fell she had betrayed the confidence of the world, which had complacently counted upon her. Hence the profound sympathy for her during the Battle of France changed into bitterness against her at the time of surrender. Hence the reproach against her, her people, and the men of Vichy, those chevaliers without shame and without self-reproach, who had delivered France to the Teutonic chevaliers *sans beurre* and *sans brioche*.

The next line of defense was up to the British. Britain, like France and like the United States, had had no use for the art and science of war in time of peace. This is to the glory of all three, but when war can no longer be avoided, and the armies take the field, all three nations instantly demand miracles from their military leadership, forgetting that the neglected grow stale.

The British soldier in battle is second to none in courage and endurance, but his skill and his leadership, three years after the declaration of war, is still behind that of the trained killers of Germany and Japan. The reverses at Singapore and Tobruk lay him open to the same scorn which yesterday was heaped upon the French. The day before yesterday the heroes of the battle-fields of the First World War were looked upon as dupes of the profit motive of capitalistic industry, to-day, the long-prepared, trained armies of Russia enjoy the greatest, well-deserved popularity in England and in America, because they were able to meet the enemy with a ferocity and a skill of their own born of at least fifteen years of indoctrination and training.

In war more than in any other sphere of life, nothing succeeds like success and nothing fails like failure. It is easier to see Tobruk in the eyes of the British, than to remember Pearl Harbor or the Aleutians in one's own eye. What is even worse it would seem that it is easier to see the mote in the eye of an ally than the beam in the eye of the enemy.

Although the United States was blessed with an administration more far-sighted than the governments of Europe had been, although President Roosevelt called the turn with unerring judgement, the all-out effort could only be recommended to the people of America, it could not be imposed. At the start of the war the Neutrality Law had been amended to permit the Allies to buy war material in this country and carry it away in their own holds, but although the restricting fetters of the law were still drastic, these could not be removed before the Presidential elections. Both candidates agreed on all-out aid to the Allies. The European war, nevertheless, dominated the debate. In a democracy the executive has to wait upon public opinion. The lend-lease law could therefore not be introduced before the country had pronounced itself.

Though the R.A.F. defeated the German air force after Dunkirk, the victory was only a defensive victory. The danger of a German victory over Britain was real, palpable, and menacing. Yet President Roosevelt was still suspected by diehard isolationists of being anxious to get this country into war for the sake of war. They demanded that the initiative be left to the enemy. Reluctance to offend the susceptibility of the aggressors dictated such ludicrous practices as flying planes to the border of Canada, landing them, and pushing them across the frontier so that they could take to the air again, in obedience to the principle of cash and carry.

Congress imposed upon the armed forces of the United States a far greater handicap by refusing to fortify Guam in order not to offend Japan. For more than fifteen years Japan had refused to inform the League of Nations what she was doing in the mandated islands. The League failed to insist. Had the United States been a member of the League the roster of government official members of the club would have been increased by one more representative subject to the will of Congress and of a peaceful public opinion at home. The United States which did not fortify Guam in her own defense could hardly have been of a firmer state of mind as a member of the League. Relations between Japan and the United States provide a close parallel to the relations of Great Britain with Germany. One can do business with a totalitarian state only by giving without demanding anything in return. One-sided concessions become appeasement.

The inveterate isolationists who continued to oppose aid to England after the fall of France were not opposed to American rearmament, but wanted American weapons kept at home. They failed to see that unused modern weapons grow rapidly obsolete, as the fifty over-age destroyers which were given to Britain in exchange for bases leased to America in the western hemisphere. "Had you but known," said Mr. Bernard Shaw, "we would have given you these bases for nothing." Guilelessly he invited the United States to build bases for its navy on the British Isles at Liverpool and Plymouth. England would ask nothing in exchange. Had the American people followed the advice of the isolationists to keep the obsolescent weapons at home, the United States would have found herself in time at the same disadvantage as France. The enemy conqueror of the European continent would have had Africa for the asking. The Japanese would have conquered China and the rest of Asia and they might have taken Australia as well. With these trifles in hand Germany and Japan could have organized a new air force of the type recommended by Major de Seversky.

Meanwhile both powers would have remained at peace with the United States, biding their time for a super *Blitz* to be staged at a moment of inferiority in American airplane design. The United States, like Europe, would have been confronted with the choice of trusting the enemy, appeasing him, and doing business with him, or remain eternally on the alert, devoting the total energy of her people to beating the productive capacity of hundreds of millions of slave labor under Axis domination. That was sound advice, given by people who were apparently jealous of the happy state of France. They wanted to see the enemy on their soil; look into the white of his eyes before they would consent to shoot, and this in a world of long-range submarines and flying fortresses.

Kept at home, American weapons would have been not only militarily useless but economically unproductive. Lend-leased they might yield large dividends in consumer goods after the war. For sheer ingenuity the lend-lease idea tops anything that the Axis countries have invented. It removes in advance any danger of repetition of the futile and barren controversy which raged between France, England and the United States after the last war over the war debts. But its greatest merit of immediate importance was this, that it prepared United States industry for mass production of planes, tanks, guns, and ships and thus materially reduced the time needed to strike back at Japan.

Hampered by the continued free demand for consumer goods, American rearmament proceeded slowly. But the pace at which the United States rearmed can be described as slow only in relation to the great potential of industrial skills and resources of the American industry. Upon Germany American rearmament, even under conditions of business as usual, imposed a severe strain. Germany had reached peak production before she went to war. The rigidity of her totalitarian state was tempered only by the willing coöperation of her people. German industry showed great flexibility. Though German combat plane and tank models had been frozen to permit assembly-line production years before Germany went to war, the industrial skill of her workers and managers permitted the progressive adoption of improvements. Hitler did not boast when he promised before the attack on Russia that Germany would have better weapons in 1942 than she had in 1941, but the degree of improvement which could be built into the German war machine was limited in scope.

Anticipating the arrival of American ships in the Atlantic and planes and tanks on the battle-fields of Europe and Africa, Germany was confronted with a difficult choice. To meet the American challenge, Germany could have stopped the mass production of her implements of war to reorganize her assembly-lines for the mass production of radically improved models of long-range bombers. But such action would have rendered her vulnerable in time to an aërial Blitzkrieg gathering momentum in the British Isles, and even more vulnerable to a Russian attack by land. In the long run Germany knew that she could not match American industry. The United States is to-day the only country in the world which can establish new assembly-lines for the production of the latest models of all implements of war without having to slow down or even reduce the mass production of the old. The other alternative open to Germany and the more promising one from her point of view was to try to beat the United States in the battle of space by organizing a two-front war against her shipping, and to utilize to the full her war machine in order to conquer for the German Reich the resources of Russia.

Anticipating that Germany would attack American shipping, President Roosevelt moved Iceland into the western hemisphere by executive order as it were, and instructed American warships to shoot on sight, or rather on sound, at any German rattlesnakes to be heard in the vital defense zones of the United States. American forces were landed in Greenland and took over from the British the defense of Iceland. The Icelanders showing better sense than Norway, Holland, and Belgium, had not made any audible objections to Canadian aid and now welcomed the American troops. By protecting the bridge of shipping the United States prepared to win the Battle of the Atlantic. American industry could win the battle of time with comparative ease, but that would avail little if the battle of space were lost. The three thousand miles of ocean which separate the United States from Europe, once conceived as an unmitigated blessing, are a severe handicap in a war which can only be won by a well-timed offensive.

While the timely action taken by President Roosevelt in the Atlantic won the opening bout for the United States in the Battle of Europe, in the Pacific the first round went to the enemy by virtue of Japan's geographical position and the structure of her state, permitting her to make full use of the technic of the surprise attack. The American expeditionary force arrived in time in the Atlantic; for the Philippines it was too late. The loss of the Battle of Bataan gave the United States a hero in General MacArthur and a moral victory to her colonial policy but it gave the Japanese the free access to raw materials which, in time of war, is the ideal of all aggressor nations.

The speed of the German victory over France had alarmed Japan as much as the United States. The people of Japan had been receiving, in return for their sacrifices to the state, regular parcel posts of the ashes of their sons and fathers who died incidentally in China. The struggle had lasted for years with no end in sight. They now demanded to know why they had not been given such shining and effective toys with which to play as the German state could give to its subjects. The Japanese totalitarians were able to supply the answer in exactly eighteen months.

There was much speculation on the question whether the Japanese attack on Pearl Harbor and Malaya, the Philippines, Singapore, and the Dutch East Indies was synchronized with German plans. To be sure both Japan and Germany would have much preferred to be independent of each other and to rule the world alone, but necessity makes bed fellows of East and West. The presence of a vast army of technical and tactical German experts in Japan, months before the attack on Pearl Harbor, argues that a marriage of convenience similar to the Russian-German pact of 1939 had taken place. Germany had learned much from Japan, but the Japanese in turn must have received the full benefit of German science for their war industries. The *Blitz* in the Pacific bore the stamp of the German masters, though it is conceivable that the lightning struck in a direction not desired by Germany, but more suitable to the Japanese thunder.

To meet the American challenge, Germany had not only decided upon a submarine war against American shipping but also upon the conquest of the Russian space. Had she succeeded in reaching the Caucasian oil fields in 1941 she would have prolonged the war for many years. The loss of the Caucasus to the Allied cause would have eliminated the Russian armies as a major factor in this war. Had she succeeded in destroying the Russian armies Germany could have driven the British out of the Middle East. In the vast spaces of Russia, Germany could have hidden her war industry from British bombing attacks as well as the Russians hid theirs from the knowledge of the Germans. Britain and the United States combined might still have been able to resist, but the defeat of Germany would then have become a task to be accomplished only in a thirty-years' war.

When the German Army invaded Russia, President Roosevelt followed the example of Churchill in supporting Russia. The controversy which had raged for so long in the western world about the respective merits of Fascism and Communism was rendered idle by the Nazi peril. Compared with the reality of the aggressor versus the victim of aggression, ideological controversies are pointless. Germany having failed in her clever scheme of organizing a crusade against Bolshevism was thus forced to lavish all her love and devotion upon the Japanese.

In sight of the Russian Caucasus and victory, it is difficult to conceive that she coached Japan for an attack upon any other front than the Russian front, for a quick victory was of the essence to her. Germany probably planned an attack upon Pearl Harbor by the Japanese Navy to force the American fleet out of the Atlantic, while the Japanese Army was to attack Russia in Siberia. But an attack upon Pearl Harbor and the Philippines was bound to bring a declaration of war from Great Britain on Japan. In possession of Singapore, Britain could have exercised a long-range blockade and the resources of the Dutch East Indies would still have been at the disposal of the democracies. If the Japanese drive was mapped by Germany and carried out according to plan by the Japanese, it would imply that Hitler had resigned himself to a long war and was willing to wage a war of attrition until Japan had rounded out her Empire in Asia and could come to the assistance of Germany in the war on Russia.

Six months after Pearl Harbor the American correspondents who were in Germany at the outbreak of war returned to the United States. Mr. Oechsner reported that after the extension of lease-lend aid to Russia a Japanese-German conference took place in Berlin, when the attack upon the United States was decided upon.

German U-boats began sinking American ships in answer to Japanese demands for proof that Germany would follow suit with a declaration of war on the United States.

Hitler could hardly have taken this course with a light heart. Up to then he had managed to avoid a declaration of war, leaving the "onus" of having done so to Britain and France. Now he was compelled to extend the war and thus to confess that a possible victory was removed into the far-distant future. The attack on Russia was a failure in 1941, because the Russians took the *Blitz* out of the German war, and Hitler had to go to any extremity to prevent American supplies from reaching Russia.

"We had no idea," said the Fuehrer ingenuously, "of the extent and the immensity of Russian preparations."

Long before the Japanese attack upon Pearl Harbor, the jockeying for position in the totalitarian race for world domination, had made it clear that the war would be world-wide in its extent. On the seventh of December Japan attacked and the global war was on. When the Japanese bombers stumbled or glided to the attack it nevertheless came as unexpectedly as the German attack on Norway. They thus illustrated better than words could do that "defense won't win this war." "Remember Pearl Harbor" is a cry against negligence, but in justification of all who were lulled into easy confidence, it must be said that to be constantly on the alert night and day against a stab in the back will always be beyond human capacity for endurance. By their very existence totalitarian states impose a strain upon the nervous system of peaceful people which renders life not worth the living.

Though American rearmament had been hampered by the absence of a sense of urgency before Pearl Harbor, the preparations of American industry to aid Britain now bore rich rewards for the United States. Six months after Pearl Harbor the United States air force supported by the navy was able to neutralize the loss to the American Pacific fleet, by inflicting severe punishment on the Japanese in the Coral Sea and at Midway. Admiral Nimitz was able to say that the United States had advanced midway to victory. A statement quite different from one made in another period and a different world. When Chamberlain returned from his first flight to Berchtesgaden he said that he would meet Hitler again, this time at Godesberg. The Fuehrer had thus shown that he was willing to meet him half way.

In the battle of time and space the United Nations have reached the half-way mark. The United States has become the arsenal of democracy in fact and not only in promise. At the same time, Great Britain's war industry has reached peak production. The tanks, planes, and guns are rolling off the assembly line in impressive quantities. Only three years after the outbreak of war in Europe is it possible to plan a counter-offensive. Only when the tools of victory are on hand can there be any world strategy, any master plan for the defeat of the enemy. From now on it will be possible to coördinate an offensive in the west with a counter-offensive in the east, to create a unified command, to wage a genuine coalition war, and to concentrate the striking force on the weakest link in the armor of the enemy. Hitherto all demands made for a second front in Europe and a supreme strategy council were reminiscent of the mice who planned to hang a bell on the cat.

In June, 1942, the United Nations agreed upon the necessity of opening a second front in Europe. Germany was designated as the principal enemy, to be defeated first. Once she is defeated there will be sufficient industrial capacity and equipment, man-power and transportation on hand for the defeat of Japan. As the United Nations are fast overtaking Germany in the output of the sinews of war, there may be in short order sufficient material on hand not only to hold Japan but to equip the armies of China, Australia, and India and to start a counter-offensive in the Pacific with the support of the American Navy even before Germany is knocked out of the war. Where, when, and how a front is to be opened in Europe concerns most intimately only the military strategist, not the historian, and for this he is grateful.

The Mediterranean Front

The tide turned in November, 1942. The series of unbroken victories for Germany was ended. It was now her turn to suffer from a shortage of victory. In Egypt the British struck heavy blows at the German Africa corps which fled to Tripolitania. At the same time the greatest amphibian force in history invaded the French Empire in North Africa. That invasion was planned in June. The execution of the plan itself thus required some five months, but the basis for this plan was laid in the winter of 1940, when Winston Churchill, addressing himself to the United States, cried: "Give us the tools and we shall finish the job."

Between the beginning of lend-lease in the spring of 1941 and the invasion of French North Africa, a year and a half had to pass before the first Allied victory could materialize. It can thus be seen that the decisive factor in this war is the time element. The tools were no sooner on hand than all the other factors worked in favor of the United Nations. The attack came as a surprise, a Blitzkrieg which struck in an unexpected direction. The coördination of Army, Navy, and Air Force, the unity of command among the Allies, the contact with the anti-Vichy French, all had been well prepared and worked perfectly. Many French officers in the colonies were taken into the confidence of the Americans, and none failed in his devotion to the cause of liberty. Even the weather, once an unfailing ally of Hitler, was favorable to the landing force. The intelligent rats in the Vichy camp scurried to leave the sinking ship.

The initiative having passed to the Allies, Hitler was forced to conform his moves to those of his enemies. He invaded the rest of France, still leaving Toulon unoccupied to induce the French fleet to remain. The resentment of the French Navy against Great Britain for the Naval Pact of 1935 may be measured by the fact that the French fleet remained at anchor at Toulon and that in Morocco it fought the invading American troops. General Eisenhower, commanding the American-British forces, was thus compelled to deal with Pétain's man, Admiral Darlan. The deal saved human lives and gained precious time, but the long arm of the past marred the frank joy of liberation for the French as well as for their liberators.

For fully two years the reactionary element in the French Navy was torn between resentment for their former ally and hatred for the real enemy. Hitler finally managed to break the deadlock by invading Toulon. The French Navy command redeemed its honor by blowing up its ships as a final gesture of defiance.

While the Allies were closing in on Tunisia and Tripolitania, the Amercian Navy in the Pacific chalked up an immense victory over the Japanese fleet at Guadalcanal, and the Russian armies, still intact, passed to the offensive after a long retreat to the Caucasus and Stalingrad, where they fought a battle of Verdun. Once Germany had a wide choice. "Encircling" her were virtually unarmed nations any one of which she could strike down without effort. She had but the trouble to choose. Henceforth she can only strike at starving Spain or at roadless Turkey. Germany has lost the economic resources of French North Africa, and the countries she has occupied she has already robbed of their substance. The blockade is growing tight, and the air offensive against her communications and production centers will increase in weight and effectiveness.

Perhaps the worst blow struck against her by the liberation of French North Africa is a psychological one. Hitherto Germany was able to rely on her enemies' adherence to the principle of non-interference in the internal affairs of the neutrals, while she was free to violate the most elementary principles of international decency. Strict adherence to the principle of non-aggression on the part of the democracies was Germany's principal asset. Now, however, the United Nations have invaded the territory of a country with which they were at peace and with which the United States entertained friendly relations: Vichy France. Germany can no longer be certain that the Allies will not invade Spain and Portugal. There is, after all, as good a moral cause for the liberation of Spain as for the liberation of France. But if Hitler invades Spain, this time honestly in order to forestall an Allied invasion, he will merely thin out his troops. France might pull a Darlan and go over to the Allies, and in any case the task of opening a front in Europe will be thereby facilitated. The Allies will have the wide choice which once was Hitler's alone.

The military machine now at the disposal of the United Nations is an improved model of the German Army. The nature of the offensive in Egypt against the German Army and the American invasion of the French African Empire was dictated by the character of that war machine. It had to be a coördinated Army, Navy, Air Force offensive; but the advice of Major de Seversky, certainly the most convincing of all special pleaders, should not be forgotten. It may be too late for the United Nations to put his theories to the test, for to do so would require some two years of industrial preparation. But it should not be forgotten that the production of an Air Armada with adequate range to reach Germany and Japan and with sufficient striking power to cripple their vital production and communication centers was advanced in this war. Short of total defeat, the enemy will remember this proposal, as he remembered the tanks which spelled his doom in 1918. If the German state survives, the Germans will apply the principles of de Seversky in the next war as they applied the principles of de Gaulle in this.

15

Psychological Warfare

ONLY after years of hard labor could the German war machine, once set in motion, be stopped by nations which had long neglected the arts and the economics of war. The sweeping German victories of 1940 seemed unbelievable. Since the secret of their might and power was as yet unknown, the wildest tales of treason, secret weapons, nerve gases, death rays, and so on, gained credence, particularly when the astounding fact was revealed that the German High Command, far from lying itself into victories, was actually indulging in understatements. For the first time in its history it was withholding the full story of the magnitude of its successes.

Americans who had never set foot on French soil experienced the sensation of personal bereavement. A neighbor told me that he would wake up at night in a cold sweat from the nightmare of the German juggernaut advancing over the fair land of France. The shock of the French defeat felt throughout the world was profound enough to affect the nervous system and consequently the judgment of sober people.

The aberration of judgment went beyond the error of attributing the defeat to treason. The momentous discovery was made that some French statesmen had mistresses, and even military analysts succumbed to the temptation of joining in the hue and cry that this was a vital factor in the French surrender. The slight difference between English and French customs of matrimony assumed world-shaking importance. The mistresses of Monsieur Reynaud and Monsieur Daladier made

317

this kind of history: for want of a nail the shoe was lost . . . for want of a marriage license . . . France was lost!

It took some time after the fall of France, when the English had proved that they were unimpressed, for sanity to return and to permit of a calm examination of the causes of the German success.

By 1939, the German war industry or rather all German industry, had labored for six years to create the war machine. It was poised for action and rarin' to go. On the other side of the barricades the chosen victims for the years 1939–40 lived under what was for all practical purposes a total peace economy. In the Far East a similar phenomenon had made its appearance—Japan confronted a totally unarmed Asia with a totally developed war economy. Throughout history all world-shaking conquests were based on similar radical divisions of labor between conqueror and conquered. The vast conquests of Egyptian pharaohs, Assyrian kings, Alexander the Great, and Cæsar were made possible because the armies led by these conquerors possessed weapons which were vastly superior to those which could be pitted against them.

The classic division of labor in the history of conquest was that between agricultural peoples and nomads. The once-free peasantry of Europe, bound to the soil by the nature of their occupation and ignorant of mobile warfare, were reduced to slavery by hordes of nomads who came from the east.

The pastoral tribes had acquired their science of warfare as an incident to their economic occupation. They learned to ride on swift horses and developed skill in the use of deadly weapons in order to protect their herds from beasts of prey. When a genius warrior such as Attila arose among them and united them, they became a perfect instrument in his hands for the conquest of the defenseless peasantry of Europe.

Unlike the huns who had developed their method of warfare as an integral part of their economic life, the totalitarian nations of our time acquired their war machine as a militant religion for its own sake as it were. To it they sacrificed 80 per cent of their productive capacity, corroding the soil upon which they lived and doing without, so that the machine might grow to be invincible.

The most primitive of the early barbarians slaughtered their victims—men, women and children—and made off with such wealth as they could find in those non-accumulative days.

But conquerors at higher stages of civilization realized that a live peasant is worth more than a dead one.

Alive he could work and be forced to pay tribute. He was therefore left in possession of his tools, so that his productive capacity might not be impaired. At this stage of civilization the conqueror began to feel the need of morally justifying his action. He claimed tribute in exchange for protection granted against other marauding tribes who might take all. The racketeer unions of our own time invented nothing. At a still higher stage in civilization the conquerors settled among the conquered, constituting the governing class, until a series of revolutions deprived them of much of their power or drove them out.

The spirit of the present totalitarian conquerors in Asia and Europe is a throwback to the oldest form of primitive conquest. It is not only a reaction against the ideals of the French Revolution. Aiming at the abolition of liberty, equality, and fraternity as a social ideal, it does not only want to reëstablish the feudal system which the French Revolution abolished but it wants to secure its victory forever by destroying the conquered.

Japan and Germany do not uniformly slaughter their victims for the time being. Final victory has not yet been achieved and Germany in particular is careful to let those of the conquered subsist who can run war factories and produce food for the German Army. But the extermination, systematic and relentless, first of the Jews in Germany and then of the conquered nations who have no specialized industrial skills useful to the German war machine, the mass starvation of the Greeks, the Yugoslavs, and the Poles is merely a dress rehearsal for the mass extermination of the western nations. Since they want their domination to last a thousand years, which for all practical purposes is eternity, the Nazis have indeed no choice. If they let their victims live revenge will inevitably come.

The Nazi superiority in industrial production could not be maintained for ever even if Germany wins the war and deprives all conquered peoples of industrial equipment. Revolutions by unskilled laborers and peasants are not unknown. Corruption of the rulers always sets in, particularly when the conquered possess a higher civilization; not to mention the fact that the danger of intermarriage is an obsession with the Fuehrer.

Hitherto all European wars, since the Thirty Years' War, were fought for limited objectives and failed to alter materially the national boundaries of Europe. The balance of power was such that the opponents in these wars were for the most part evenly matched. In spite of victories and defeats France remained France, England remained England and Germany remained Germany. Even the innumerable nationalities of the Austrian Empire and the Balkan peninsula—the Poles divided between three empires, never lost their national identity and sooner or later were bound to free themselves in a war of liberation. The Nazis are well aware of these facts and know the danger. They must be trusted and believed when they threaten annihilation of the subjugated. Lest they be doubted, they are doing it now. Nevertheless they still feel the need of moral justification for their action: Unless they exterminate their victims, the Germans are told, these victims will exterminate them. Consequently what they are doing is merely an act of self-preservation.

All They That Take the Sword . . .

Though the secret of the Nazi war machine is out of the bag, and although the material conditions for the victory of the United Nations is now clear, the cohesive power of Nazi morale and the degree of popular support which the Nazis enjoy in Germany is still dangerously underestimated.

A 1942 Gallup poll showed that 75 per cent of the American people believe that they are fighting only Hitlerism and not the German people. This idea has considerable bearing on post-war reconstruction and what is of even greater immediate importance it exercises a profound influence on American propaganda directed at Germany.

The British have a different opinion on the subject, since they experienced the action of the Nazis by the impersonal method of bombs falling from the sky. Seventy-five per cent of the British believe that they are fighting the German people and not only their government. The peoples under the Nazi yoke finally know, every one of them, that they are fighting all of Germany.

Joseph Stalin in his address to the Red Army on the twentieth anniversary of its creation said that Russia is fighting Hitlerism, but that the German people and the German state will remain. However, a few months later he told Germany that the crimes committed against the civilian population in Russia will not go unpunished.

The American people who have, as yet, suffered little from the war are most prone to fall victim to the comfortable idea that once Hitlerism is destroyed there will emerge from beneath its insufferable rule a German people unaffected in its basic qualities, ordinary folks, no better and no worse than the rest of the world, ready to work at the reconstruction of their country and perhaps grateful to the victors for having liberated them from the Nazi yoke.

At the same time there exists a widespread belief that Wilson's fourteen points contributed mightily to the undermining of the German war morale in the last war. (Wilson's promise of national self-determination hastened the disintegration of Austria, chequerboard of nationalities, and thus brought nearer the military defeat of Germany. It is to this fact that the error is due. The collapse of Germany and of Austria are confounded as one and the same.) It is this confusion which colors American broadcasts to Germany. Germany is told that the American people are not fighting the

German people but only their government. Hope of freedom and well-being is held out to them as an inducement to help in the overthrow of Hitler.

Even people who are convinced that the Treaty of Versailles was too mild and that a future treaty must make certain that the Germans are deprived of the means of rebuilding a war machine believe that by promising a "better" treaty now the German people can be induced to revolt. They admit that this is not quite honest, but in war one must not be too squeamish about the methods one uses to win through to victory, given the fact that every day of the war takes its toll in human lives, and misery. *C'est la guerre!*

But in order to wage psychological warfare on the enemy, the nature of his war morale must be fully understood. As far as the Nazis are concerned that offers little difficulty. The rank and file of the Nazis are sustained by the knowledge that the enemy is weakened by moral ideals and that he is therefore in no condition to visit retribution upon them in case he should be victorious. Hitler and his immediate collaborators may suffer severe punishment, but the rank and file are certain that they will escape. There is safety in numbers, and they number millions. Thus Nazi barbarism differs from primitive barbarism not in degree but in kind. It is the barbarism of a degraded civilization.

The primitive barbarian who exterminated the men, women, and children of the tribes which he conquered knew of no moral principle in his victims if, indeed, any was present. He fully expected to be treated with equal cruelty if perchance the battle were to turn against him. But the unrestrained fury of the Nazis is born of anticipated immunity in case of defeat. This knowledge confers a sense of security upon them which drives them wild with lust for loot, conquest, domination, and mass murder. This, too, is the essence of the Nazi conception of a *Herrenvolk*, a master of the whip and the executioner's ax. A savagery sustained by the knowledge that the enemy will be merciful if he should be victorious is new in the recorded history of mankind. Even the mythology of antiquity offers no analogy. As such it pertains of the fabulous, and is as inconceivable to peaceful people as was, in the days of the fall of France, the juggernaut which advanced over the fleeing Belgian population and drove them into the fire of their own armies.

If this is Nazi morale, what of the German people as a whole? Are they to-day uncorrupted by victories and brutalities perpetrated upon the conquered? Are they at least what they were in 1933, when some 60 per cent of the population were not for the Nazis? We can assume that a good part of the 40 per cent which did vote the Nazi ticket were not necessarily heart and soul with them, but feared the Communists more. Can we assume that they are at least no worse than they were then?

The American correspondents who returned to the United States six months after Pearl Harbor have reported that the civilian population in Germany is repeating parrot-like what the Nazi propaganda machine has blared over the loud-speakers since the Russians took the *Blitz* out of the *Krieg*—to wit, that the victors intend to annihilate the German people if Germany should lose the war. In the six years of hard gruelling labor which were imposed upon them before the outbreak of war, the German people manifested no sign of revolt. When the Nazis proclaimed to all the world that the pogroms were spontaneous expressions of the indignant German people, and that the victims of the German people were being taken by the humanitarian Nazis in protective custody, there was no protest from the people of Germany. Though they knew that the Nazis lied, smearing their good name in the world, though they knew that they had never hated Jews, Protestant parsons, and Catholic priests to the point of smashing their shop-windows and of accusing the leaders of the churches of dark vices and political treasons, they nevertheless allowed the Nazis to associate them in the moral responsibility for those crimes.

To-day, the German people are still willing to associate themselves without protest in the Nazi program of extermination.

While their victims are still disarmed, the people of Germany
beg them to suspend the judgment of Christ. They plead with
their victims not to draw the sword lest Germany perish.
The hypocrisy of the Nazi claim that they are annihilating
their victims only because these victims were planning to do
thus to Germany is also the hypocrisy of those who informed
the American correspondents that Nazi crimes are justified.

A Voice of Protest

Unless we win this war, Germans say, we will be an-
nihilated. Do they believe it? Have they a genuine premoni-
tion that the victorious United Nations will herd women and
children or even men into freight-cars in the dead of winter
and transport them to some barren region of the world without food or clothing to die en route or at the point of destination? Do they believe that German children will be put before
a firing squad and machine-gunned by the thousands as the
Nazis have done to the children of Yugoslavia?

Alex Dreier who left Germany a few days before Pearl Harbor provides evidence that they do not. He tells that he asked
his taxi-driver in Berlin what he thought of Hess' flight to
England. The taxi-driver turned round and laughed: "Mister,"
said he, "if this taxi had wings would I not fly there, too."
Hess himself, whatever his motive in flying to England, had
no expectation of being torn limb from limb; he was even
outraged to find that the British Government was not willing
to treat him as a plenipotentiary of the Reich, to be granted
extra-territorial rights, an Ambassador at large, as it were. At
the same time, according to Mr. Dreier, a doggerel was making the rounds of Berlin, something to the effect that a man
is called crazy by the Nazis when he flies away from trouble.

Is there any evidence that the war morale of the German people has been imperiled by misgivings about Nazi
bestiality perpetrated in the conquered countries? Do they
fear that the enemy, under the impact of Nazi fury, has lost
some of his propensity for humanitarian slosh and mayhap

after victory is won will do unto Germany as Germany has done unto them?

The Nazis are violating the most elementary principles of humanity and doing it with apparant relish, visiting death and destruction upon the conquered lands, leveling Rotterdam to the ground after Holland had surrendered, looting, mass-murdering, shooting hostages, and destroying the village of Lidice in Czechoslovakia in retaliation for the death of one hangman. They might commit their deeds in secrecy; instead they trumpet them without hesitation and without shame to the world, with the evident intention of binding the people of Germany ever closer to their own fate. Yet no protests are heard from the German people. There is no evidence of even a single courageous German voice having been raised against these cowardly outrages, unprecedented in the cruelest epoch of modern history and matched only by Japan.

That a protest could be voiced, if there were a genuine will to voice one, can be deduced from the secret radio station "Siegfried." There is a voice of protest. Up to the time when this voice was first heard, one could assume that the Nazis represent the very lowest level to which a perverted people can fall, in thought and action. By no means. Siegfried has gone them one better. The Nazis are not Nazi enough to his taste. He protests against Nazi inefficiency, in language so vile that its publication is impossible and in a German which surpasses in violence the violence of the Nazis. His radio station is powerful enough to be heard in the United States and he broadcasts twenty-four hours a day. He is also fully informed on every detail in the Nazi organization and instantly described the confusion caused in Cologne during the British mass air-raid owing to corruption in the Nazi police organization.

The protest of the German bishops published in full in the United States concerned itself exclusively with the violence done by the Nazis to German Christians of the Catholic faith. Thus not even these courageous bishops have raised their voice against the violence done to their brethren outside of Germany in the conquered lands. At the same time they extolled the heroism of the German soldiers, taking pride in the "many decorations" bestowed upon them and attributing their deeds of valor to their devotion to the fatherland, the Church, and love for the teaching of Christ.

Most astounding of all facts, passing strange: The concentration camps of Germany are filled with hundreds of thousands of prisoners. What of their families and friends? It has been argued that they are not rebelling because of the terrible punishment which would be visited upon them. The Gestapo practising vicarious justice would destroy not only the assassin, saboteur, or agitator, but all the members of his family unto the third generation and unto the third, fourth, or fifth removed cousin. But that is precisely what the Gestapo and the German armies are doing in the conquered countries, and the more they are doing it the more resistance they meet, everywhere except in Germany.

Before the Nazis seized power I met, in the house of a friend in Berlin, a woman in his employ who had lost her only son. He had been induced by his school friends to join the Storm Troopers of Captain Roehm. The Nazis in those days were engaged in hunting Communists. Wherever the opportunity arose they would break into meetings of the Communists in beer cellars or assembly halls, engage in fist fights, flash hunting-knives and exchange revolver shots. The woman told me that her boy participated in one such expedition, but after that he was sick with the sight of blood. Though he had received no wounds he lay in delirium for three weeks. He tried to withdraw from the party as soon as he had recovered. A few days after his "resignation" his friends came to her flat, charming, friendly, full of smiles and sympathy for her sensitive boy. He went out with them for a beer. Days later his mangled body was found in the Grunewald, the pine forest near Berlin. His face was completely disfigured and she was able to identify his body in the morgue only by his ring, which the assassins had overlooked. This happened under the Weimar Republic at least as frequently as a bootlegger was taken for a ride by his fellow-merchants during prohibition. Naturally, she gave the name and addresses of his friends to the police, but nothing happened. There were no arrests and no trials.

The woman assured me that she lived only for the day of revenge. She had decorated her room with a large picture of Hitler lest she forget. In her purse she carried the names and addresses of the boys who had been the friends of her son.

There must be uncounted numbers of such men and women in Germany. Sheeplike they let themselves be slaughtered by the Gestapo, and though the survivors live with bitterness and loathing in their hearts, there is no action. Yet that same nation goes to war with a ferocity and a self-sacrifice unsurpassed in the annals of history. Is there any other nation on earth that has shown at home such submissiveness to assassins decorated with the lying emblem of authority, and such courage on the battle-field against a foe chosen by their masters?

The behavior of German soldiers can be exemplary or brutal according to orders received.

When the French saw them well behaved and polite with the formality of the obedient robot they were astounded. Failing to recognize in them their invaders of old, they marveled: "But these Nazis, they are correct." The Germans were looting the country with faked currency, a technic employed in Germany by the Reichsbank under the Weimar Republic, and it took the French populace some time to find that out. When it was discovered, the Germans dropped all pretense and demanded collaboration. The conqueror at the point of the gun ordered that his job of looting be facilitated by the willing coöperation of the victim.

There being no evidence of any active opposition movement in Germany, not even any noticeable degree of direct action from individual enemies of the régime, the drawing of a sharp line between the people of Germany and the Fuehrer can be only of theoretical value.

Now as in the early days of the Nazi régime the opposition,

dissatisfaction, and grumbling, with few exceptions, is directed against the hardship which the totalitarian state imposes upon its subjects, but by no means against the plan of conquest, particularly since Goering promised that it would be easy and that no bombs would fall on Germany. The German armies have since passed through the first winter in Russia, one of the coldest in history, according to the Fuehrer. It was so cold, said Goering, that the flesh of one's hand stuck to the metal of the guns. The Germans were without sufficient warm clothing and often without food. Time and again the supply system broke down, leaving them exposed to the enemy without ammunition. There were Russians in front of them, Russians around them and Russians behind them. To be sure there must have been some mutinies. Goering begged the Germans not to believe wild rumors, but said that the Fuehrer in his goodness was forced to take stern measures to prevent disaster. These stern measures, when used on the conquered, invariably produce more revolts. But when used on Germans by the Fuehrer they find the German Army loyal in the spring and ready to start an offensive with the same devotion and self-sacrifice as of old.

After the last war, Hitler damned the Kaiser as a fool. He had lost the war because he had expended the lives of German soldiers in driblets over a period of four years. He, Hitler, would throw in all his forces at once, lose two million men in one go, but win the war, instead of losing four million over a long period of time, and lose the war. That was good strategy and humane to boot. In war it does not pay to be economical with money or lives. In Russia Hitler is following this principle and his army is taking it. A national army conscripted to the last man is identical with the nation, and the record does not argue for any division between Fuehrer and people. It would seem rather that the Nazis have told the truth with their slogan: One Volk, One Reich, One Fuehrer.

In Russia and Libya, the Germans have met their equals in fighting spirit and the intuition of the Fuehrer has misfired.

He has lost more than two million men in Russia and final victory is farther away than ever, since the declaration of war on the United States. At home the German people are being bombed worse than the English were in 1940–41, yet Germany is taking it. How is this to be explained except on the supposition that they are desiring a final victory with their whole heart and soul as ardently as the Nazis on the battle-field and are as determined to get it as the Fuehrer. No one who saw the German Army in action in 1914–18 and in this war can deny them their due. They are as devoted to conquest as their victims are devoted to the defense of their hearth and home.

Though their sufferings are great; though they have labored exhausting hours, for poor food; though they are treated little better than their enslaved "fellow-workers" imported into Germany from the conquered lands; though they have grumbled and complained; though the taking of Paris fell short in grandeur of anticipation; though the words of the Nazis are listened to with less enthusiasm than in the past—the promise of power which is held out to them tops anything that the Allies can offer as a price for revolt. The Nazis can promise to make each German a leader over ten of those slave people in Africa and Asia who will be allowed to live, because no revolt is feared from them and no corruptive influence. Germans will be set as leaders over hundreds and as leaders over thousands. Each German can look forward to command over subjugated people. The unskilled German laborer will be a foreman and the skilled a manager. Every German will be a functionary of the German state when Germany has conquered the world and will lord over the teaming millions of Africa and Asia. The greater the hardships imposed upon the people of Germany in the pursuit of this magnificent goal the better it steels their spirit. The anticipation of being able to take out on the conquered the kicks they have been receiving from their masters these many years, exercises an allure which the German finds utterly irresistible. Such a spirit does not bend, it can only be broken, as it was broken in 1918, by force of arms.

The Prodigal Son

It consequently serves no purpose when American propaganda, based on United Nations war aims attempts to offer the German people something better than the Germans hope the Nazis can give them. There is nothing better than freedom that Germany can be offered, freedom from fear and freedom from want. But if the Germans are victorious they will be free from fear and free from want, or that at least is what they are promised by the Nazis and they will have the glorious freedom to lord it over others to boot. It is peculiar to those who thirst for power that slavery itself is sweet, since it permits the slave to identify himself with his master, much as adolescent youth sees in the movie hero an image of himself. Whereas the freedom we offer is based upon reciprocity, and equality, supplemented by a fraternity, when all the present white heat of hatred, which the Nazis evoke wherever they have practised their new order, will be forgotten.

It serves no purpose to tell the German people that we are fighting only their government. As a matter of sober fact that is not true at present. As long as the German people fight for Hitlerism with a faith and a devotion which can hardly be surpassed, it *is* the German people the armies of the United Nations are fighting and not only their government. As long as the German people identify themselves with their government they are bound to see through the stratagem of those who would tell them differently in order to persuade them to abandon their Fuehrer. To tell them that they are better than the Nazis is to flatter them. "Flatter the varlet and he will stab you, stab him and he will love you."

I quote from one broadcast directed at Germany from the United States. Having discussed the crimes committed by the Nazis in the conquered countries, the propagandist has this to say: "Not all Germans probably know about the crimes committed by the Nazis in the conquered territory. Frequently enough the army command has tried to oppose the Nazis but has invariably been overruled. We here believe that these crimes are the work of the Nazis only. We here in America do not wish that feelings of hatred lead to injustices after the war." This is intended to act as a wedge between the German soldier and the Nazis. The flattery intended is obvious, silly and insincere. Its probable effect is to strengthen the German faith in the veracity of the German High Command's pronouncements, as distinct from Nazi lies.

It is as dangerous to underestimate the intelligence of the enemy as it is dangerous to underestimate his fighting spirit and the striking power of his weapons. It has happened that the propagandist goes so far, as to tell the German radio audience that the heart of the American people is filled with pity at the thought of what American flying fortresses are going to do to them, but the propagandist begs them to remember that it is all Hitler's fault. This propaganda line must sound like brazen hypocrisy, and not only to the German ear.

One script sent out regularly by the American propaganda service deals with the post-war world. Germany is informed that Americans are realizing more and more that America was at fault in withdrawing from European affairs after the last war. In future, however, this mistake will not be repeated. Once victory is won, America will not side-step her "duty" but will continue to take an active part in European affairs, and see to it that Europe is reconstructed properly; then all will be happier.

Listening to this particular script which crops up with variations at least once a week, one is reminded of the fable by La Fontaine, *The Pest Strikes the Animals:*

Not all died, but all were afflicted. The very turtle doves fled each other. There was no love, hence no joy. . . .

The animals concluded that heaven had sent them this dread punishment for their crimes and the Lion, king of his realm, urged each to confess so that the worst criminal might expiate. He sets the example by telling of his own misdeeds. He has devoured many sheep who had done him no harm and sometimes it so happened that he ate the shepherd to boot. These are his crimes; they are grievous, but let others speak after him. The fox immediately tells his majesty that he is really too good. It could hardly be a sin to destroy such stupid worthless breed as sheep are. On the contrary his majesty did them much honor by deigning to feast on them. As to the shepherds, who did they think they were, attributing to themselves a pretended ascendancy over the animals. No one dared to examine too closely the confessions of the other beasts of prey. To believe them they were all little saints. Finally the ass speaks up for a share in the guilt. And what was his crime? He recollects that once passing the meadow of a monastery, tempted by hunger, opportunity, the tender leaves, and he thinks also, some devil pushing him, he gobbled up a patch of grass the size of his tongue. If the truth were known he had no right to do that.

In the fable the beasts of prey fall upon him and tear him apart, but, resurrected he still goes on braying his *mea culpa* short-wave to Germany.

This script reveals the propagandist as oblivious to the fact that he is not talking to the late isolationists, but broadcasting to Germany. If the script were addressed to the conquered nations of Europe thinking of what might have been, if the United States had not withdrawn from Europe it might serve to give them courage and stamina. But addressed to Germany its effect in the conquered countries is appalling. It creates dismay and fear in the countries under the Nazi heel where German is understood. In Alsace, Luxembourg, Holland, Poland, and Czechoslovakia, people who hear this must conclude that the period of appeasement is not yet ended and that after the war they may have to face a reconstructed Germany, free to shape a policy of her own.

It tells the Germans who listen to foreign radio broadcasts at the risk of their lives that not they or their government are responsible for the present carnage, but the United States, because she refused to join the League of Nations, and because she failed to insist upon a better deal for Germany in 1918. It also tells them that in continuing to support Hitlerism without a protest Germans risk nothing at all. If Germany is victorious the German people will be masters like the

Nazis over the conquered people. If she loses, they will but have lost that which never did belong to them—dominion over others. It would be difficult to imagine a program better calculated to give aid and comfort to the enemy.

Germany is also being told that if she gets rid of Hitler and Hitlerism, soon she will receive better treatment, but if she persists in the error of her ways, she can expect no mercy. This belongs to the category of underestimating the intelligence of the enemy. The Germans know quite well that their enemies—at least their democratic enemies—are civilized in comparison with the Nazis (and this is an understatement). They also know, and do not have to be told, that if they overthrew the Nazi régime they would be treated like a prodigal son on his return home. Every nation on earth would slaughter a fatted calf. There would be feasting and rejoicing throughout the world. But what is a fatted calf in comparison with world domination? Of what use is the fairest treaty when defeat has to be swallowed first? Those who have basked in the glory of conquest can be offered no compensation that could begin to reconcile them to its loss.

That the overthrow of Hitler, in case all is lost, is on the minds of ambitious army officers few who know them can doubt. Such a course is held in reserve. When Hitler and the rest of the Nazi leadership will be constrained to acknowledge defeat some one will step forward, as Scheidemann and Ebert did in 1918 and demand a prize from the victor for having made a "revolution." But until then no promise of a golden future can have any other effect upon Germany except to sustain her war morale.

It is unwise to assume that the Germans do not know of the standards of international ethics to which democratic people adhered in the days of appeasement. On the contrary. Such respect for the rights of other nations which prevented annexation of the Rhineland by France, rendered the reparation payments, imposed upon Germany, profitable to German heavy industry, and forced a withdrawal of the French troops from the Ruhr were regarded by my German schoolmasters and classmates when I went to school in Germany, as proof of military weakness and decadence. Well aware of the good faith of people in England and America, the Weimar Republic constantly urged the victors to mitigate the rigors of Versailles in conformity with the principles of fair play and the outstretched hand to a beaten opponent.

The course followed up to now by American propaganda is simply a continuation "with other means" of the appeasement policy on which the Nazis waxed fat and powerful under the Weimar Republic until they were able to kick the democrats out without a fight. Since German war morale thrived on appeasement to what possible purpose is it being fed more of it now?

The effect of this kind of humanitarian propaganda upon the fighting spirit and the determination of the United Nations —themselves not yet under the Nazi heel—may be disastrous. People whose native hue of resolution is sickled o'er with the pale cast of thought can be no match for the totalitarian beast.

After the fall of Tobruk James Aldridge sent a despatch to the New York *Times* from Cairo describing the B.B.C. propaganda broadcasts and their effect upon the British soldiers away from the hell of war for a brief breathing spell. He wrote: "The average B.B.C. programs for the desert might sound fine in London, but it is an insult to the intelligence of the men who are looking death in the face, out in the worst country on earth." The soldier on leave lacks good recreation, but worse than this lack his morale receives no new stimulus. The correspondent tells that in one camp established for soldiers on leave outside of a town, he saw an open-air movie: "The picture I saw was a bad Pacifist picture from the United States. It was about the last war. The picture ended with a woman opening a letter and her soldier husband's identity disk dropping out of it. It was all to show the hopelessness of war; the audience was to move to the front next day."

I do not wish for a moment to suggest that Germany be offered the sword instead of honeyed words. Where the sun shining warmly down upon the traveling warrior fails to make him shed his armor, the storm will be equally ineffective. It would do no good to tell Germany that the victors mean to exterminate every man, woman and child in Germany and scorch the earth over them, unless they rise in revolt against the Nazis this very instant. Because unfortunately the threat of capital punishment does not work as a deterrent on the criminal or on the accessory after the fact. It will neither stop the Nazis nor will it induce the German people to put a stop to them. In the time of Queen Elizabeth pickpockets were hung for stealing as little as a shilling, but their colleagues plied their trade unperturbed among the dense crowds watching the hangings. Human imagination does not reach far enough to permit a man to visualize his own extermination. Both the British and the Germans are standing up well under the merciless bombings. It is said that unless a bomb carries your name on it, it will do you no harm.

The Polish and Czechoslovakian governments in exile have proposed that the Nazis be brought to trial after the war, and that those proven guilty of murder be convicted and executed. This proposal recalls a similar one of the last war. The Kaiser was to be hung and the responsible army officers brought to trial. It does not seem likely that the idea will prove more durable after this war. Every Nazi identifies himself with the army and the German government. If brought to trial he will plead that he has merely carried out the orders given, the way a soldier obeys his commanding officers. The technical difficulties of such a trial alone would render the idea fantastic as soon as peace is reëstablished.

The cases would run into the hundreds of thousands not to say millions. Courts would have to be set up on the model of chain stores throughout Europe. The firing squads would be kept busy day and night to carry out the judgment against all those who, according to law, deserve capital punishment, nor would there be prisons enough to take care of the rest.

Such a bloodbath would revolt the conscience of the world after the end of this present slaughter. It could be carried out

only by an internal revolution in Germany itself. Revolutionary tribunals have been very efficient at this kind of work and
only in civil war are passions strong enough to deal in this
fashion with those who are willing to surrender. But there will
be no civil war in Germany.

It is not impossible that the Nazis have succeeded in rendering the peaceful nations of Europe such implacable enemies that they will come and seek them out in Germany after
the war. But at this distance it is difficult to conceive of such
lasting hatred, and it can be taken for granted that neither
the Nazis nor the civilian population in Germany are anticipating any such future for themselves. By this time the bombing of non-military objectives in enemy lands, the shooting of
hostages, the leveling of villages, etc., is routine matter to
them, as was the sinking without trace of neutral merchant
ships in the last war. They would be most astounded to learn
that such acts are sincerely regarded as atrocities by their
victims. Thus they feel secure in their innocence and interpret
the indignation of the propagandist as sheer hypocrisy, and the
promise of a trial as proof that he does not mean what he says.

Sufficient Unto the Day . . .

It is imperative that at this time as much care be given to
an intelligent homogeneous propaganda program to be sent to
Germany as goes into the construction of a flying fortress, for
the lives of soldiers, sailors, and flyers of the United Nations
may well depend upon it. The propaganda weapon intelli-
gently used may shorten the war by undermining the morale
of Germany, while at present it tends to lengthen the war by
sustaining her morale. American propaganda is still in the
stage in which the British were when they threw leaflets to
Germans. The wits claimed at the time that the British were
doing that only reluctantly. They were afraid that an unopened
package might fall down and hurt some one.

The present confusion is due to the fact that the propaganda
weapon is conceived of as inevitably and inextricably linked to

war aims. The war aims of the United Nations to date are
rather vague and nebulous. They are so of necessity because
of possible divergencies of interests in the post-war world.
As long as the war aims are in process of evolution and
clarification it is impossible to use them authoritatively as a
clear-cut and forthright offer to the vanquished, even if the
psychology of the foe were more accessible to reason.

The stages by which victory can be won are clearly defined.
In point of time the all-out offensive must wait on the production of weapons and the training of the armies. Use of the
propaganda weapon likewise precedes the defeat of the
enemy and should be designed to undermine his morale, to
soften him up for the final blow. First things must come first.
There must be the strictest economy of timing. We have not
yet shot the bear and can not sell his skin. The resounding defeat of Germany is yet to come. Any discussion of peace terms
with her people, any pledge of the victors to adhere to humanitarian principles in the treatment of a vanquished Germany must wait upon victory. And it is this irreducible obstacle
which alone should be allowed to sharpen the propaganda
weapon.

Sufficient unto the day are the evils thereof. Divorcing
the propaganda weapon from post-war aims opens a perfectly good alternative to the Allies. It can be taken for granted
that Germany will collapse within twenty-four hours after it
has dawned upon the German people and leaders that they
can not win. In this one respect the aggressor is at a disadvantage. The victim of aggression fights to the end, because
right and justice are clearly on his side and because he knows
that life is not worth living under the yoke of the conqueror.
The unprecedented Nazi terror in the conquered countries
has served only to consolidate the victims amongst themselves.
The bitterest political enemies of yesterday have become one
and indivisible. Catholics and reactionaries in France have
become reconciled with the old Communist cells which
came in handy as a nucleus of organized resistance to the
German occupation. The French Communists themselves, but

yesterday bent upon using their cells for the purpose of undermining the war effort, are now truly revolutionary in spirit. No longer the willing tools of sterile Moscow propaganda, they have developed a spirit and ingenuity of their own which makes them one with the revolutionary spirit of France.

But while those who have justice on their side can not be broken short of total extermination, the aggressor has no staying power after he has become convinced that he can not reach his goal. The story of the *Bismarck* as told in *Harper's Magazine* is a faithful forecast of what will happen to German war morale when the armies of the United Nations will be ready for the kill. As announced in advance by the German propaganda service, the battleship *Bismarck* had sunk the *Hood*, largest British battle-cruiser afloat. After such a feat British seamen would have cheered, a round of rum would have been issued to the men and congratulations would have arrived from the Admiralty for a job well done.

On *Bismarck* there was hysterical elation. "The top deck, empty during the action, was filled with officers and men singing and embracing each other." There was "a triumphant and fiery speech" by Admiral Luetjens to the crew. "An exultant message and decorations arrived from Hitler . . . over the ether." However, "the exultant mood of victory can not be maintained indefinitely, there is an inevitable reaction. With the German crew it came about the second day after the sinking of the *Hood*. They realized that they were being hunted. When the *Bismarck* was trapped misgivings among the crew gave way to depression as hysterical as the elation had been." Instead of turning back after the victory Admiral Luetjens had fallen victim to a *crise de grandeur*. Against the advice of more sober officers he had collected the crew and told them that he was leading them on to further victories. The *Bismarck* was now alone, the *Prince Eugen* having turned back. British torpedo planes appeared and launched their missiles.

When the *Bismarck* was crippled, Luetjens "sent a message to Hitler: 'We shall fight to the last shell. Long live the Fuehrer, the Chief of the Fleet'; after that he cracked badly. He was heard through his door, shouting hysterically: 'Do what you like, I am through.'"

Though the *Bismarck* went on firing to the end, the morale of the crew had cracked as badly as Luetjens'. In the end there was panic. Those rescued showed, days after they had rested, the effect of moral shock. They had believed that they were invincible. Now their universe was shattered.

This story as told in full by Edwin Muller should be required reading for all script writers of the short-wave broadcasts beamed at Germany.

In propaganda silence is often worth its weight in bombs. Winston Churchill's speech warning Germany against the use of gas was magnificent both for what he did not say when addressing himself to Germany as well as for what he did say. He invited the civilian population to make off to the fields if they want to escape bombing, "and watch the home fires burning." He did not offer to reconstruct the homes for them after the war. It is to be hoped that following the Churchill precedent all references to a post-war Europe be rigidly banned from American short-wave broadcasts beamed at Germany. They are giving as much aid and comfort to the enemy as if we were broadcasting the movement of our merchant ships, our troops, and our warships to the German submarines in the Atlantic Ocean. The entire propaganda barrage must be directed for the here and now and not for some nebulous hereafter. This is but common sense. America is at war: out to destroy the enemy in a war which Hitler has declared. Extermination and annihilation is going on now: it can only be stopped by victory for the Allies, and it is the duty of the propaganda weapon to herald this advent in advance: blow the trumpet to help batter down the walls of Jericho.

To repeat: *Any propaganda, to be effective, must meet with the predisposition in the listener to believe what he is being told. He must react instantly with the feeling that the propagandist is merely putting into words what he himself has hoped or feared all along.* In spite of Nazi propaganda to the contrary the legend of the productive capacity of the United States is still very much alive in Germany. America is the land *"der unbegrenzten Moeglichkeiten"* (of unlimited possibilities). No secret should be made of the quantity of weapons the United States is producing. It could hardly stimulate the enemy to greater effort since he is doing his utmost anyhow. His spy system is very efficient. The German Government, it can be taken for granted, knows exactly what is being produced here better than the American people. But the rank and file in the army and in civilian life in Germany do not know. It would benefit us if they should be informed.

That would be the opening wedge through which the German radio audience can be weaned away from the disposition to believe in a Nazi victory, but it is only the thin end of the wedge. It is being used but the thick end is yet to follow. It must be brought home to Germany that the American people are no Caspar Milquetoasts, but that by heaven, they are fighting mad. The Yanks are coming and millions strong, every one of them a Paul Bunyan. Germany has declared war on the United States of America: woe to the aggressor.

Some of that strategy is being used, but *c'est le ton qui fait la musique.* It can not be overemphasized that it fails to impress the German listener as long as it is richly flavored with bleeding-heart humanitarianism. Such appeals to the good sense and heart of Germany are as effective as the preaching of purity in a red-light district. Propaganda as a weapon used by free men excludes the lie, nor is there the faintest reason why recourse should be taken to it. The truth is a formidable weapon against the wicked, provided it is used like cold steel aimed at the heart—as Winston Churchill uses it—not like a bundle of hay to attract a donkey. The slightest deviation from the swift and the merciless, blunts or breaks the weapon as if it were used to cut stone.

As soon as it is realized that propaganda directed at Germany does not have to be linked up with post-war aims a wide variety of subject matter is provided generously day by day by the Nazis themselves. Rex Stout is demonstrating this every Sunday in a radio program which would be most effective if it were sent to Germany. The Nazis are not nearly as great in propaganda as they claim to be. They have benefited for long by being the only ones in the field. Up to the outbreak of war it was regarded as bad form to tell them how stupid and disastrous was their game. Diplomacy forbade it. Nazi "statesmen," with the mentality of barkers at a fair, were treated to the ceremonial prevalent in diplomatic circles. The whole array of gangsters, paperhangers, and champagne salesmen, with their criminal mentality, were treated like princes by a world regarded by Germans with envy for its externals; everything that could be done was done to confirm to the Germans their judgment that they were governed by a great Fuehrer, the first since Bismarck—who was a genius in politics—that mysterious science which the Germans have always regretted they do not understand.

References to war aims in broadcasts beamed at Germany can have a beneficial effect only if it is made crystal clear to Germany that our only vital concern in the post-war world is the well-being of the people against whom aggression has been committed and not the people of the aggressor nations.

For twenty years and more Germany has held the center of the world stage. Upon her has been lavished all the care of every one in the world who was concerned with the building of a just and a durable peace. For her sake France was isolated by the United States and by Britain at Versailles and after. All that could have been done by any power other than by the German people themselves to reconcile Germany to the well-deserved defeat of 1918 was done. With the result that she gave herself a Hitler and started the same process all over again.

There is not the slightest reason in the world why she should not be told now that the last to be considered in the coming peace will be Germany. All the victim nations will be put back upon their feet; all the hungry and undernourished children of Norway, Denmark, Belgium, Holland, France, Yugoslavia, Greece, Poland, Luxembourg, and Russia will be nursed back to health; the economic life of these nations, their cooperatives, their industries, and their agriculture will be reconstructed; and hospitals will be provided for all the millons of prisoners and enslaved workers who are being starved in the labor camps of Germany. If Germany wants to regain prosperity she will have to make the effort to dig for treasure in her own vineyard. We shall see to it for the sake of Germany's neighbors, and for their sake alone, that she safeguards the physical and mental health of her population. This would be a broadcast worth sending to Germany every day, so that the conquered peoples under the Nazi yoke may know that there is no aid and comfort for the enemy being prepared in the United States of America. It is only the peaceful peoples who have a claim upon the charity of the civilized world. They must have the security and the assurance *now* that they will not once again be delivered to an enemy reconstructed with the capital of the western world, who paid back the way Germany repaid.

Beyond that, civilized men can not go in words, and it is not likely that they will go that far in deed. To be sure, the German armies have now invaded Belgium and France for the second time in twenty-five years. One can not safely assume that the population of these countries will let them go home in peace. Poland and parts of Russia in turn are likewise experiencing their second German invasion in one generation. In Norway and the other countries, which are having German occupation for the first time, the Nazis have done their level best to make up for the omissions of the Kaiser. The allied governments may once again grant Germany an armistice while her troops are yet on foreign soil, but the people of the conquered countries will not. The Belgians are said to have sworn each other their sacred honor that no German will get back to the fatherland alive, if they can help it. However, such action would still be part of the war. The enemy within your gate can not expect or demand that you let him depart in peace.

The drawing up of a blue-print for a post-war world does not belong to the duty of the historian any more than the conduct of the war. But all history is written with the future in mind and since the past projects itself into the future an essay at a forecast may be made.

16

What of the Future?

THE victors of the last war can say with the Common Prayer Book: "We have left undone those things which we ought to have done and we have done those things which we ought not to have done."

While the democratic governments exercised totalitarian powers during the last war, they intervened in the Russian Revolution, contributing in no small measure to stem the tide of expanding liberty in Russia. In aiding the Russian advocates of dictatorship to reverse the trend of the revolution they helped to set totalitarianism on its triumphal march through Europe. That was doing those things which it would have been better to have left undone.

In 1918, during the war of intervention, the Russian poet Alexander Blok, famous for his song: "The Twelve" in which he celebrated the revolution, also sent this warning to the western world:

> Yea Russia is a Sphinx, exulting, grieving,
> And sweating blood, she cannot sate
> Her eyes that gaze and gaze and gaze
> At you with stone-lipped love for you, and hate.
> . . . .
> Go all of you, to Ural fastnesses.
> We clear the ground for the appalling scenes
> Of war between the savage Mongol hordes
> And pitiless science with its massed machines.
>
> But we, we shall no longer be your shield.
> But, careless of the battle-cries,

Will watch the deadly duel seethe,
Aloof, with indurate and narrow eyes.

We will not move when the ferocious Hun
Despoils the corpse and leaves it bare,
Burns towns, herds cattle in the church,
And smell of white flesh roasting fills the air.*

Let no one say that prophets are to be found only in the old testament. Alexander Blok himself fell victim to the Allied intervention and the counter-revolution in Russia. He died in 1921 at the age of forty-one.

The democracies paid the price for their intervention in Russia when Joseph Stalin concluded his non-aggression pact with Hitler in 1939, and touched off the present world war. It is to be hoped that the price has been paid in full. Though Russia watched "aloof with indurate and narrow eyes" she, too, was finally attacked by the ferocious Hun. Inescapably her destiny is linked to that of the western world. The Russian people are now fighting on the side of the democracies against the common enemy. There is an unhoped-for opportunity now to make amends for the sins of the past. The all-out aid now being given to Russia by the democracies, the eventual opening of a second front, the present comradeship of arms against the common enemy must establish a bond firm enough to outlast this war.

A bond which must convince the Russian people, that after victory is won they may compel a switch-over from war production to peace production in Russia, without fear of thus laying themselves open to foreign attack. If all the totalitarian states surrounding Russia in the west and the east are destroyed, the Russian people, after nearly a quarter of a century of untold sacrifices, will insist upon the way of life for which the Revolution was fought. To-day the people of Russia are the army of Russia. If it returns victorious from this war, it will constitute a force which even a totalitarian régime may not be able to suppress. There may be a burst of new

* Translation by Babette Deutsch and Avrahm Yarmolinsky.

freedom. The hostility of the western world throughout the years between the wars gave the Russian régime an excuse for the deprivations which its totalitarian armament plans imposed upon peasant and workingmen alike. Even then the danger of foreign attack was not judged great enough by the people to make them willing and enthusiastic slaves. At no time were they enamored of foreign conquests. The Communist dictatorship has never held out as an inducement to the Russian people the glory of conquests abroad, of loot and pillage in foreign lands. Such a promise would have fallen on deaf ears, striking no responsive chord in their hearts. The Russian rulers have never offered to the people of Russia lack of *Lebensraum* as an explanation for the poverty and want which they had to endure. Such an argument would have been given no credence in Russia. If the Russians endured their privations for so long they had the memory of the war of intervention when, like England after the fall of France, they fought alone, and for three years, against the entire world which had united against their Revolution.

No effort should be spared to-day, before this war ends, to get the message of the western world to the people of Russia, that after victory is won the United Nations can count upon the resolution of the democratic peoples to prevent another attack upon any nation in the world from any quarter whatsoever.

Much is at stake. If Russia can not find the courage to give herself a free and productive economy after victory is won, a return to total peace production in the industry of the rest of the world will be impossible. No nation will dare to fall behind in the technic and in the economy of war. A new rivalry of arms production may develop and thus remove the basis for any effort at the attainment of freedom from want throughout the world.

Dogmatically stated the entire world has to choose between world-wide total war production or world-wide total peace production. With the swift and irresistible progress in industry and invention business as usual and preparation for total war can no longer be carried on side by side. Thus freedom from fear must precede, in point of time, the attainment of freedom from want.

Fortunately the people of Russia can fall back upon the resources and the spirit of the Revolution. All history shows that a revolution of such depth and intensity as the Russian Revolution can never be wholly suppressed by subsequent reactions, however violent and ruthless. It lives on even in the institutions of the totalitarian state. The framework of the Soviets has been preserved, and, before this war the government of Russia felt impelled to promise a democratic constitution. Though the constitution remained on paper, a basis for popular demands of free elections in the Soviets has been provided. The history of the Russian people's opposition to totalitarianism; the beneficial effect of victory after so great a fight, as they are now waging against the mightiest army in the world, which they have proved to be not invincible; the sense of security which such a victory may give them justifies optimism for the future of internal liberty in Russia.

Future Frontiers

There can not be any faith in the foreign policy of the present Russian régime after the war. To be sure there is not the slightest reason to doubt that the Russian Government will keep its pledge to fight to the end and that it will never consent to a separate peace with Germany. But the people of the western world who have set up checks and balances to the power of their own elected governments—checks and balances the operations of which are jealously watched because no man can be trusted with unrestricted power—can not be expected to trust unreservedly a foreign government which is free from all popular control.

The Russian Government has asked the United Nations to give their consent to the reëstablishment of the pre-1914 Russian frontiers on the ground that these frontiers are vital to Russia for strategic reasons.

That is not a good argument. What is sauce to the goose is sauce to the gander. If Russia, covering one-sixth of this earth, must have Lithuania, Latvia, Esthonia, and part of Finland for her defense, what of these diminutive countries themselves or even of any other country in the world? Should not Luxembourg have the right to parts of France and Germany for strategic reasons? There would be a much better reason to give to Finland part of Russia so that she may be enabled to defend herself. Lithuania should have Poland, and so on.

The world which will emerge from this war will have shrunk to the size of a country no bigger than Australia. The landscapes of the two warring camps are dotted with airplane factories and airdromes. All means of communication and transport have received a maximum of development under the impetus of war. After the war the two systems developed separately in the two warring camps will merge and the obstacle of space in war or peace will have been radically reduced. The evolution of a new and swifter world-wide system of transport and communication is a potential force for good as much as for evil, for peace as much as for war. Nor will the development stop when peace comes.

Utilization of the airplane for transport and exchange of merchandise will receive a new impetus from the opening up of markets now closed to the trade of the world by enemy occupation and blockade. The war potential of all industrialized countries will continue to expand in time of peace. Every industrialized country will soon be potentially able to realize Major de Seversky's blue-print of an air force to span the globe, with a radius great enough to reach any point from its base and able to carry a bomb load large enough to wipe out any industrial center in a surprise attack.

The menace of such an air force, in possession of an aggressor nation, to the security of all countries is so great that it is slightly unrealistic to insist upon "strategic" frontiers. For protection the sky will be literally the limit.

In such a world the only possible protection against war is the possession of peaceful neighbors, and in the post-war world every one will be the neighbor of every one else. The only possible guarantee of peaceful intentions which the nations of this world can give to each other remains their internal organization, the economic and social liberty of their members. Only the free are non-aggressive and non-invasive.

Failure of recognizing this fact is the main reason why the victors of the last war left undone what they ought to have done. They intervened against the Russian effort of broadening the scope of internal liberty, but they failed to intervene when the state in Italy, Japan, and Germany wiped out even that relative liberty which the people of these countries enjoyed. And they failed to intervene when these states set out to destroy liberty abroad.

In the years between the wars, the democratic governments, members of the League of Nations, and the United States remained faithful to the principles of self-determination for all nations proclaimed by President Wilson in the fourteen points. Adherence to this principle must be regarded as the main cause which rendered the democracies defenseless against the propaganda of the totalitarian state before it was armed, against the threat of war by Germany when her armaments had progressed far enough, and against the German attack when it came. Respect for the rights of Germans and Japanese to renounce their liberty and to give themselves the form of government they chose made any counterpropaganda and any counteraction impossible. It prevented the democracies from parrying the threat of war, forcing them on the defensive materially and ideologically.

Hitler's remilitarization of the Rhineland was justified by the appeasers and by the pacifists on the principle that he was merely exercising the sovereign rights of the German people over their own territory. When Austria was threatened, the democracies could not have established bases in Austria for their air forces even if they had disposed of any before Germany marched in. Such a precaution, which to-day appears elementary, could not have been undertaken even with the consent of Austria, because it would have been denounced as an act of aggression by Germany. Czechoslovakia was accused of having built air bases for the Russian air force, and she had to defend herself against so horrible an accusation. It was pleaded for Germany that the Sudetens had a right to national self-determination and incorporation in the Reich. When Poland was being threatened it was still argued that Danzig, being a German city, should not be denied the right to rejoin the Reich. It mattered not that Danzig was governed by Nazis, in any case, appointed by Hitler. It mattered not that the Sudetens enjoyed full national rights in Czechoslovakia, and individual rights which they were bound to lose under Nazi rule, the principle of national self-determination was given precedence over the rights of the individual.

The peaceful nations and the League granted Germany the time to give herself an army powerful enough to conquer the world, an army which was bound to attack as soon as its equipment was ready. It was not perceived that the totalitarian state can perform no other function than the total production of armaments, and that no nation could meet the challenge without vesting totalitarian power over production and distribution in its own government.

The enemy is the totalitarian state. The nation, or people, who set up such a state, fall subject to it, or sustain it after it has been set up, commit a clear act of aggression against the liberty of the world. To wait, as the League of Nations was bound to wait, until the armies of a totalitarian state crossed the first neighbor's frontier, was to invite disaster.

Nevertheless Point Three of the Atlantic Charter reads as follows: "They (the United Nations) respect the right of all peoples to choose the form of government under which they will live; and they wish to see sovereign rights and self-government restored to those who have been forcibly deprived of them."

In view of the probable state of mind of the Germans and the Japanese after a crushing defeat is administered to them, it is imperative that the meaning of Point Three be clarified before the end of the war.

It can be taken for granted that the vanquished nations will interpret this point to mean that the victors are pledged not to intervene if at a time of their own choosing they renounce the elementary human rights to life, liberty, and the pursuit of happiness of their individual members and give themselves once again a totalitarian state. If this should be also the meaning of this point in the eyes of the victor nations it is not difficult to predict that once again the peace will be lost and that the sacrifice of life and fortune will have been made in vain. Our children will grow up to find that we, too, tried and failed and with the continuous progress in industry and invention they may not have to wait twenty years for the next global war. And that war will take place on a much smaller planet. The entire civilized world will suffer the fate of France, in that war and there will be no western hemisphere, no last refuge of liberty, which will be granted the time to prepare a counteroffensive.

If to-day we can not be certain that a victorious Russia, free from anxiety for her security, will give herself a peace economy, it would be folly to presume that a defeated Germany or a defeated Japan will of their own volition renounce for ever the dream of world conquest. The wolf cubs are more likely to grow into perfect wolves, watching carefully until the shepherds have left their huts.

Cervantes on Germany

The historian who writes of the present can not escape the charge of personal bias; much less can one hope to escape that charge when attempting a forecast of the future. It is, therefore, necessary to state the facts of one's own personal feelings with regard to Japanese and Germans. I can be objective about the Japanese because I have no knowledge whatever about them that does not come from books and newspaper articles. The only Japanese I have ever known is the painter Fujita, a delightful companion and a source of the most entertaining anecdotes for the entire Montparnasse and

Latin Quarter in Paris. But objectivity born of ignorance is a very poor variety of that finest of all attributes in the historian. What I read about Japan reminds me most vividly of my school days in Germany. Though the bitterness of the German mind was due to defeat and although the Japanese have not yet been defeated, the similarities between the two mentalities are striking indeed. Apparently the Japanese hate the western world for the same reason the Germans hate the west. It frustrates their desire for power and conquest.

I left Germany in 1924 as soon as my school days were over without any hatred for the country or its people. Although all my classmates belonged to the Nazi youth organization before the occupation of the Ruhr and before the inflation, I believed them to be foolish rather than vicious. Nor am I aware of any prejudice now. Our little boy, born in the United States, was named after John Peter Altgeld, governor of Illinois at the turn of the last century, an American born in Germany who sacrificed his office and his career for the sake of justice.

That Germany has given birth to one Altgeld, if no other man of courage and devotion to the common good, should be proof sufficient that ultimately the enemy is the totalitarian state and not a race or a people. If one were to despair for ever of salvaging the people of Germany one must at the same time abandon hope for the future of the human race. But ultimately we are all dead and the fact that the descendants of German immigrants in the United States in the environment of the new world have given to this country men of courage does not create a new environment in Germany, where the conditions for an emancipation of the German spirit are absent.

What the desire for power and for a still better reason, the possession of power, does to character is best told by the great writers of imaginative literature.

The universality of their appeal, the immortality of their work is the best test of the veracity of creative writers.

Cervantes, for instance, has a treatise on power interspersed in his *Don Quixote.*

Hitler, seeking to spread evil with the same intensity of faith which inspired Don Quixote to attempt the revival of the noble traditions of knighthood is the very antipode of Cervantes' hero; but he found in the German people his Sancho Panza. Don Quixote induced Sancho to join in the crusade by promising him the governorship of an island. Now Sancho was a realistic fellow totally devoid of any romantic impulse to fight for lost causes. He knew his master to be mad. Unlike Don Quixote he never mistook a windmill for a giant, a herd of sheep for a hostile army, or a procession of priests for a gang of sorcerers and perjured rascals. But he wanted to become governor of an island. That promise stirred his imagination. It was the only notion of his master which he took seriously.

And his wife pleaded in vain that he stay home and tend to his children and his farm, assuring him that he could live without being a governor: "The devil take all the governments of this world," said she, "You came from the belly of your mother without government, you have lived to this day without government, and when it pleases God you will be carried to your final resting place without the aid of government. There are so many people in this world who live without government and for all that they do not tire of life and are looked upon as human beings."

Sancho, like the German people, received no wages from his master and suffered more rough treatment from enemies Don Quixote made at every turn, than did his master himself. But through all his trials and tribulations, through all the beatings he got and the hunger and the thirst he suffered, Sancho was sustained by the promise of power made to him by a man who called nothing his own except an old nag, a helmet from the basin of a barber, and a mad desire to set the world aright.

Finally, a Spanish Grandee, bored with his wealth and the ceremony of his court, found Don Quixote highly entertaining and made Sancho governor of a city as a practical joke and a source of merriment to his Duchess and his court.

Governor Sancho was attended by courtiers, political, military, and medical advisers who were instructed to make his life miserable with endless rules and regulations. They performed their task so well that Sancho handed in his resignation, finding the job of ruling more arduous than serving his master. But, says Cervantes: "Sancho, though he hated his job of governor, nevertheless wanted to regain his commandment to see himself obeyed. The exercise of authority invariably produces this evil result, even when the authority was only a sham and a joke."

To compare the German people with Sancho is the most charitable view one may take of them. Though Sancho thought the windmills useful, while his master saw in them instruments used to squeeze taxes out of the peasants, at least Sancho knew that there was no harm in Don Quixote.

Every German soldier has exercised command in the conquered countries. If they did not all rise to be corporal as Hitler did in the last war, they have all commandeered the goods of their neighbors with fake currency, and every one of them, like Sancho, carries the promise of rulership over an island in his knapsack. The poison which is now in their blood stream is likely to be far more virulent than it was in 1918.

The best conceived peace treaty, after such a glorious expectation, must taste like the bitter bread of charity and be as humiliating to boot.

Those who are diseased with alcoholism can be deprived of the bottle but that does not stop their craving. Prohibitions written into the treaty against rearmament, pledges signed by the diseased, a Volstead act on a world wide scale will avail nothing against the German craving for power. There are men who can carry their alcohol like gentlemen, but there are also kindly and generous men who go berserk when they are drunk, and knowing it, yet find it impossible to abstain. Power is a far headier liquor than alcohol, and neither Germans nor the Japanese are able to carry it.

Germany and Japan's easy conquests have brought global domination within the reach of their governments and of their people. Both nations have shown in their past that they can not learn to cultivate their own vineyards. It will be utterly useless to conclude any treaty with the governments they may give themselves after defeat. These governments will have no solid support from the nation, their pledges and their word will be of no greater value than the pledges of Hitler. It would be criminal foolhardiness to trust that, after defeat, Germany and Japan will automatically have acquired the ability to husband their own resources, to impose upon themselves a severe priority rule in favor of a consumer-goods industry. The terrifying deficiency in constructive ability of the German people has been manifested to the outside world throughout the last twenty-five years. The Weimar Republic, devoid of totalitarian powers, appeared weak to the German people because it could threaten no one. Under its liberal institutions the Germans were unable or unwilling to give themselves a workable economy. And their reactionaries were perfectly right in suspecting that the Allies were supporting German democracy merely because it kept Germany militarily impotent.

Under Hitler those who were thoroughly disappointed and disillusioned by his ruthless régime explained freely to non-German friends that they could not overthrow him because there would be nothing to take his place. They were afraid that there would be a vacuum. This ludicrous fear of a lawless vacuum which, compared with Nazi rule would have been a blessing, is the most striking manifestation of the deficiency of the German mind. A people of eighty millions trained in all sorts of industrial, agricultural, and commercial skills, inhabiting a territory rich enough in resources to permit the construction of the most powerful war machine in the world were afraid of a vacuum if the cancer which had festered in their body politic were cut out. Clearly the vacuum is in their minds.

And equally clearly that vacuum can not be filled by the outside world. Defeat is no cure for such a deficiency. Defeat will rob them of the prey with which they tried to fill their vacuum, and leave them emptier and more embittered than they were after 1918. It is, therefore, an illusion to assume that defeat will liberate the people of Germany or Japan. Such a result may be hoped for only from the Italians, and even in their case it is by no means certain that they will greet the victorious allies as liberators.

Captives whose bodies are enslaved but whose minds are free, the French, the Belgians, the Dutch, the Danes, and the Norwegians, can be liberated by force, but those whose minds are enslaved can not be freed. If victory is looked forward to as the end of war, this global war will have been fought in vain, and the post-war world will once again furnish an object lesson of the futility of war as a reform movement.

If the aggressor nations can not be liberated from their own deficiencies they can and must be prevented from trying once again to establish their domination over others. That can be done, effectively, only if the structure of the German state is destroyed. The Weimar Republic promised a radical land reform to the peasantry of Germany and failed to keep the promise. Hitler gained their votes by promising the expropriation of the Junkers and naturally failed likewise to keep that promise. The victorious United Nations can bring home to the Junkers the knowledge that aggression does not pay only by expropriating them and by giving title to the land to the peasantry.

Franz Oppenheimer writes that "the agricultural population of Germany, including farm laborers and their families, amounts to seventeen million; so that, assuming five persons to a family and an equal division of the farmlands, each family would have twenty-five acres." Twenty-five acres of the poorest land to the family were enough in the time of the migration of the barbarians "to feed and fatten into giants the immense families of these child-producing Germans." Not so long ago Joseph Chamberlain campaigned in England for three acres and a cow to each British farmer as an ideal which he offered to fulfil once he was elected. He never did, of course, but the land in Germany is not poorer than in England. It can be seen, therefore, that there is plenty of *Lebensraum* in Germany or would be if the peasantry were not cut off from access to the land.

Division of the land among the peasantry would create for the victors at least one class inside Germany which would have reason to be grateful for the defeat. It would, of course, have been a thousand times preferable if the Germans could have freed themselves, but since their enslavement to the Junkers is one of the primary causes for their pugnacity and brutality in war, the impulse for reform must come from without.

The same lesson can be brought home by the expropriation of all German industrialists without compensation. Furthermore there must be a summary dismissal of all school-teachers, and all civil servants, whether Nazi appointed or inherited from the Weimar régime whether they are known to be Nazis or not.

There need be no anxiety for the economic future of the individuals belonging to these classes. They can learn some useful trade like the Russian aristocrats who fled to France after the revolution. These did very well as taxi-drivers, cooks, waiters, and dressmakers. It would be the better part of wisdom to demand no indemnities from Germany for the havoc which she has wrought. The temptation to do this after the experience of the last peace will not be great. It is common experience that it is impossible to get payments from those who are unwilling to pay. The victors acting as judge in their own cause would be wise to decide that the two contestants should each carry their own costs. Though right and justice were clearly on our side, the loser has nothing with which to pay, having exhausted his resources in the trial. No one, after the experience of the last peace should be tempted to put Germany back upon her feet so that she may grow powerful enough to try the case again. Once again Germany would look for aid from abroad to enable her to pay, and if she got loans on the capital markets of the world the history of the Weimar Republic would be repeated. She would use the capital to reconstruct her industries and then default on her foreign debt. Sulking

over her defeat, she did not wish to coöperate with the rest of
the world. It would be better next time to show her people
that the world can get along without their coöperation.

Thus Germany would bear alone the consequences of her
impoverishment through the war she has waged. If it is made
clear to her that she can not count on easy money and aid
from abroad, she will learn to feed her population on her own
ample resources. Ultimately, it may be hoped that her people
can take their place again among a concert of peaceful nations
but this is a problem for future generations. It has been suggested that Germany be deprived of all industrial equipment,
so that she may never again have the resources to reconstruct
a new war machine, but doing unto her as she has planned to
do and is doing unto others will not necessarily be adequate
protection for the future. The United States ammunition industry has been built from scratch in two years, and if the
vigilance of the world is ever again relaxed war industries will
spring up in Germany like mushrooms. A much better protection
against German rearmament can be obtained by safeguarding
the right of the individual to choose the goods upon which
he would want to spend his earnings. That constitutes the only
security against the creation of a totalitarian war machine. Deprived of the totalitarian state Germans will not spend their
substance upon armaments, for even in Germany total rearmament can be achieved only by government coercion.

It is the reëmergence of a totalitarian state against which the
world must remain on its guard.

World War III?

Clarence Streit has proposed a union between the United
States and Great Britain as a nucleus for a world democracy
to embrace all free peoples who wish to join. He weakens his
argument unnecessarily by pointing out that in an Anglo-
American super-congress America would still have the majority. That will, of course, appeal more to Americans than to
the British. One can not renounce national sovereignty and

have it, too. But even if all the delegates to the new congress make abstraction of their nationalistic feelings and are guided in their votes by the merits of the issue alone, such a super-congress of the Anglo-Saxon world would not by itself constitute any guarantee against a new war and a possible defeat.

The British Empire was large enough. But for its complete decentralization it could not have been governed at all; in all probability the dominions would have fallen away from the motherland like the original thirteen colonies. The British have been unable to defend themselves alone not because the British Empire was not large enough, or lacked the resources in material goods and acquired skills, but simply and solely because they were unarmed and because their government granted the grace of time to the enemy to arm for total war.

Precisely the same difficulties were encountered by the League of Nations. For all practical purposes the League embraced the world. Even though the United States was not a member, she nevertheless coöperated faithfully in all important decisions made by the League; yet the League was helpless, because its machinery was defective, and because its members were not prepared to make full use of that machinery until it was too late. The League was pledged not to apply sanctions or to declare war until the aggression had been made indisputable, that is to say until the enemy attacked in full force.

All proposals for world government suffer from the same difficulty. The size of a state does not by itself prevent aggression. If the League of Nations had been a sovereign state, a world government with highly centralized power, it would have faced the same problems created by totalitarianism without being better prepared to cope with it. Like the League of Nations a world-wide democratic federation would fail to preserve the peace if it refused to designate the enemy and time the attack upon him, before he has built up his war machine to launch his own offensive.

To-day the solution is possible. The revolution brought about in the economic process by assembly-line production permits beyond any shadow of doubt to designate the enemy at the very instant when he makes his appearance and years before he is ready for the assault. It is at that instant and not when his armies have crossed some neighboring country that the act of aggression has been committed. It is then and not when he is ready to march that he must be attacked and destroyed.

The revolution in industrial preparation for war by the development of assembly-line production has rendered the nations whose industries are devoted to peace production virtually defenseless if they permit the aggressor to prepare for war in time of peace.

Any new world organization must therefore have as its principle article binding upon all its members, that the emergence of a totalitarian state anywhere in the world is an act of aggression against all.

The nation which gives itself a totalitarian state thereby designates itself as the aggressor and its neighbors, that is to say, all nations of the world, if they wish to survive, must attack and destroy such a state.

Such an immediate intervention in the internal affairs of other nations is vital, and it is justified by the clear threat to the liberty of the world which a totalitarian state constitutes. Every one's liberty is necessarily limited by the liberty of one's fellowman or rather, liberty can find its full realization only in coöperation with others. The nation which gives itself a totalitarian government signifies that it will not coöperate but intends to dominate, if it is given the time to realize the only objective for which the totalitarian setup has any utility. Owing to the revolution effected by assembly-line production, nothing more than an armed force, a national militia on the Swiss model, need be retained by any nation in order to cope with a totalitarian state.

At the moment of its inception such a state is still unarmed and can be put out of business forthwith and without any bloodshed. Inside that state there will still be millions of citizens willing to aid in its overthrow before their minds are totally poisoned by the spiritual fare of totalitarianism. Non-toleration of the suppression of freedom anywhere in the world is a principle of universal application. The imperialism of pre-war days in Asia and, it is to be hoped, in Africa is ended for ever. But the people of Asia and Africa may find that in losing their foreign masters, room has been made for the growth of native despotisms. That would be falling from the frying-pan into the fire. Thus the checks and balances which every demo-cratic nation sets up within against the arbitrary will of elected rulers must in an interdependent world find application with-out as well.

The setting up of international organizations whose task would be the establishment and application of these checks and balances thus becomes the principal task to be realized in the post-war world.

If the principle of national sovereignty is maintained, a re-turn to peace production would be tantamount to committing suicide.

Every sovereign state would have to keep its war indus-tries working on the same scale as to-day, and every nation of the world would have to remain for ever slave to it. There would never again be more food, clothing and shelter than is absolutely necessary to maintain life for any one and no hope for a better order. Though defeated the totalitarian states would have won the war because they would have imposed permanent totalitarianism upon the entire world. Now, as in the past, every nation must indeed be free to give itself the eco-nomic and social organization which corresponds to its needs. But the interdependence of the world which has made of this war a global war will inevitably be intensified after this war is won, and in such a world nations are no longer free to do at home as they please without regard for their neighbors. More accurately they are no longer free to renounce their freedom.

Such renunciation of freedom as the Nazis and the Japa-nese have practised is of mortal danger to the free people of the world, regardless of the distance at which they are situated from the machine of destruction which a totalitarian government invariably develops. Nor can there be any guarantee written or otherwise that the totalitarian state will refrain from intervening in the internal affairs of other nations. On the contrary.

By its very character such a state is compelled to practise what it does not preach. Between it and the free peoples of the world there can be no reciprocity, no collaboration, no faith in treaties signed and in the given word. The totalitarian ruler is compelled to produce armaments exclusively, if he wants to survive internally, and he must try to survive in office since he can resign only at the price of instant death.

From the day of their inception the smokestacks of totalitarian industry are visible on the horizon of the entire world, bellowing forth the smoke of the fire which it is laying. Unless the free peoples of the world can instantly summon all their energies to put such a national trust of war production out of business, the story we have told in these pages will be repeated word by word. History will repeat itself in World War III. The very next generation, the children now being born, will read the story of our time with the terrifying realization: "This is where we came in."

Index

Action Française, 169,201, 255
Africa, 287-288
Airplanes, freezing of, 8
  future of, 348
  German, 40, 157-158
Albania, 235
Aldridge, James, 334
Alexander, King, 160
Alfonso XIII, 165
Altgeld, John Peter, 352
America First Committee, the, 283
American Expeditionary Force, 241-242
American Legion, 293
Anarchism, principles of, 168, 212 n
Anarchists, Spanish, 32
Anarcho-Syndicalists, 168, 212
Anglo-German Naval Pact, 157-161
Anti-Bolshevism, 206
Anti-Fascist newspapers, 94
Anti-Semitism, 196-206
Appeasement, 1, 28-30, 113-179, 268, 333-334
Archduke of Austria, 15
Argentine, the, 292
Armada, 119
Armaments, 45-48, 53, 56, 191, 207, 232, 243
Arras, 129
Assembly line production. See Mass production.
Association of German Industrialists, 26, 27
Atlantic Charter, 1, 350-351
Australia, 121
Austria, 78, 157, 172-174, 188
  Nazi party in, 78

Austrian gold stock, 225-226
Austrian Socialists, 32

Bakunin, Michael, 168
Balance of power, 132-135
Baldwin, Stanley, 155-156, 161
Baltic states, 234
Banque de France, 59
Barbarism, Nazi, 181, 182, 322-324
Barthou, Louis, 159-160, 188
Bataan, Battle of, 310
Battles. See under separate names.
Battleship, English, 105
Baudelaire, 125
B.B.C. programs, 334
Beer-Cellar Putsch, 22-23
Belgium, 80, 117, 157, 342
Benes, Eduard, 266
Bercovici, Konrad, 134
Berlin Diary, 43
Berliner Tageblatt, 128
Bernanos, 169
Bernsdorff, Count, 121
Bismarck, 21, 93
Bismarck, the, 11, 338-339
Black shirts, in England, 227
Blitzkrieg, 6-8, 41
Blok, Alexander, 344-345
"Blood bath" of June, 1934, 66
Blum, Léon, 144-145, 154, 166, 167, 253, 265
Boer War, 109-110
Bohemia, 233
Bolshevik Party, 209, 215-216
Bombings, civilian, 279-280, 335
Books, burning of, 202

(1)